When Silence Hurts

by

Anne Frehill

ORLA KELLY
PUBLISHING

"One may smile, and smile, and be a villain."
Hamlet by William Shakespeare.

(Act 1, scene v)

Dedication

In memory of my dear parents
Delia and James Mc Carthy.
Also, my loyal companion Lassie,
a beautiful border collie.
Who snored gently beside me,
as I chased words around the page,
until she ran out of time at the grand
old age of 15 years.

Acknowledgements

My grateful thanks to: my husband Liam and my daughter Olivia, who were game for a laugh as I learned about the intricacies of various guns, over dinner. And a few special individuals who offered me their unstinting encouragement down through the years.

I also wish to acknowledge the kind and invaluable help of Orla Kelly.

Prologue

OCTOBER 1947

It was a perfect night to be out on the town in Dublin. Above the city, the sky was a mesmerising midnight blue dotted with a million stars.

In Sackville Place, revellers were starting to drift outside. Some to collect their bicycles from among the rows propped against the nearby walls before the rush started and others, in the first flush of love and lust, because they could not wait any longer to be alone in the dark with their partner.

Inside Clerys Ballroom, the sparkling rose coloured lights concealed the sweat on the brows of the dancers and the slippiness of the floor.

She sat beside her cousin on the women's side.

Val shouted into her ear to be heard over the sound of the trumpet.

"Forget Stevie, he is just a two-timing bastard."

She shouted back.

"I know but it's only three weeks ago since I caught him with his tongue down Marie Connelly's throat."

"Just find someone else and in a few months, you won't even recall his name."

Soon the music ended, and a hush fell on the ballroom

"Ladies, and gentlemen, that's all for tonight! Safe home!"

The bandleader winked at the two pretty, young girls sitting along the wall near the stage and in an impromptu move had a quick word with his fellow band members.

"Change of plan! This is a special one, for the two young ladies to my right. Gentlemen, seize the moment!"

Seconds later the strains of "Boogie Woogie Bugle Boy" reverberated around the ballroom as the couples on the floor gave it their all.

Out of nowhere, a big man, with frizzy fair hair and broad shoulders had appeared at Evie's side.

"Come on gorgeous dance with me!"

He leaned over her.

"It's too warm and there are too many on the floor. Go away!"

"I won't take no for an answer."

She rolled her hazel eyes.

"No, means no."

He gave her a cheeky grin.

"There is plenty of space to dance near the door, follow me."

She turned to the left to exchange a bored glance with her cousin but realized that Val had taken to the floor with a pimply-faced lad and she was the only one left.

She nodded at her admirer.

"After you!"

He flashed a smile at her.

"You won't regret it, I am Kevin, Kevin Moore."

For many years to follow she replayed that scene over and over in her mind. And then tried to imagine how her life might have worked out if Val had not danced with that pimply-faced youth and she had not cared about being dubbed "a wallflower" at 23 years of age.

Contents

Chapter One

(1958)

It was one of those dog days in August when farmers and townspeople alike longed for rain. For almost a month the sun had beaten down relentlessly, and Redmills Urban District Council had limited the water supply to designated times every day, to prevent water being wasted on car washes and gardens. Daring, young boys waded knee-deep in the perilous water of the Bree river, well outside the town and away from the prying eyes of adults. While a group of little girls, searched in a shallow stream behind the abandoned workhouse, hoping to fill the empty jam jars in their hands with pinkeens.

An unkempt young teenager with freckles and a bold grin watched them from the mossy bank nearby.

"Those little fish will die if you take them out of the water."

A girl in a crumpled blue frock eyed her.

"Shut up Bridget Mc Ginley, they won't die - because we will fill our jars with water before we take them home."

"I bet you a halfpenny they will die in this heat."

A child with the hem of her skirt tucked under the elastic of her pink knickers screamed.

"Stop gawking at us, you tinker!"

Suddenly, the clippety-clop of horses sounded as they passed by.

Bridget took off at a break-neck speed across the grass and climbed a rusty, iron gate. She was just in time to catch sight of two magnificent white horses pulling a wedding carriage. Her young heart seemed to skip a beat, she had heard her Ma saying that there was a swanky wedding in the Protestant church.

Inside the packed church, with gothic arch doors and windows, the wedding guests, all aristocrats, and VIPs from Dublin or London were restless, eager to escape under the shade of the ancient yew trees. While the Very Reverend Charles Campbell intoned traditional prayers before leading the couple through their wedding vows, the gentlemen loosened their ties as sweat dripped down their foreheads and the ladies shifted uncomfortably under their wide-brimmed hats, hoping that their make -up would not run down their cheeks.

Outside, Evie twisted the thick gold band on her finger as memories came flooding back of her own wedding, ten years earlier. Resting her back against the grim wall which encircled the church and cemetery, she gave a little sigh of relief. While the emerald green gabardine dress with white contrasting collar and cuffs, accentuated her hazel eyes and glossy, black hair, it was too heavy for a summer's day but she had chosen it after much deliberation because it concealed the horrible blue-black marks on her upper arm. Even her favourite black suede shoes were squashing her toes while the new nylon stockings, purchased from Porters Drapery Shop, were clinging to her legs as the prickly heat filled her with the impulse to run out of the churchyard.

Glancing to her right and left, she saw that small cliques of onlookers were gathering, she knew them all, but she remained a little apart. Weddings filled her with misgivings, and she was not in a mood, to stomach gushing comments from bored housewives and flighty young girls as they marvelled over every detail of the elaborate nuptials between this high society man and woman. If anyone invited her to join one of the groups, she would politely refuse, asserting that she was in a perfect vantage point to see the newly married couple when they emerged from the tiny porch, which was bedecked with flowers. Even at a distance, the heady smell of the lilies and orange blossom filled her nostrils. Longing for a smoke, she rummaged in her oversize leather handbag while a tiny voice in her head mocked her.

Hypocrite! You can't bear to be in the same room as the bride because she treats you like some servant.

To her disgust, she could not find the cigarette packet amidst the lipsticks, comb, powder compact, purse, and a collection of pencils, pens, and small notebooks.

She heard a tinkling laugh and looked up to see Helen Jones from the Drama Society

"Fancy seeing you loitering outside a Protestant church, with a gaggle of old nosey biddies and starry-eyed youngsters." Helen raised her eyebrows.

Evie smiled.

"Needs must! The bride is a daughter of Mrs Ryder-Lee, I work for her as a personal assistant, so I decided to have a look at the wedding just to keep her happy. They will live in England."

"I was cycling by when I noticed you, I just wanted to tell you that Tom has decided to bring forward our AGM to the first Monday in September, he has asked me to spread the word."

"Thanks for telling me, I will be there," Evie said.

"We are hoping that this year you might take a bigger role in our production, it seems a waste to just have you in a walk-on part." Helen gave her a sideways look.

A frisson of excitement shot through Evie's body followed by one of apprehension as she thought of Kevin's views on her involvement in acting.

"I will think about it, now I think the newlyweds are about to emerge."

Glancing at the door of the church, Helen grinned.

"You are right! I must go!"

"See you."

Evie watched her slip out through a tiny gate at the side. Then to the strains of Mendelssohn's Wedding March, the newly minted viscountess emerged, on the arm of her viscount, followed by the bridal party. A palpable gasp went through the onlookers as they beheld the magnificent floor-length tulle gown in creamy-white with a long delicate veil. In her hands, she carried a shield-shaped bouquet of lily-of-the-valley, blush pink roses, and myrtle, while the five bridesmaids were attired in delicate pink dresses. The whole effect was stunning, and Evie watched as the photographer began to arrange the couple in a formal pose. From the corner of her eye, she saw Mrs Ryder-Lee, on the arm of a sallow-skinned man with a regal bearing. Tall and elegant she seemed to glide over to where her daughter Gloria was having her veil arranged by a young flower girl. Evie marvelled at her glamorous appearance in a pale green silk coat and dress with matching hat, the sunglasses which she always wore outdoors only added to her air of mystique.

She was just thinking of leaving when she felt a tug at her elbow, she knew without turning around that it was Hilary Byrne from the corner shop, as the telltale scent of her 4711 Cologne assailed her sinuses.

"Aah Mrs Byrne."

"You must be disappointed Mrs Moore that you were not invited and you so well in with the bride's mother. I hear that a whole team of experts were flown in from London to deck out Richmond House and keep the gentry in the style to which they are accustomed."

Evie replied in a voice dripping with ice.

"Do remember I am merely an employee, I have only met the bride once, she has lived in London for years."

Mrs Byrne leaned in closer.

"I always think that Protestants have much nicer weddings than our lot."

"I don't agree, it's all about money, anyone can have a big splash if they are wealthy. I have to go I have lots to do at home, but I haven't the bike."

"Good, I'll walk as far as the shop with you, I don't really trust young Bridie, she would let her pals fill their pockets with my sweets in a flash," Mrs Byrne replied.

When they had edged their way around the snow-white horses and the wedding carriage blocking the gate, they walked down the sloping side street which led to the town centre.

The older woman remarked.

"It's not busy today, they must be all in the bog bringing home the turf like my three lads."

Evie nodded.

"It's August so a lot of people are on holiday in Salthill or Bray."

She gave Evie a furtive look. And Evie had seen similar looks passed between other local women when she was waiting in Byrne's shop to be served.

"That frock must be killing you on a day like this!"

Evie lied.

"There is a good lining in it, and it keeps me cool."

Mrs Byrne stopped suddenly just a few yards from Sam Guiney's butcher shop where a queue of women was snaking its way out through the large doorway and onto the footpath, in anticipation of his famous freshly made pork sausages.

"I thought you looked a little flushed and then that heavy dress. Now, it all makes sense, you are in the family way."

Evie was aware that heads had turned, and several pairs of eyes were examining her shape.

She dismissed the comment with a wave of her hands.

"Mrs Byrne, do you think that for even one hour you could try minding your own business?"

Then she hurriedly crossed the street, almost colliding with Eamonn Rafferty, who along with his pony and cart, was making his way home from the creamery.

However, she realized when she reached the other side that Mrs Byrne was in hot pursuit, gesticulating wildly, as she shouted.

"Evelyn Moore, don't you run away from me, I want an apology."

Evie stopped outside the offices of Burke Reilly & Company, which had a large sign with *Closed* hanging in the window.

Mrs Byrne, who had caught up with her, shouted angrily.

"How dare you make a show of me in front of that crowd outside the butchers, who do you think you are?"

Evie scoffed at her remarks.

"You are the one who put me on show, making snide remarks about my dress and my condition. You started all this, and I was just defending myself."

Her accuser harrumphed.

"You have a twisted mind, I just thought that you were expecting a baby, after all these years and I was delighted. I feel sorry for your husband, he is such a fine man and a gifted veterinary surgeon by all accounts."

Evie's blood was almost boiling with rage, but she managed to respond.

"The subject of having or not having children is entirely our business. Anyway, do not project your thoughts onto my husband."

"Any fool can see that he would love a few strong sons like himself, he would be marvellous with kids."

This was said with an air of triumphalism as if she had hit the nail on the head.

A group of young boys with fishing rods appeared from around a corner and ran past them, allowing Evie to think of a fitting retort.

"Look here Mrs Byrne if I were you, I would mind my own affairs and keep a close eye on your eldest boy, Packie. I heard that he was caught in Hannifan's haybarn on Wednesday night with Molly Feeney from out the Mill road. Apparently, old Francie had to get a bucket of water from a barrel to separate them, they were like two dogs in heat."

Evie watched smugly while her opponent's mouth fell open with shock but a few seconds later she regained her composure and ranted.

"Lies, all lies! I distinctly remember what happened on Wednesday night, Packie was tired and went to bed early as he had been up at dawn helping his father round up cattle for the market in Dublin. My other two lads did not go to bed until well past ten because they were working late at the mill. So, they would have told me if Packie's bed was empty as they all share the same room."

Grinning from ear to ear, Evie's reply was cutting.

"All that talk about children and you don't know what your own are doing behind your back. If I were you, I would get my own house in order first!"

She watched as if in slow motion as the embattled woman said.

"Evelyn Moore, you will regret this day, mark my words!"

Then, mopping the sweat from her brow with a flowery handkerchief, the shopkeeper hurried off.

Looking around her, Evie noticed that several doors were wide open further down the street, there was no doubt about it, curious residents of St. Hyacinth's terrace would have heard every word of their argument on this hot, humid day with not a puff of wind.

Chiding herself for engaging in a shouting match with Hilary Byrne, she hurried down the street until she reached Cobblers Lane which would take her on a short cut to the bicycle shop on the other side of town, where she had left her bike for repair. She hoped and prayed, as she nodded to passers-by that Kevin would not hear about her run-in with that awful woman. From her honeymoon, when she had witnessed his violent temper over a lost room key, she had tried to appease him as much as possible. There was no knowing how he might respond to the news that she had brought their marriage and childlessness under the spotlight of the whole town.

Chapter Two

Tentacles of sunlight were weaving through the slit in the heavy blue curtains when Evie awoke the next morning. Through the half-open sash window came the sound of church bells from the town, heralding the first mass of the day. In her mind's eye she could see the parish priest Fr. Philip Gandon, fingering his rosary beads in the vestry until he was satisfied that it was precisely 7 o'clock when he would sashay out onto the altar in his vestments and begin the Latin mass. Although she had studied Latin in school, there were some words which she did not know, and she wondered how the congregation were supposed to follow it given that many in the local community were still illiterate.

There would be another mass at 11 o'clock but she decided to skip it, she was not going to take the risk of some busy body remarking on her argument with that ogre Mrs Byrne.

Stretching, she got up and wrapped a long blue dressing gown around her slim body. In the room across the landing, her husband was still snoring, reminding her of an old train riding the tracks and then rising to a crescendo when it gathered up speed. She padded across to the open doorway and watched for some minutes as he slept blissfully on.

A familiar yet annoying pang of disappointment hit her as she studied his weather-beaten face and fair hair. His rugged appearance at 43 still made him attractive to other women but often she felt that they were like two strangers who happened to share a house. The same old feelings of guilt assailed her, had she made the biggest mistake of her life three years earlier, insisting on moving to her own bedroom. The fact that he was called out regularly during the night to attend to sick animals had caused a lot of friction between them. Not only was she awakened when he went out but also on his return. And he was usually so exhausted that he fell into bed without washing properly which meant that a curious mix of disinfectant and animal musk came from his hair and lingered on his body.

Suddenly, a tiny voice rebuked her.

Blaming yourself for all that has gone wrong between you, but he only latches onto that excuse to cover his own failings.

Sighing, she turned away, hurrying down the 15 steps of the stairs which had a dark wine carpet running in the centre and bare varnished wood at the sides. In the kitchen, she took out a big, heavy frying pan and placed it on her electric cooker, a recent purchase, bought with her own money. She would make a big fry for breakfast as she always did when he had a day off work, it never failed to put him in good humour.

Half an hour later, he appeared dressed in a grey suit, his hair still wet after a bath and his face freshly shaven.

"That lovely smell of rashers got me out of the bed."

He grinned sheepishly as he took his place at the table. She put a large plate packed with bacon, eggs, sausages, black pudding, and fried bread in front of him.

"There is nothing like a big breakfast."

She replied as she poured strong tea from a large willow pattern teapot into two matching cups.

"I hope old Jack's hens were locked in last night."

He remarked ruefully.

"Why."

Feigning interest, she took her place at the opposite end of the table, thinking that the expanse of oak wood between them might as well be an ocean.

"My last call out was over at Hartley's old place, so it was past twelve when I arrived home. As I got out of the car, I saw a young fox cutting through our hedge and into the pathway that leads to Maguires."

She shook salt and pepper over the two soft eggs at the centre of her plate and then enquired.

"Did you try to scare him?"

"What do you think I am, a bloody scarecrow?"

A smile played at his lips as he stirred sugar into his tea with gusto.

"She chose her words carefully.

"I just hope his hens are all right. Poor old man, he is all by himself in that rundown place."

He sighed.

"Look, it's his own fault, if Philip Maguire wasn't so attached to that land he would pass it on to his nephew and then he would have plenty of company. Mickey has a wife and three young kids but just ekes out a living as a cobbler."

Evie nodded.

"Yes, but he is probably afraid that he will lose his independence if he allows them to move in with him."

He cut the rashers into pieces and chewed them quickly.

"Then to hell with him! He cannot have it both ways."

For some minutes only the sound of Doris Day singing in the background filled the kitchen. "Who's the broad?" He enquired.

"Do you have to use American slang?"

He slurped his tea and then replied.

"It's just a word."

But with you, it's about denigrating women.

She remained silent.

"Hell's fire! Can my own wife not just give me a civil answer?"

"Doris Day."

He wiped his mouth with a cotton napkin and then used a match to remove a piece of grizzle from between his teeth.

"You had better hurry up if you want to make mass at 11 o'clock, it will take you a while to put on your face."

She ignored his sarcasm.

" I am not going today, I have a headache, I got too much sun yesterday, besides I have a lot of preparations to do if I am to have a full meal ready for our guests."

He eyed her for a moment while her heart seemed to beat louder than usual. If she told him that she was avoiding mass, she would have to spill the beans about the insults which she had traded with Hilary Byrne and he would be furious that his name had been dragged into a public showdown.

"Kevin, you go ahead, don't worry about me I will be fine once I have a nice, relaxing bath."

She gave him her best smile.

Much to her relief, he agreed.

"If that's what you want. I must get a bottle of Scotch on the way home for Andrew, I have to keep the boss happy, you know."

"Great, can you get Schweppes soda water and some red lemonade, I have a lovely menu planned for them."

He pushed back his chair from the table and winked at her.

"Right! God forbid that the Rev. Gander is saying mass, I will be slipping out at communion."

Her face softened.

"His sermons seem to go on for hours but if he hears you calling him by that name you won't have to worry about them anymore as he will have you excommunicated."

He guffawed loudly.

"See you later."

"Try to be home by 2 o'clock as they might arrive early."

She said, aware that when he went to the Pub, he often lost track of time.

She watched from the window as his jeep rattled down the drive, took a right turn at the gate and after a few moments, disappeared in a cloud of dust. Then fiddling with the knobs on the Radio she turned up the volume until the sound of Dean Martin's voice filled the entire house with *That's Amore*.

Singing in tune with him, she rummaged in the drawer of the big dresser and took out a neatly folded sheet of paper where she had planned her menu with military precision. Allowing her eye to scan through it for one last time before the real work began.

Starter
Stuffed garlic mushrooms with crisp lettuce and
olive oil dressing

Main course
Roast duck with baked apples, carrots, and
mashed potatoes

Pudding
Compote of Pears with whipped cream
Followed by a cheeseboard

A smile lit up her features, she was glad now that she had spent so much time pouring over recipe books, she wanted to impress Andrew and Elizabeth Boxer, an English couple who had taken over the main veterinary practice in the county, following Leo Mahon's retirement six months earlier. Kevin along with a younger colleague covered all the sprawling countryside which made up the practise while Andrew confined his work to elective surgery at his clinic. She knew Kevin's work was difficult and it was the reason she often made excuses to herself for his mood swings and abusive behaviour. Rolling up the sleeves of her dressing-gown she flung open the windows and the scent of rosemary, parsley and thyme from the herb plot filled the room. Then she set about preparing the duck for the oven, massaging dried cinnamon, coriander, and butter into the breast.

By half-past one, everything was prepared, while in the dining room the table spread with white linen sparkled with her best cut glass and silver-plated cutlery. She was proud of the centrepiece, having copied it from the lavish dinner parties Mrs Ryder-Lee gave for her illustrious guests. Nestled in green foliage an array of pink roses and purple clematis entwined with baby's breath made an eye-catching arrangement.

Choosing a frock had been the most difficult, in the end, she opted for one in navy with polka dots. It had not seen the light of day for the last three scorching summers because of the long sleeves with frills at the cuffs. Yet today she welcomed the sleeves because they would hide the bruising on her right arm and neck where Kevin had grabbed her with force on the previous Monday evening. Now, standing in front of the ornate mirror over the fireplace in the dining room it all flooded back to her. The way his features had changed into a distorted shape when she announced that she was taking a week off to coincide with his annual leave so that they could stay at a hotel in Galway. She had pleaded with him for the sake of their relationship to take some time out with her, but he had ranted about wanting time away on his own. Then seizing her by the arm and squeezing her neck he shouted.

"For God's sake woman, it's all arranged, I am going to stay with my brother in west Cork, to do some fishing, now shut up about it."

Squirming, she had protested.

"You are hurting me."

And after a few minutes, she managed to get away from him but not before he had left the traces of his fingers on her skin.

Why the surprise? It's not the first time.

Her inner voice mocked her.

You know about his temper.

Unable to bear it any longer, she turned on her heel and went back into the kitchen where an aroma of roast duck mingled with that of garlic mushrooms filled the air. Checking the time on the wall clock her stomach knotted.

How in God's name am I going to get through this charade.

She uncorked a bottle of expensive white wine from the refrigerator and poured a large glass. The off-dry golden liquid gradually calmed her as she sipped it slowly.

Things were going smoothly, Andrew Boxer was a loud, opinionated man while his wife who had a patrician appearance, was happy to sit back, now, and then interrupting with anecdotes about her beloved horses and their bloodlines.

Kevin was giving his best performance as the attentive husband and they were all in agreement that Evie's cooking was every bit as good as the food in Jammet's, Dublin's finest restaurant.

"Where did you learn to cook?"

Elizabeth asked as she chased the last piece of pear around her dessert bowl with a spoon.

Evie laughed.

"I actually worked in Jammet's for over a year, following my Leaving Certificate examination. I learned a lot there about food preparation."

Andrew raised his eyebrows.

"May I be impertinent and ask why you left?"

Evie fiddled with her used napkin.

"It's a long story, suffice it to say that I wanted to attend Miss Pimm's Academy and I worked for a year to save up enough money for her fees. It is a prestigious course that prepares girls for a variety of careers both at home and abroad."

"Ah, I see, like your husband you have many talents. Kevin is not only good with animals, but he has a way of endearing himself to even the most belligerent farmers?"

Evie sat back in her chair and glanced at Kevin who was stuffing his mouth with cream.

"Oh, I know he is great with animals."

She would not concede any more.

Andrew turned his full attention to Kevin.

"You are lucky to have picked this coming week for your holiday. I hear it will be a scorcher."

Elizabeth shot Kevin a look of envy.

"A holiday! Kevin, where are you taking this lucky lady?"

Evie sipped from her wine glass as silence reigned for a few minutes. Then, pushing back his chair loudly Kevin stood up while he declared gleefully.

"If I told you that I would be ruining the surprise for my lovely Evie, my lips are sealed until tomorrow morning."

"Well, aren't you just a total romantic!"

Elizabeth exclaimed while her husband put his finger to his lips in mock horror.

"I suppose you could call me an old fool for walking myself into that trap, I guess I will have to do something similar for my wife when September comes around."

"You certainly will!" She replied while they all laughed.

Although Evie joined with them in their moment of gaiety her anger was smouldering at the barefaced lies of her husband. On his way to the sideboard to get a packet of cigarettes, he left a kiss on the top of her head as he said.

"Thank you darling for such a lovely meal."

"Yes, Thank you, Evelyn."

The two guests smiled indulgently at her, while she felt that she would throw up her meal if she did not escape from the stifling atmosphere of that space. Making an excuse she fled to the kitchen.

Later that evening, she was putting away the last of her favourite china when her husband came into the room.

"Evie, leave those until tomorrow, join me for a brandy in the sitting room, there is a replay on the radio of today's semi-final in Croke Park, Tipperary hammered Galway."

She stole a hurried look at him, she knew by his soft low tone that he was hoping to get into her good books after a few brandies.

"Why did you tell such a blatant lie, pretending to your boss that you have a surprise holiday arranged for us. How dare you!"

Her face was glacial.

He threw his head back and chuckled.

"You have to admit that I came up with a good excuse."

"It's just all window dressing with you."

He moved closer to her and took her hands in his.

"Evelyn, you know that my workload is difficult, out day and night in all kinds of weather to pay for our lovely house and comfortable life. Surely, I am entitled to a week away to clear my head."

She dropped his hands while her face reddened with frustration.

"And what about me, it's not easy working for a renowned writer, keeping editors, agents, the Press and all her fan clubs happy."

He loosened his shirt collar.

"I know but some days I seem to battle against death and disease in vain and it gets to me. I just need a week fishing with Pat to recharge my batteries."

A strange look came into his eyes as if he were far away. She relented.

"It's just such a pity that Pat is a canon, otherwise I would go down and stay with you in the Presbytery."

"You know that you are always welcome there."

He gave her a surreptitious glance as he flicked back his mop of reddish-fair hair.

"And you know that his housekeeper hates my guts since the time I cooked that four course meal for the bishop when she had flu."

He threw his head back and sniggered.

"True, you showed how basic her cooking skills are!"

He edged nearer and kissed her.

"Evelyn, I love you."

She swallowed.

"Ditto!"

He pulled her closer, when they kissed, she felt his body stirring but she drew back, as her mind raced.

You are not going to give in to him that easily, while your arm is still black and blue.

"I am tired, and I need to finish clearing up, tomorrow I am going to Dublin to stay with Valerie for the week."

He reacted as if he had been stung by a bee.

"Right, it might do you good – you are very uptight – I want to hear the match."

She studied his broad back as he retreated. Only when she was alone again with the sink filled with encrusted dishes did she allow the tears to flow.

Chapter Three

Back gardens displaying rows of cabbages, scallions, and potato plants flashed by as the train picked up speed and headed for the open countryside. She loved to look at the patterns of the fields, some dotted with livestock while in others the threshing was in full swing, with men, women, and children all lending a hand. Their motley assortment of ragged straw hats and colourful handkerchiefs tied in four knots on big bald heads, to protect against the blazing sun, made her smile.

The only other passenger in her carriage was a man in a pin-striped suit, who was lost in some book titled *Jungian Psychology*, he had barely glanced up when she embarked on her journey in Redmills station. Settling back into her seat she thought about her marriage.

Maybe he is right, a break away from each other might be just what we need to move us out *of our rut.*

Despite her resolve the previous evening to avoid sex with him, he had come to her bed during the night, the smell of brandy heavy on his breath. She had awoken from a deep sleep to find him lifting her nightdress and too tired to resist, she gave in. It was always the same, wham, bang, and over in a few minutes. Spent, he fell asleep, while she tossed and turned until dawn, agonising over his twisted idea of lovemaking.

After ten years you know that he has no regard for your needs.

A tiny voice admonished her.

She stood up suddenly, to open the window, wincing as her head hit a sharp point on the rack above her seat. The smell of sun-kissed hay and wildflowers rushed inside and made the man opposite sneeze. There was something wet on her forehead and she saw that it was blood as she wiped it with her flowery handkerchief. The trouble was that the more she wiped it the more that flowed and tiny spatters of blood were all over her hands.

"I happen to be a doctor may I assist you?"

The man was now beside her, his blue eyes full of kindness.

"Keep this pressed to the wound."

He offered her a folded crisp white square from his top pocket.

"I must have scraped it on a nail." She explained.

He brought over a medical bag from under his seat and sat beside her.

"Here, let me have a look at that wound, I will clean it up and stop the blood flow. You just relax and close your eyes."

He worked quickly, his touch so gentle that she scarcely knew he was disinfecting the wound and five minutes later he had not only cleaned up her face and hair but applied a neat bandage.

"You are most fortunate that you don't require stitches but let me say that if the wound were any deeper, I would be sending you to the nearest hospital on reaching Kingsbridge station. I am giving you this bottle of antiseptic and some bandages to keep it clean and dressed three times a day for about 5 days."

She opened her eyes and smiled up at him.

"I cannot thank you enough, I feel rather foolish for causing you all this trouble. "

"No trouble at all but look here I can feel a long nail sticking out when I run my finger along this rail."

He bent down to study the protruding object while she studied his long pale fingers, with neatly manicured nails so different to Kevin's hands.

"I will report this when we reach our destination, otherwise some other poor soul will suffer."

To her surprise, she heard herself say.

"And that poor soul may not have a kind doctor on hand to heal the wound."

He laughed and his whole face lit up to reveal perfect white teeth.

"Come now, anyone would help a lovely lady in distress. By the way, my name is Robert Nash."

She took the hand he extended towards her as she replied.

"Mine is Evelyn Moore, but my friends call me Evie."

For a few seconds, he held her hand before releasing it.

"It is a pleasure to meet you. I can see beads of sweat on your brow, may I suggest that you remove your heavy jacket, it is very humid in this carriage and we don't want you passing out with heat exhaustion."

Her face turned crimson while she struggled to find a good excuse for not removing it but feeling a little light-headed, she decided it was best to take his advice.

She was wearing a pretty, sleeveless red dress in cotton with a white belt at the waist. His eyes followed the soft line of her neck, the swell of her bosom and then to her horror rested on the black and white bruises on her upper right arm and neck.

Flustered, she came up with a crazy excuse.

"My husband is a vet and last week I went to visit him while he was dosing cattle, one of the bullocks escaped and he had to grab me and pull me out of the way."

For a few deafening minutes, she was aware only of the screeching of the engine as it raced towards Dublin.

Then he spoke.

"I see. Do you mind if I have a look at them?"

"Not at all, but they will disappear in time."

He gently probed the four black finger marks which seemed to Evie to be more pronounced than ever in the glare of the noonday sunshine. She could feel his hot breath on her arm and his aftershave smelt of lemon and pine, reminding her of a forest.

His eyes narrowed.

"Are you sure that is what caused this hematoma or bruising, it is quite deep?"

She nodded, unable to speak due to a lump in her throat.

"What are you putting on it?" His tone was concerned.

"Just Zambuck," she said quietly.

"That's not for bruising, I have a small pot of ointment in my bag, you must have it and apply it four times a day."

While he searched through the contents of his professional bag, she enquired.

"What is it made from?"

"Oh, it's been around for hundreds of years in one form or other, it's from the arnica plant."

"Now, put your arm out straight while I rub it in."

He removed a green top from a fat tub of cream and his fingers worked deftly until he was satisfied that all the bruising had been treated. She pretended to look out the window but all she could think about was his dark, wavy hair greying at the temples.

"Remember to use it four times a day."

He sealed the jar and handed it to her.

She took out her purse,

"How much do I owe you for the disinfectant lotion, bandages and Arnica?"

"Nothing, I would be insulted, put that money away."

His eyes twinkled as he looked intently into hers.

She felt as if she were 16 years old again, eager to have his attention for as long as possible. Throwing caution to the wind she said.

"Well, in that case when we reach Dublin, do you have the time to join me for some tea and cakes in the Phoenix hotel, it is just a short walk from the station. I simply must thank you in some way."

"If it makes you happy, I will accept but you owe me nothing."

He looked from under his eyebrows which reminded her of two caterpillars.

"Right, that's settled."

She surreptitiously eyed his fingers and noted that he had no wedding ring.

One hour later, in the old -world drawing room of the Phoenix hotel, they chose a table by the large bay window with a panoramic view over the river Liffey. The hotel was famous for its giant palms reminiscent of late nineteenth century parlours. With all the doors and windows flung open the palms seemed to sway back and forth in the gentle breeze. Robert studied his surroundings for a minute before perusing the menu.

"I must say this is the perfect place to cool off after the humidity of the train and it is so rarefied after the hustle and bustle of the railway station. When we disembarked it seemed like the world and his wife were all departing the city for some more salubrious location."

"Yes. It's like a whole different world here. When I visit, I always imagine that the palms are whispering among themselves about the comings and goings of guests and staff. It's an oasis in the centre of the city."

He leaned across the table in her direction.

"And I cannot help but notice that some of the most opulent palms are placed in strategic corners where one can gossip to one's heart's content without being overheard."

He paused as his eyes twinkled and then he added mischievously.

"One could even plan to overthrow a government, commit a murder or have an extra-marital affair, no one would notice."

She rolled her eyes upwards.

"Maybe, you should try one of them."

His reply was nonchalant.

"Maybe, I can see that old philanderer Edward VII frequenting a place exactly like this."

In a hushed voice, she said.

"I work for the novelist Iris Ryder-Lee, she is currently researching the life of Edward when he was Prince of Wales, as she is planning a historical novel about the Edwardian period. I sometimes come here with her."

"How interesting! You are a lucky lady to be employed by such a colossus of the literary world."

"There is never a dull moment, not forgetting the temper tantrums! In public, she is a prima donna but in private she is really not so bad!" She conceded.

"Good!" He exclaimed as the waiter approached.

They both ordered iced tea with petit fours, then she sat back and studied the other guests who were mostly couples, marvelling to herself how she had ended up on such a sultry afternoon, in her favourite hotel with a convivial and handsome stranger.

"A penny for those thoughts!"

He exclaimed in a teasing tone.

She looked up at him.

"Sorry, I was miles away, I was just thinking how lovely it is to be in Dublin, away from the pettiness of a small town like Redmills. I grew up in Dublin, near Glasnevin Cemetery and it was almost surrounded by fields then."

Chuckling, he said drily.

"I would never have mistaken you for some country bumpkin!"

She knew that he was studying her face closely for a reaction.

"Obviously, I would never have moved to the wilds of Meath except for Kevin. Veterinary medicine is tough going and some practices do not pay well contrary to public perception. He was working in the city when we met but his old boss was a skinflint, then a vacancy arose in Redmills Veterinary Practise and he jumped at the chance. We got married a short time later."

He rubbed his chin,

"That must have been a big shock to move to a small town where little or nothing happens apart from a man of the cloth ranting from the pulpit about the evils of close dancing."

She nodded.

"When I moved to Redmills, a local gossip felt it was her duty to tell me about a list of young girls who had left good jobs, down through the years and never returned. Of course, she implied that they all had conceived outside marriage and were sent away by their families to give up their babies, and have their wicked ways worked out of them by the nuns."

He looked out the window for a few moments, before replying.

"The stigma of illegitimacy in Ireland towers above everything else. Church and state are so busy repressing anything to do with sex that they fail to see the biggest problem of all, is poverty. When I returned from Africa, I was shocked to find abject poverty among so many of my patients. During my time away, having been confronted with life and death every minute of my working day, I glossed over the socio-economic problems here."

"Yes. There is massive unemployment right across the country, for all his rhetoric Eamonn De Valera and his government have not addressed this problem. I know that at least eight girls and twelve boys from my national school days, have emigrated. You just have to look around you on the back streets to see the men loitering at the corners and the kids dressed in filthy clothes."

He made a sniffing noise.

"I never had much time for De Valera, he is too cerebral, he should have stayed in an ivory tower teaching higher mathematics to middle-class scholars."

Evie gave a wry laugh.

"They say that he has his eye on Sean T O'Kelly's position!"

Robert looked around the room to see why the food was slow in arriving and then replied. "No doubt about it, he will take his place next year as President of this country when O'Kelly's time is up."

Stop talking like a pair of socialists and ask him about himself.

For a moment, the voice inside her silenced her, then she cleared her throat.

"Enough about politics, you must tell me all about yourself. Where is your medical practise and do you have a wife and children?"

He hesitated while the waiter placed the drinks and cakes carefully on the table and then departed.

"I shall answer your last question first. My wife died 11 years ago, and my two sons live overseas. Roger is a doctor in South Africa and Peter is in New York, he is a radiologist."

Evie's face reddened as she tried to take in the fact that he had no wife.

"I am so sorry to hear about your wife, but your sons must be a great source of consolation to you."

He gave her an enigmatic look.

"I married June while I was still a medical student, she was pregnant with Roger at the time and it was a big struggle to finish my studies. We were too young, she was just 19 while I was 20, and to complicate matters Peter arrived the following year."

She felt tongue-tied.

"Sorry for asking."

He waved a hand in the air to dismiss her apology.

"You could not possibly know the story. After the second birth, June began to suffer from depression, and I think it is fair to say she never fully recovered. Despite being treated by two of my colleagues who specialise in psychiatry, she jumped from a bridge one evening while she was staying with her sister in Waterford."

Evie bit her lip.

"Oh, my God, that's so sad. The poor soul must have been in a terrible state to end her life like that!"

He pursed his lips.

"We thought she was happy to stay with her sister for a holiday. I could not watch her for every second of the day and night."

His face clouded over, and she longed to reach across and leave her hand on his. Instead, she said in a gentle voice.

"Please don't upset yourself any further. Let us change the subject, tell me are you a dispensary doctor?"

He blew his nose and then spoke in a gentle voice.

"I worked in St. Cecilia's hospital for many years, after my boys finished their medical studies, I resigned and spent four years in the heart of Africa. It was an eye-opening experience following the antiseptic world of a Dublin hospital"

"Well done! Did you manage to see much of that vast continent?"

"Well, I took six months off to travel around before I returned home, and I work now as the official doctor for dockers, and sailors. Yesterday, I travelled to Drogheda, a man was injured at the port there last week and I had to assess his condition."

"But what of the local hospital there?" She asked.

"They are doing their best, but I recommended that they move him to Dublin, where he will get specialist attention and his insurance should cover the costs."

She smiled.

"So, you spent the night in Drogheda?"

"What else would I be doing? Now, enough about me. Do you have children?"

It was a reasonable question, but she felt like a black cloud had come into the room and eclipsed the golden sunlight.

"No, no children."

She shook her head and took a long drink of the chilled tea.

He watched her, it was a look like her mother would have given if she suspected that she was hiding something.

"Would you think it impertinent if I asked if this is by choice?"

A long silence followed as she took a cigarette from her bag and searched for matches.

The waiter appeared with a Connemara marble lighter and lit it for her.

"Thank you."

She said, aware that an old couple at the next table were watching her.

Suddenly, Robert assumed a glacial countenance which he aimed at the man and woman in question. Immediately, they turned away while Evie burst out laughing.

"Better to be your friend than your enemy, what a sour face you made at them!"

He winked.

"Nosey old codgers!"

Her face grew serious again.

"Given, that you are a doctor I will answer your question. We have been married for over ten years and we never did anything to prevent conception, if that's what you mean. I had an examination in the Rotunda hospital, but they could not find any problems."

With a sombre expression, he asked.

"What about your husband?"

"He refuses to be tested as he believes that the fault as he sees it must lie with me."

She pulled on her cigarette and exhaled slowly.

"One would imagine that a vet would know better having studied animal reproduction."

He drained his glass.

"Indeed, but the mere suggestion that he might be the infertile partner is seen by him as a gross insult to his manhood."

"I suppose that just about sums up the attitude among many males." He conceded.

She lowered her voice.

"Indeed, his pride is everything."

"While I was training, I spent one year on a gynaecological ward. If you wish, I can write to the professor and have his secretary pencil in an appointment for you, he has a long waiting list, but he might be able to talk some sense into him."

Her face lit up.

"Thank you, I doubt if he will agree to it but I can give you my full address."

"No problem at all."

He took out a small black notebook with a fat gold fountain pen and handed it to her.

"Now, your full name and address here please."

While she was writing he excused himself and left the room.

Some minutes later he returned along with a waiter who was carrying a tray of drinks from the bar. The young man quickly cleared the table and left two large glasses of gin and tonic with ice and lemon, resting on coasters showing the hotel's phoenix emblem on them.

After he had gone, Evie, with the pen still in her hand, protested.

"You are far too generous, ordering these drinks, after all, I invited you here to repay your kindness on the train. Now, I must get the bill for the tea and cakes."

He grinned like a boy.

"Forget it, I have settled the bill in full. You owe me nothing Evie except, perhaps…"

His voice trailed off, while he lit a slim cigar.

Her head turned to survey the new arrivals in the room, a family of four, but from underneath her lashes, she watched his steady hand and his square jaw.

When he had finished, he inhaled deeply and then blew the smoke out in circles.

"You were saying?" She ventured.

"I am guessing that you will be staying here for a day or two?"

She looked at him directly.

"Yes, my cousin Valerie is a nurse in the Mater hospital, I opted to stay here, it's only a ten-minute walk. She is on night duty and it will be tomorrow evening before we can meet up, Kevin is fishing in Cork for a few days, so I am taking a break!"

"In that case would you join me for dinner this evening? I have started to write a book about my time in Africa and I wonder if you would consider typing the script, organising my notes and so forth. I confess that I am drowning in a sea of paper at present, I would pay you well."

She did not hesitate.

"Certainly, I would be happy to have dinner with you and we can talk about your script then."

He guffawed.

"Let's just say that it won't be an easy task to compress the notes on my African adventures. Now, that's settled. I need to go home and change. I live in Rathgar, I will book dinner on the way out, what time suits you?"

She heard herself speak in a measured tone.

"Say eight pm, I have not even checked in at reception yet and I need a bath after the heat of the train."

He gave her a broad smile.

"Excellent. Don't forget to treat that wound on your head and the bruises too."

For a second her chest felt constricted at the mention of the bruising, but she kept a calm exterior.

"Certainly."

Then she raised her glass in union with his and as the glasses tinkled, her eyes met his deep blue eyes.

For a few minutes, they chatted about a striking oil painting on the wall which depicted a winding path through a forest. He told her about his interest in art and she revealed how she sometimes painted the wildlife along the banks of the Boyne.

While he was a great conversationalist, Evie's head was filled with questions.

What are you playing at?

Soon, their glasses were empty, and they went their separate ways, agreeing to meet in the foyer later. From her place in the queue at the front desk, she watched while he negotiated the revolving doors. She reckoned that he must be at least six feet tall and when his straight back and broad shoulders disappeared amidst the pedestrians outside, she could not stop herself from smiling.

Chapter Four

The sommelier poured a taster of the dark red wine from a bottle bearing the Mouton-Rothchild label, Evie took a few sips and nodded her approval.

When the waiter had departed, Robert raised his glass to her.

"I must say that I am impressed with your knowledge of wine, how did you come to be such a connoisseur?"

She laughed.

"Too many lunches spent with Mrs Ryder-Lee, they often get boozy if she has an agent visiting. She keeps a fine collection of wine!"

He chuckled.

"Do tell me, I promise not to repeat anything you say about her."

Over the starter of liver pate on toast, she found herself telling anecdotes about various soirees which her boss had held. And as she talked, he gave her his full attention as if the dining room were empty apart from themselves. This was a novelty for Evie who was used to Kevin continuously checking out new entrants to every restaurant that they visited. Often, she had drawn his attention to his irritating habit, but he always defended it by saying that he was well known and had to be sure to keep his clients onside.

When his main course of roast loin of pork with pear and potato puree arrived, Robert exclaimed.

"I really should try to eat more fish, but I am hopeless in that respect, I like my meat!"

"So, I see. A typical Irishman!"

She exchanged a wry smile with him as the aroma of herb encrusted salmon with creamed potatoes and petis pois rose from her plate.

Later, before they emptied the tall dessert glasses filled with strawberries and cream, Evie agreed to help him with his manuscript. He had confessed to having several notebooks and at least a hundred pages of loose notes about his time in Africa, all in scrawling handwriting.

With a boyish grin, he explained.

"I have an introduction done and one chapter, but at times I cannot read my own writing and it frustrates me as I lose a sense of where the book is going."

"Look, post them to me and I will try to make a filing system for you and type up as many as possible. I am good at deciphering writing. Once you get them back it should be easier for you to structure the whole project and plan your chapters. Then after the actual draft is finished post it back to me, I can type it up properly."

"What a relief to have some help with it all! You know it is nearly three years since I returned from Africa and the more time that passes the less likelihood there is of me having it published. I am so grateful, do you want me to pay an initial fee now?"

She drained the last drop of wine from her glass before answering.

"Not at all, I will not accept money at this stage. You have been most kind to me, when you get the book accepted by an agent, then we can talk about money."

"Ah! Evelyn, thank you very much, but once you get stuck into it, I shall insist on paying you regularly."

She loved the way he pronounced her name in his deep voice which still had the traces of a Waterford accent.

"You are so welcome. One good turn deserves another."

A clock somewhere in the foyer was chiming 11 and he signalled the waiter.

"It's getting late and I have an early start tomorrow, I am going to a conference for the rest of the week in Kildare. No doubt, you are looking forward to meeting up with your cousin."

"Yes, it will be nice to see Valerie." She stifled a yawn. "Apologies but I was up early this morning, there is so much to do before going on holiday."

She was beginning to regret drinking four glasses of wine as the wound on her head was throbbing. However, when he had paid the bill, she insisted on walking with him to the front door where a taxi was waiting to take him home. Outside, the night was still warm, and a group of young men and women dressed to the nines laughed and joked with each other as they passed by, leaving a trail of perfume in their wake. Robert wrinkled his nose like a puppy, and she burst out laughing.

Suddenly he kissed her on the lips and for a few seconds she responded.

Then, looking into her eyes, he whispered.

"I must go but I will remember that."

Her reply was barely audible.

"I hope so!"

He jumped into the taxi and called out.

"Enjoy the rest of your holiday."

A tiny sprite-like voice in her head goaded her.

You fool, you let him slip away.

Biting her top lip, she waved as the vehicle edged into the line of cars going over the bridge.

At five o 'clock the next day, Evie stood at the narrow front door of Val's small cottage and hesitated for a few minutes. She still felt a mixture of confusion and excitement over her encounter with Robert. When she had taken a few deep breaths, she lifted the highly polished brass knocker and allowed it to strike the plate attached to the door. It made a deep sound that seemed to echo through the narrow street. Then the door opened suddenly, and Val appeared, in her dressing gown and with her long red hair, still damp after a bath, spilling across her shoulders.

"Evie! It's great to see you."

"Val It's great to be here!"

The two cousins embraced and then Val said with a knowing smile.

"Come inside before the old wind-bag across the road sees me still in my night attire at this hour. And do tell me what happened to your head."

Evie giggled as she stepped indoors.

"It's nothing, the overhead rack on the train had a nail protruding, I just grazed my skin. By the way, thanks for swopping shifts at the eleventh hour to spend some time with me."

Val cleared her throat.

"No problem! I was delighted when I got your message, but I thought you seemed upset when I rang you back about Kevin going off to his brother for a holiday."

"I was but I am over it now, his work is physically and emotionally draining, and he just wants to switch off from the busy world with some fishing."

Evie felt like an observer in her own life as she heard her own contrived matter-of-fact tone.

Val gave her a sympathetic smile.

"I am glad to hear it."

Evie followed her into a small living room and chose a green armchair chair near the window.

"Val you look wonderful, like some Titian beauty in a Rembrandt painting."

"Do you hear who's talking! Evie, when I saw you on the doorstep, I thought you looked like that beautiful movie star Julie Adams, who starred in the film Creature from the Black Lagoon."

Evie burst out laughing.

"In that case why am I still slogging away for Mrs Ryder-Lee?"

Val joined in the laughter.

"For the same reason I toil in the hospital, no one has noticed us yet! Now, make yourself comfortable, I will bring you a drink to pass the time while I get dressed. Feel free to take off your cardigan, its hot in here."

Go on, get it over with! Tell her the lie you told Robert about the bruising.

She quelled her inner promptings and removed her fluffy cardigan as she spun Val the same story about Kevin pulling her to safety from the bullock's path.

Val inclined her head sideways.

"Veterinary medicine is a tough career, but someone has to do it. Fortunately, you escaped with just a few bruises."

"Yes, that's true. I want to tell you that I have booked a table for seven pm in a new restaurant called Bourrides, it specialises in fish."

Evie felt relief that she had managed to change the subject.

Val paused at the doorway.

"That sounds interesting, I always like dining out. Have a look at today's newspaper, some old I.R.A. groups want to have Nelson's Pillar removed from O' Connell Street because it is reminiscent of the British Empire. Do you remember how we used to sneak off and climb up all the steps to the top?"

Evie nodded.

"It was great fun, I loved seeing all the rooftops."

Val disappeared and re-emerged a few minutes later from the kitchen with a tall slim glass filled with whiskey and soda water.

"I shall be tipsy before I even reach the restaurant!" Evie said.

"No chance of that!" Val replied with a wink.

While Val was dressing, a copy of "Woman's Own" magazine on the table caught her attention and she thumbed through it, published in England it was not available in Redmills. A page with a weekly advice column caught her eye, it featured a letter from a reader titled; *My husband abuses me.*

A feeling like nausea gripped her but she continued to read.

To her horror, the letter detailed the litany of abuse that the husband inflicted on his wife at random intervals including dropping a brick on her foot for some real or imagined hurt. Suddenly, an image of Kevin brutally grabbing her by the arm came back to her and she began to shake all over.

Is there worse to follow?

She emptied the contents of her glass in one go and tried to read the response from a woman named Flora, who dispensed advice in the weekly column. However, the print seemed to blur in front of her eyes, and she abandoned the magazine.

When she heard footsteps in the hallway, she grabbed her handbag and was powdering her nose when Val entered.

One hour later, the first rain in weeks fell, as they entered the restaurant. When all heads turned to look at the two glamorous young women, Val said in a low voice.

"This place is divine!"

Evie agreed.

"It has prices to match but it's good to treat ourselves now and again."

The strains of classical music from the private dining room upstairs floated through the air while the waiter showed them to a table by the window which overlooked St Stephen's Green. Minutes later, Evie took a mouthful of a Tuscan red wine and swilled it around in her mouth while a haughty waiter hovered.

"Delightful!"

Evie exchanged a look with Val while the wine was poured.

Once he was out of earshot, she said.

"This place is so elegant, it's a long way from our childhood."

Val gave a sentimental nod.

"When you think of the humble road where we grew up, just a few cottages and old Mrs Butler's dusty sweet shop."

Evie pursed her lips.

"I always felt so lucky that we were best friends, I even told you the truth when Sean ran away from home. Of course, my parents kept up a front and told everyone that he had gone to live with a distant relative in Boston."

Val emptied her glass.

"True, it was our secret. Other girls were so jealous of our friendship because most cousins fought with each other. I shared everything with you too including my first kiss with that fat boy called Eddie Fagan."

"You were a wild one! You must have been about twelve then."

Val whispered.

"I was always getting into trouble with my parents for hanging around the streets with boys, do you remember how I cried and cried one evening up in your bedroom after Fred Tuohy coaxed me into a field and pulled down my knickers."

Evie smiled knowingly.

"Oh, I remember it all, and the way we used to steal apples from Murray's orchard and swap our tattered comics with the Kellegher twins."

Yet, even as she spoke, a nagging thought kept recurring in her head.

Then why not share your worries about Kevin with Val?

But as the evening unfolded and dessert was served, she did talk about Kevin's refusal to go for tests and his dogged determination to blame her for their infertility.

Val's face grew red with exasperation.

"It really annoys me that he is behaving like some ignorant old farmer especially with his knowledge of biology.

He treats human reproduction like animal reproduction. That is a shocking mindset." Val declared.

Evie leaned across the table and whispered.

"As I told you before, he has always been abysmal with lovemaking as he is so selfish, it's all over in a rush."

Val considered this for a moment, then she left down the silver-plated spoon and pushed away a bowl of Black Forest Gateau which she had barely touched.

" I got a shock the last time I visited, do you still have separate bedrooms?"

With a flick of her eyelashes, Evie verified the matter.

Val looked at her friend with an expression of disbelief.

"This is 1958! You should not have to tolerate his self-centred idea of sexuality. He needs a good lesson in how to treat his wife with respect and care."

"He keeps thirty shorthorn cattle in the fields near our house and I think that they get more attention than I do," Evie admitted.

"Did he read even one of those books from London I sent to you a few years ago about love-making?"

"I tried to discuss them with him but he refused and so I left them in his room, a few days later I found them in the dustbin," Evie explained.

Val took a sip from her glass.

"I am sorry Evie, but I do not know why you stay with him."

Evie cleared her throat.

"Do you know I ask myself the same question …?"

The over-attentive waiter hovered nearby as Evie wiped a tear from the corner of her eye with a small hankie.

Val addressed him in a firm tone as she nodded at the empty bottle on the table.

"More wine, please."

When he had gone, she said softly.

"Evie, you cannot go on much longer like this. You both need to talk with a professional who will tease out the major problems in your marriage, that should be done before children arrive."

"Perish the thought that you will ever see Kevin admitting that we have problems to a third party, no he is stuck in the past and thinks that all marriages should be like his parents, where the husband is the head of the house and the wife is just an uncomplaining little woman, who does his bidding."

Evie exhaled loudly while Val said.

"That's what I like about London, it is so cosmopolitan. Of course, I knew nothing about sexuality until I went over there as a student nurse at 16."

Evie shook her head sadly.

"Count yourself lucky, I was still a virgin on my wedding night and Kevin's cold attitude to intercourse scared me, when it was over, I cried myself to sleep. My parents never spoke about sex and when I got my first period my mother just said it was a sign that I was growing up."

Val smiled.

"Do you remember how the nuns used to tell us to keep our legs crossed when keeping company with boys?"

Evie giggled like a schoolgirl and then muttered *sotto voce*.

"Even at Miss Pimm's fancy college, there was no direct reference made to sex education except a few oblique remarks warning us to behave like ladies when dating men."

Val's eyes twinkled.

"So did Miss Pimm's never hear that Victorian ladies liked nothing better than a romp behind the heavy drapes with some randy Earl?"

"Val, you are incorrigible! That reminds me, how is your love life?"

"Great! I have no complaints."

"Lucky you!" Evie said.

Then they laughed, which drew the attention of the waiter, who refilled their glasses.

When he left their table, Val continued.

"Aarush is just such a caring person and so considerate in the bedroom, not like some men I meet."

Evie took a sip of wine.

"I envy you! Tell me again what his name means."

"First ray of the sun, he is an engineer but adheres to the principles of Ayurvedic medicine and lives such a holistic life."

"You are blessed! You mentioned in your last letter that you took him to Fairyhouse for the racing on Easter Monday."

Evie tried to dismiss a hint of envy that was bubbling up inside her.

There was a long pause while Val drank from her glass. Then she hunched her shoulders and whispered.

"Yes, he came over for a week, it was his first time in Ireland, and he found the countryside very beautiful but not so the people!"

"Really!"

"Yes, a man in a dark wine suit and bow tie stepped up to him just before the start of the Grand National and shouted.

"The only good Indian is a dead one. I was mortified and shouted back at him."

Evie turned pale in the face.

"That's terrible! What did you say to him?"

"I reminded him that in certain parts of America and England, some people say the same about the Irish. He was so blinded by prejudice that he called me "a nigger's slut."

"That's pure racism! What did Aarush say?"

"Nothing, he is a gentle soul. But worse was to follow, on the last night before he departed, we were walking home from the Abbey Theatre when a bunch of corner boys in O'Connell St. started to sneer as we passed by. Then one of them approached us and said,

"Go back to Calcutta, you filthy fucker."

Evie's face puckered as if she were about to explode with anger.

"What happened next?"

"Nothing, we both ignored them and hurried on as we were mindful that they probably had knives."

Evie sat back shocked by her friend's revelation.

Then after a long silence, Val spoke.

"Look, it's happened to us in London too but somehow it seemed worse in my own city. And don't forget there are signs in several residential parts of London stating.

No Blacks, No Irish, and No dogs.

Evie's eyes were full of empathy.

"It's just appalling to hear that individuals are still acting like people from the Dark Ages.!"

Val nodded.

"I know, but I have to say that I miss London and when my contract is up in the Mater, I will return. I just came home really two years ago because I was offered that place on the specialist course in Pulmonary Care."

Evie played with her wedding ring.

"Of course, I will miss you but that won't be for some weeks yet, I hope."

"I don't know, I have to sort out a few details before I can say for sure."

Evie's eyes sparkled.

"Good, now I must tell you about the gorgeous doctor who came to my aid yesterday on the train, he was just so kind and handsome, I had dinner with him last night and a parting kiss."

Val topped up their glasses.

"I am all ears you have to tell me everything! This is just what you need, a bit of diversion."

Evie downed a large mouthful of wine and giggled.

"At least you are not shocked by my behaviour, and I a married woman!"

"Married woman my foot! Do continue."

"Well, for a start I hope to see him again as I have agreed to help him with a book which he plans to publish about his time in Africa."

Val paused while she took out a packet of cigarettes and offered one to Evie.

After the headwaiter had lit their cigarettes with a flourish, Val teased her friend.

"Mrs Evelyn Moore you are a dark horse! Now, tell me everything you know about this charming man!"

"Ah," said Evie with a broad smile, "I don't know a lot about him yet but give me time …"

Chapter Five

The days passed quickly. Every morning they ordered coffee and a three-tiered china plate, stacked with mouth-watering pastries, in Bewley's on Grafton Street. There they lazed for a couple of hours while they observed their fellow diners. Young lovers, barely able to keep their hands off each other, eccentric spinsters with severe, old fashioned hats almost as stiff as their faces, animated students from Trinity College and a lanky academic with rimless glasses and a Fainne pin on his corduroy jacket, which proclaimed his fluency in the Irish language. With whole idle days stretching in front of them, they enjoyed each other's company and in the afternoons wandered around the shops and the nearby Art Gallery. Evie loved browsing in the various department stores and in Switzer's treated herself to a suit in a soft lilac shade and two pretty cotton dresses for social occasions.

On Saturday, their last day together they took a steam train which chugged alongside the coast all the way to Wicklow, while the salty air rushed in through the open window. Later that evening, when Evie had taken her leave of her friend she returned to her hotel and stopped at reception to collect her key.

Suddenly, the porter, a stout man with a red face hurried over.

"Ah, Mrs Moore a delivery of flowers arrived for you this afternoon. I put them in water and had them placed in your room with instructions to leave a window open, the fresh air should help to keep them fresh."

Evie could not hide her delight.

"Thank you so much."

He grinned as he clasped his hands together.

"Your husband knows his flowers! If I may say so, they are a magnificent arrangement."

She smiled.

"I am glad to hear it and thank you again."

She headed for the sweeping stairway, taking the steps two at a time while chastising herself for having spoken in such negative terms about Kevin to Val. He had obviously missed her, and this was his way of apologising for going off on his own on holiday and for the bruises on her arm. Her fingers were trembling when she put the key in the lock, and as soon as she opened the door the sweet scent from the flowers filled her nostrils.

A small round table with two chairs stood near the window and on the centre of it, a large arrangement of flowers rested in a beautiful wicker basket. She rushed over to admire the stunning arrangement of white hydrangeas, delicate lily-of-the-valley, white peony roses, white orchids and the most eye-catching of all, pale pink camellias. Overcome with emotion, she sat on a chair to admire their beauty while musing to herself that Kevin must have spent several pounds on them. He had not sent her flowers since their short courtship.

Then her eye spotted a tiny card tucked into the bottom of the basket with neat unfamiliar handwriting in black ink. A smile lit up her face while she tried to extricate it without disturbing the flowers, Kevin must have given the florist the message that he wanted written on it. Moments later, she quickly read aloud the words, but her hand automatically went to her mouth and she gasped in shock, it was not from Kevin. The card slid to the soft Axminister carpet on the floor before she managed to retrieve it. She reread it several times while her heart seemed about to explode against her ribcage.

> To Evelyn,
> I cannot stop thinking about you!
> I hope to see you soon,
> Robert.

Several minutes went by as she tried to take in the significance of his message. In the distance, a peal of bells from Christ Church Cathedral sounded above the roar of the traffic and she checked her watch, which showed 10 pm. Each night during the week, she had listened to the sound of the bell ringers practising, because it transported her back to medieval times where she visualised monks being called to prayer. Now, closing her eyes, she allowed her mind to rest and her breathing became more even. When the bells ceased, she felt calmer and picked up the telephone. Dialling one for reception, she spoke gently when the phone clicked at the other end.

"Good evening, I would like a treble brandy with ice and soda water sent to my room.

The clipped tone of the receptionist answered.

"Certainly, Madam. A treble brandy, as well as ice and soda water. Is there anything else?"

"No. That will be all. Thank you. Good evening."

Replacing the receiver, she paced the room until she heard the light tap of the porter at the door bearing her order on a silver-plated tray.

When he had departed with a smile and a generous tip, she kicked off her shoes and sat cross-legged on the bed while she sipped the golden liquid. She hated to admit even to herself that she was thrilled about Robert sending her the flowers.

Then her conscience chided her.

How can you be so excited about flowers from a man you hardly know?

Suddenly, she jumped off the bed and pulled a beautiful pink camelia from the basket. Then placing it in her dark hair she studied her reflection in the mirror before her eyes took on a faraway expression. Rightly or wrongly, now that she knew Robert felt the same, she longed to meet him again and next time she wanted more than a snatched kiss from the man with the intelligent, sky blue eyes.

She rose early the following morning, her sleep had been fragmented, filled with dreams where bulls were chasing her across fields while Kevin stood idly by with a smirk on his face.

She had breakfast brought to her room. Her mind was reeling, on the one hand, she was filled with trepidation about going back to her life with Kevin while on the other she was excited about Robert.

At precisely 11am the taxi arrived, and the sinewy driver helped her with her bags while admiring the flamboyant floral arrangement which she was carrying.

He exclaimed in a strong Dublin accent.

"Lovely flowers, that cost your admirer a week's wages."

She looked at him sharply.

"I want to go to Glasnevin Cemetery where my parents are buried. It will only take about ten minutes, so I need you to wait for me as I have a train to catch at 1.30 pm in Kingsbridge Station."

Hurriedly, he piled in her shopping bags marked with the distinctive grey and white stripes of Switzer's store.

"I beg your pardon I meant no offence I had no idea that your destination was the cemetery in Glasnevin!"

"Don't worry about it."

She remained stern-faced as he held the door open and she took a back seat. The truth was that she hated having to part with the flowers but to bring them home was to invite not only Kevin's suspicions but his wrath upon herself. After over an hour of agonising the previous night, she had settled on placing them on the graves, consoling herself that they would not be wasted.

Torrential rain was falling by the time they reached the cemetery, but the taxi driver had a large black umbrella which she borrowed. She picked her way through the rivulets of water hurtling down pathways and across the sodden grass until she came to an old grave under an oak tree marked with a tall Celtic cross.

No matter how often she visited it, her eyes always misted over when she saw the inscription.

> In loving memory of Edmund Sherlock,
> Beloved husband and Father,
> Who departed this life on June 12th 1936, aged 50 years.
> And his wife Catherine.,
> Who died on November 10th 1944 aged 48 years.
> Greatly missed by their daughter.

Hastily, she removed old dead leaves and flowers and placed her basket in the centre of the grave, offering a silent prayer for their souls. Then she took out a tissue and cleaned away the bird droppings which had hardened on to the stone. Looking up into the tree above, where the pigeons were sheltering from the rain, she shook her head sadly.

Since her brother had run away at the age of 16, following a beating because he had impregnated a local girl, he had never been heard of since. His disappearance had caused great distress at home and according to medics had contributed to her mother's early death from a massive stroke. Sometimes, when things were particularly bad between herself and Kevin, she hated Sean with a vengeance, blaming him for the fact that she had rushed into a hasty marriage. With both parents dead and Sean nowhere to be found, a searing sense of loneliness drove her to search for a husband and build a new family. Her first boyfriend, a silver-tongued secondary teacher had made a fool of her with his cheating ways. So, she had been overjoyed when Kevin had swept her off her feet and proposed to her after just three months. Excitement at the prospect of marriage blinded her to his controlling attitude and the insidious way in which he gradually cut her off from the friends she had made at Miss Pimm's Academy.

Suddenly, a distant rumble of thunder startled her and brought her back to the present. She said a quick prayer followed by the sign of the cross and headed back to the waiting taxi. The wipers were making a loud grating noise as she approached the vehicle, while the driver sat bolt upright, struggling to see through the fogged-up windscreen.

"The heavens have opened with all this rain! Next stop, Kingsbridge Station!"

He turned up the collar of his raincoat and opened the door.

She handed the umbrella back to him and got in quickly, muttering a curt.

"Thanks".

As the taxi made its way out through the grim, high gates onto the main road, she closed her eyes lost in her thoughts.

Chapter Six

When she arrived home, there was no sign of Kevin other than the lingering smell of rashers and a sink full of dirty dishes, telling her that he had returned from Cork and gone out again. The grandfather clock which had once belonged to her mother ticked away the minutes in the hallway, as she poured herself a stiff whiskey. Then she sat on the bottom step of the stairs and sipped her drink, allowing her mind to wander back to those first few exciting weeks after they had moved in as newly-weds. Full of plans and dreams for the future she had spent most of the money from the sale of her mother's cottage on redecorating this spacious house complete with pantry and outdoor dairy. Suddenly, great sobs shook her body as she acknowledged that now the house often felt more like a jail than a home because she spent most of her time there either waiting or listening. Waiting to hear the crunch of his tyres in the drive or the slam of a door as she made sure that everything including food was to his liking. Or worse still, straining her ears to the sounds of the old house which acted as warning signs for her. When she retired to bed early with a book, she listened for the creak of the second last step of

61

the stairs, a sign that he was going to bed. And then during the dead of the night, she was often awoken with a start by the loud creaking of his bedroom door, an indication that he was on his way to demand sex. However, feigning sleep never deterred him as he was hell-bent on satisfying his urges. The gurgling of the hot water pipes told their own story, a protracted hot bath at weekends made him more dangerous than ever as he compiled a mental list of all his grudges against the world. While the slam of the heavy sash window in his room was a portent that his shirts were not ironed to his satisfaction or his collars had too much starch.

After a long time, she wiped her face and went to her room, where she unpacked and sorted out her outfit for the next day. Mrs Ryder-Lee was fastidious about clothes and expected Evie to dress elegantly even on those days when she was just attending to basic office duties.

By midnight she was beginning to worry that Kevin might have been involved in some sort of road accident and her frustration grew because he had not even bothered to leave a note for her. There were so many places including pubs where he could have gone that she was reluctant to start ringing around.

Eventually, she fell asleep in the kitchen, wrapped in a rug. Later she heard his key in the back door and for a few moments, he stood framed in the doorway, while she could hardly believe her own eyes. His face was blackened, the whites of his eyes were red, his hair dishevelled, and his clothes reeked of smoke.

With a sheepish grin, he said.

"That was some night!"

She heaved herself to her feet.

"You look awful, what happened?"

He sat on the edge of a chair and ran his grubby fingers through his hair.

"I got home from Cork at about 4.30 and after a big fry-up I decided to check on the cattle and then drive over to Goff's to pay them for herding the cattle while I was away."

He paused and coughed up black phlegm into his handkerchief.

Evie could not contain her curiosity.

"What happened?"

"From the top of the lane I could see black smoke and when I arrived at the cottage it was on fire huge flames were shooting into the air. Kieran was outside throwing buckets of water on it and he might as well have been spitting at it, as the fire had taken hold of the thatch roof."

Evie frowned.

"Oh my God, was there anyone inside?"

He coughed again, a long rattling cough and she ran to fetch him a large glass of water.

When he had swallowed several mouthfuls, he explained.

"His mother Nancy, who is well over 90, was inside so I took off my jumper, wrapped it over my mouth and nose and ran inside. It was impossible to see but I heard her screaming for help in the kitchen, it was like the screams of an animal in a trap, I managed to pick her up in my arms."

He paused for breath and then cleared his throat.

"On the way out, something gave my head an unmerciful blow, but I managed to keep going and brought her outside, blazing beams from the roof were falling all around us!"

She left a hand on his shoulder.

"Kevin, you are very brave, but I think that you should go to the hospital to be checked by a doctor."

He shook his head crossly.

"For heaven's sake woman, I have already been examined, my head is fine, and they said there will be no lasting damage to my lungs."

She ignored his tone and enquired.

"Is Mrs Goff still alive?"

"Yes, she is in hospital and they are doing everything possible for her. She is such an old woman, Kieran is by her bedside, although he is well over 40, he rocked back and forth like a child when I brought her out of that inferno."

Evie smiled sadly.

"Well, he has no one else but his poor mother. It's a shame that he did not marry."

He grunted.

"Maybe, he is better off without a wife!"

She ignored the barb.

"Is any part of the cottage left?"

"No, burned to the ground. The Kennedy family across the fields spotted the clouds of thick smoke but by the time they managed to reach a telephone in Major Sanson's house and call the fire brigade it was too late."

A shiver ran through her body as she said flatly.

"Without your intervention, Mrs Goff would have been burned alive. You are such a hero! I am so relieved that you have not been harmed."

He shrugged.

"Anyone would have done the same, I did it really without thinking. So, I am your hero!"

She planted a kiss on top of his blackened smoke-filled hair.

"Indeed, you are my hero, are you sure that you are ok?"

"Stop fussing woman, now make me a hot whiskey before I have a bath and get rid of this stench."

She smiled.

"Stay where you are! A double hot whiskey coming up!"

When she returned from the kitchen, she was surprised to see that he was undressed apart from his trunks.

"Oh! Do you want to wash first and then have this?"

She left the tumbler of steaming whiskey on the coffee table in front of him.

He drank it in two mouthfuls, caught her wrist and pulled her towards him.

"Give us a kiss."

Then he put his mouth on her lips and she kissed him lightly but drew back as the smell of smoke made her cough and her eyes watered.

"Take a bath, you reek of smoke."

She moved towards the door, but he caught her by the arm and stared at her angrily for a few moments. Then with a smirk, he exclaimed.

"A few minutes ago, you told me that I was your hero now prove it."

She tried to wriggle away from him, but his grip grew tighter.

"For God's sake you are hurting me, and you stink like a rat let me go and have your bath."

His eyes narrowed.

"I need sex to clear my head all I can hear is the sound of that old woman's screams."

The stench of smoke was filling her lungs and making her want to retch.

"Right now, you repulse me, let me go do you never think about how I feel?"

Muttering to himself, he dropped her wrist and she headed for the hallway, but he pulled her back, put his two hands around her waist and threw her onto the couch.

"You are my wife, and it is your duty to meet my needs".

Then he forced her to lie back.

She pleaded with him.

"Kevin do not do this to me I am tired."

"Just shut up and relax."

She tried to knee him in the groin, but he pressed the full weight of his body down on her. A sharp pain shot up her back and she froze while he fumbled with her nightdress. It was all over in less than three minutes. Then he got to his feet and stood as if in a daze for a few moments while she grabbed the tartan rug from the back of the chair and covered her body with it.

From the corner of her eye, she saw him pull on his underpants.

"I still have an awful pain in my head from that old beam."

She did not answer.

He smirked.

"I didn't take long to do the business."

" Get out of my sight!"

He stepped over the pile of dirty clothes on the floor and went to the bathroom. She waited until she heard him running a bath and then hurrying to her room huddled in a chair for a long time until she was certain that he had gone to bed. Scarcely daring to breathe, she crept to the door of his bedroom and measured the regular rhythm of his snoring. Only then did she go to the bathroom and take a hot, soapy bath to wash away his smell.

That night she slept fitfully. When the ringing of the telephone woke her at seven, she felt troubled as the memory of the previous night came back to her. She listened while Kevin picked up the phone and gave monosyllabic answers. After the conversation ended, she heard his footsteps coming towards her room.

"Evelyn, get up! That was Kieran Goff on the phone, his mother got a turn during the night so he is staying by her bedside, he wants me to find someone who will milk the cows and look after his livestock."

She stared past him as if he were invisible.

"Evie. please help me this is an emergency my head is still pounding, and I need to attend to my own work as well as his affairs."

"Yes, so do I. Mrs Ryder-Lee will have plenty of work laid out for me to do."

She replied.

He coughed for a few moments and she noticed that both his eyes were still a deep red.

At that instant, her attitude softened a little as she recalled that he could have died during his attempt to rescue Mrs Goff.

"You should take two Anadin tablets every four hours and if that does not help you will need to call the doctor. What do you want me to do?"

He sighed, rubbing the corner of his eye with the sleeve of his pyjamas.

"I don't have time for breakfast now but if you could make ham sandwiches and a flask of tea, I can bring them with me. Luckily, I bought some groceries on my way back from Cork yesterday."

"All right."

"Thanks, Evie, I love you," he said, through a fit of coughing before he hurried off to shave.

She frowned angrily as she changed into a dress and cardigan. She had let him off the hook again for his despicable behaviour the night before, but she reasoned that it was not the time to start a row. A small voice in her head mocked her.

It's never the right time."

Later, the sun was already hot as she took a short cut and cycled in a south-westerly direction through lanes and dusty back roads until she reached the impressive entrance gates to Richmond House, an elegant three-storey mansion built in the late eighteenth century. It looked particularly resplendent on that glorious sunny morning as she sped up the long avenue lined with beech, lime, and poplar trees. Harry Ryder-Lee had inherited it, following the death of his cousin Sir George Humphries, an eccentric bachelor. While the Ryder-Lees had managed to retain the big house surrounded by 200 acres, they were forced to sell 600 acres of farmland to pay off old debts which Sir George had amassed. Mrs Ryder-Lee, who insisted that Evie call her by her first name: "Iris" when they were alone, often reminded her that had she not been such a successful writer with several bestsellers that her husband, since deceased, would never have been able to hang onto such a big property.

When Evie reached the cluster of giant horse chestnut trees she stopped, here the avenue branched into three roads. One ending in an entrance court at the front, the second led to the left-wing which had been converted into offices and a study where Iris could write and shut herself off from the main house. And the third road swung around by the right-wing and led to the back yard complete with stables and a clock tower in old stone. Wiping her brow with a hankie she then closed her eyes for a few minutes and allowed the sounds of the doves cooing in the trees to calm her mind. It was hard to believe that it was scarcely twenty-four hours since she had placed that beautiful basket of flowers from Robert on the graves, so much had happened in between.

Then in a panic, she got back on the bike and took the second road, it was almost 9.20 leaving her with just 10 minutes to change into a smart boucle suit with matching blouse. Then she would run a comb through her hair, sweeping it up into a chignon and finally, select a pair of high heeled shoes to complete the look. Image was important to Iris, being an American by birth she regularly visited New York and the latest copy of Vogue Magazine was always on hand. It was the same with all her staff, the haughty housekeeper Mrs Higgins, the cook Maisie Butler, a waitress cum kitchen maid known as Ivy, the elderly gardener Sonny Dillon, and the chauffeur cum handyman Brendan Delaney, each one was expected to have impeccable standards. Even the charwoman Tess and her daughter Babs, who cleaned and dusted under the steely eye of Mrs Higgins were badgered into wearing black pinafores with large white starched aprons and matching white caps, which proved to be counterintuitive given that much of their work was cleaning out grates and mopping floors. Invariably, they had to change the outer layers at least twice and often three times a day to maintain what Iris called "a snow-white front" leading them to call her a 'snow goose' when she was out of earshot.

Getting back on her bike she rode to the office, and quickly changed her clothes. Iris swept into the room, just as she was removing the cover from her typewriter, attired in a chic suit of deep purple trimmed with black.

"Good morning Evelyn. I hear from Brendan that your husband was quite the hero yesterday evening."

Evie smiled wryly. "Good morning Iris, my goodness, I cannot believe that news travels so fast!"

Iris ran her finger along the window seat to check for dust before sitting on it.

"In Redmills, every bit of gossip has wings! I sent Brendan for the newspapers this morning and he told me that the customers in Keoghs were agog for more news about Kevin's role in rescuing Mrs Goff."

Evie shrugged.

"He did what anybody would do in the circumstances, he heard her screams, went inside the blazing cottage and carried her out."

Then she began to sort through the mountain of post that had built up. She resented the fact that he would now be regarded as some sort of hero, given the brutal treatment which she had endured, on his return. Iris surveyed the sweep of the parkland where deer were grazing and then turned to face Evie.

"Your husband is growing more and more like a protagonist from one of my novels, not only is he good-looking and lithe but now a knight in shining armour."

She laughed at her own joke and then added.

"Someday I might even base a character on him!"

Evie felt her face burning with rage, but she tried to make light of the comments.

"Thanks, Iris, but don't praise him too much or his head will grow so big that he won't be able to enter through the door. Now, shall I go through all this mail, most of it is from fans or is there something more urgent?"

Iris got up and handed her a pocket-sized notebook that she had left on the desk.

"I have been invited to a soiree in Fitzwilliam Square this evening, some contacts I made through my daughter's new in-laws, so I plan to spend the rest of this week in Dublin. I have written down all that I want done while I am away."

Evie flicked through the notebook for a few minutes and then lifted her gaze to her boss. There is a lot here, but I will do my best. May I say that the wedding was beautiful, and Gloria looked so elegant in her bridal gown."

Iris adjusted the string of simple pearls which nestled at her neck and showed off her silver-blonde hair and navy-blue eyes.

"Yes, many of the guests remarked on her resemblance to Princess Grace of Monaco, I suppose her looks come from Harry's side, his mother was regarded as a society beauty in her day."

Evie gave the answer which she knew was expected of her.

"Iris, I think you are being too modest we all know that you are blessed with both brains and beauty."

"Well, thank you, Evelyn, I always say …"

Much to Evie's relief, a firm knock on the door interrupted the flow of conversation and then the chauffeur's head appeared around the door.

"Mrs Ryder-Lee, the car is now sparkling and ready to go. I have put your cases in the boot, and I wonder if there is anything else to be done before we leave?"

She gave him a little smile.

"No. Go and have a smoke, I need to have a word with Mrs Higgins before we leave."

"Good, I could do with a cigarette."

Minutes later, Iris followed him leaving a trail of Chanel No 5 in her wake.

As the week wore on, Evie felt more and more exhausted, Iris had left her a heavy workload which she was determined to master. Things were no better at home, Kevin complained of a nagging headache and only managed to get through his long days tending to animals by popping painkillers. However, as soon as he lay in bed at night mucous collected at the back of his throat causing him to get up continually to clear it. And nightmares in which he was locked inside a blazing stables with several animals dogged him as soon as he went back to sleep. Invariably, he ended each night by sitting in a chair where he was able to sleep albeit fitfully, without a paroxysm of coughing. Evie noticed that the lack of proper sleep was making him increasingly peevish and she asked their family doctor, a tall, bespectacled man in his sixties, to drop around to the house on Wednesday evening, ostensibly on a casual visit to congratulate Kevin on his bravery. She was pleasantly surprised when Kevin not only agreed to a full examination but requested a course of sleeping tablets and strong pain-killers to help him recover.

"Really you should be taking a week off work, but I accept that you don't want to leave your boss in the lurch so you must promise me that you will get plenty of rest in the evenings. I will look in again on you in about ten days." Dr Macey said.

Kevin raised his eyebrows. "What about my golf?"

The doctor snapped his black medical bag shut.

"For God's sake Kevin, you of all people should know that the body needs time to rest following an injury and/or trauma. To hell with the golf get yourself better, promise me that you will skip the golf for a while."

Kevin was silent for a moment, then he burst out.

"Ok, no golf but what a load of bollocks! I tried to do a good deed and now it has backfired!"

The medic gestured at the prescription and then glanced sideways at Evie who gave a quick nod of the head.

It was a long, strange week and she was relieved when Friday evening finally arrived, all she wanted to do was soak in a hot bath. Kevin was adhering to the doctor's advice and was sleeping through the night. When she arrived home, she found him dozing in the sitting room while jazz from the radio blared in the background.

She turned down the volume just as he opened his eyes.

"How is the headache?" She asked, picking up pages from the newspaper strewn across the floor.

He moved his head up and down for a few moments.

"It's the same but hunger won't help me. I'm famished."

"Don't worry, I will heat up the remainder of the beef casserole we had yesterday, and it will be ready in twenty minutes."

She forced herself to smile.

"Good, I had to put down an old horse belonging to Tommy Farrell, his wife brought me in for a big feed of bacon and cabbage, but that was hours ago."

"How kind of her."

Inwardly, she was furious with Kevin and the way he sat there like a child complaining about his hunger when all he had to do was reheat the food in the oven.

There was silence for a moment, then he looked at her curiously.

"Do you know that I am quite the hero? Every place I go be it farm or tobacconist's someone approaches me to shake my hand. And on my rounds, they all insist on making tea as if they need to feed me like some prize bull, it's hilarious."

"Great. Enjoy it while it lasts!"

She knew that he would milk the image of himself as both a hero and a macho man for as long as possible.

She was just leaving the room when he called after her.

"By the way, there is a parcel in the hall for you from Dublin, looks like books."

Suddenly, her face flushed but she replied in a steady voice as she glanced at the large, neatly wrapped package on the hall table.

"Oh, I see it, I will open it later, it's just more work. Some doctor who is an acquaintance of Mrs Ryder- Lee rang me about typing up all his old notes from his time in Africa. He intends to write a book but is finding it hard to wade through his own writing."

"Bloody idiot, I hope he pays you well," Kevin exclaimed and then added. "Hurry up with that food."

She took a deep breath, at least he had swallowed her story about Robert and Iris.

"Sure, coming right up. Would you like a small port while you are waiting?"

She asked, in a fake dutiful voice, glad that the matter of the parcel was settled.

"Good woman," he retorted smugly.

A tiny voice inside her said teasingly.

He is just short of slapping you on the bum like one of his best heifers.

However, she remonstrated with herself silently as she placed the casserole dish on the top shelf of the gas cooker.

If he thinks that I am going to continue being a dumb little wife who attends to his every whim he is in for a big shock.

Her fingers were aching to rip open the parcel, after Robert's extravagant floral gesture she wondered if he had concealed anything inside it for her. Yet, she could not risk opening it until at least the following day lest her eagerness aroused Kevin's suspicions.

Chapter Seven

Next morning, when Kevin had left for work, she opened the parcel in her bedroom. Packed into one large cardboard box were hundreds of loose pages all in Roberts handwriting, completed during his time in Nairobi, Mombasa, and Kisumu. Glancing through them at random she strewed them across the bed, print and cursive writing were all jumbled together and unless the pages were lined the writing undulated hither and thither. It was obvious to her that he had scrawled them at odd hours, perhaps after a long shift on the wards or even during the night. It was so different to what she had expected that she burst out laughing, while many were detailed medical records about patients and treatments many other pages encapsulated the raw beauty of Kenya's landscapes and wildlife. It struck her that he had at least the essence of two books in that motley collection, the first a medical book and the second a travel book.

It was only when she reached the bottom of the box that she found a small blue envelope marked with her name. Quickly she tore it open and read a note which he had written in small, careful writing, in which he thanked her for agreeing to look at his "scribblings" and requested that they meet up on a Saturday of her choosing in Dublin, to discuss the work to be done. At the end, he added his home telephone number and enclosed a cheque for five pounds.

She had just locked all his papers into a filing cabinet at the back of the house when she heard Kevin shouting her name.

His frame filled the doorway, as he brandished a copy of the Redmills Champion newspaper with his eyes blazing and the smell of cow muck coming from his wellingtons.

Looking up, she enquired.

"Did your story about rescuing Mrs Goff make the front page?"

Spittle escaped from his mouth.

"Yes, that sly reporter who interviewed me on Wednesday printed every single word I said, even the fact that I am on medication because of the blow to the head sustained inside that inferno. Now, every bloody farmer will quiz me about the state of my health."

He handed her the paper, and she took a quick look at the front page which was accompanied by a photo of Kevin in green veterinary overalls, the article was continued on page two.

"I would not worry at all, his style is flowery and effusive, but you have emerged as the hero and that is what matters. Surely, if farmers comment about your injury it will merely be out of sympathy and not in any way malicious.

He cast a thunderous look at her as she folded the paper.

"You think that you are so fucking smart just because you are working for some jumped up writer, of all the ways of earning a living it must be the most futile … fairy stories, all make-believe!"

She felt her chest muscles tighten as she reacted to his insults with derision.

"Novel writing is both an art and a craft and without creative thinking, this world would be a very drab place indeed."

He was now standing directly in front of her as he exploded into a rage.

"You are just a loose-tongued woman, with nothing better to do than start-up rows with Hilary Byrne about her son Packie."

The blood drained from Evie's face, while an interior voice said.

You thought that you had got away with it.

Trying to appear calm she replied.

"That woman insulted me, I had to defend myself."

He stabbed his finger in the direction of her face.

"I don't normally buy my papers in Byrne's, but I went there this morning to avoid the traffic because there was a funeral in the town. Well, as soon as I entered the shop Hilary started ranting at me about how you destroyed the reputation of her son and that of young Molly Feeney."

Evie did not like the way the conversation was going.

"Look Kevin, she goaded me about our childlessness … it hurt me, so I just blurted out the story about her son."

"She will take it to court. And as for our childlessness, that's all your fault, the way you lie there like an old sow."

It seemed that out of nowhere his right fist came flying and hit her on the left cheek.

She screamed in pain and staggered backwards before falling.

He was standing over her.

"You stupid fool, of all the vicious cunts in the town you had to pick on the worst one, Hilary Byrne won't stop until they get money."

She picked herself up slowly and then held onto the back of a chair with both hands. The room seemed to be reeling in front of her eyes as he watched her.

She was aware of something wet on her face and she realized that it was drops of blood from her nose.

He rummaged in his pocket and gave her a handkerchief which she pressed to it.

"Evie, I am so sorry, and I apologise wholeheartedly, but all this is your fault … Now we owe both families money to shut them up!"

"Oh, I know that I should have ignored her jibes, but I did not think."

"That's your problem, you never think straight before you open that effing mouth of yours but let me tell you that I won't pay one penny to them, you can get a loan from the bank. Now, clean yourself up, no man would touch you in that state, I have to go back to work."

Just as he walked outside, she picked up a cookery book and flung it at his back, but it missed and crashed onto the floor. Unaware that she had aimed it at him, she heard him muttering about her clumsiness.

In the late afternoon, after a long bath, she cycled over to her friend Orla, who lived on the other side of the town. She had befriended Orla, a librarian, and a fellow Dubliner, after moving to Redmills. She enjoyed Orla's company because they both shared a love of books and could talk for hours about the latest publications. Orla had revealed that she had been in a long entanglement with a man, which had ended abruptly, and had no real interest in settling down with a family. Yet, she was a feisty woman, who looked younger than her 37 years and she had a string of admirers, who took her into Dublin and wined and dined her.

Evie was so pleased to find someone else in Redmills who was genuinely interested in literature, that the friendship blossomed.

That evening they went for a cycle to the market town of Trim, some 6 miles away and enjoyed a picnic of chicken sandwiches and sticky buns washed down with cider, among the ruins of St John's castle. While Evie's face was red and bruising was beginning to show under her eye, she made light of it when Orla enquired about what had happened.

"Oh, it's nothing, I bruise easily. This morning I was up on a step- ladder but I fell and landed on the floor.

I did more damage to my china fruit bowl than to my-self."

Orla pulled a face.

"I bet that you will have a right shiner tomorrow. Last year when I went to visit my Aunt in Kerry I fell from a ladder as I was trying to clean her gutters and I had a black eye for days."

Relief washed over Evie.

"It could be worse!"

They both chortled just as two nuns passed by and gave them looks of disdain. Then for a few minutes, they sat silently in the sunshine while Evie mulled over telling Orla about her predicament with Hilary Byrne.

Hesitantly, she leaned closer and asked.

Do you know Hilary Byrne, she runs a small newsagents and sweet shop?"

Before she could finish, Orla interrupted.

"That woman and her family are the bane of my life I am locked in battle with them at present, so I have had to enlist the help of Fr. Gandon. Next Friday we are meeting in the Parochial house to sort it out."

Evie's face brightened.

"Do you mean that he has summoned her to this meet-ing?"

Orla shook her head.

"Yes, that woman is incorrigible, but she is one of those pathetic individuals, who for all their guff is in awe of the clergy."

Evie grinned as she realized that there might be a way of dealing with Hilary Byrne.

"Orla, I am going to tell you about a run-in I had with her recently, you might be able to help me."

Orla sniffed loudly.

"I will do anything I can to teach that awful woman a lesson."

When Evie had finished explaining, Orla said.

"Don't worry any more about that harridan. For months, her youngest son Bill has been systematically stealing books from the Library, most are detective stories. He has devised all kinds of ways to get them out of the building, some have been concealed in his underwear while others were up his jumper."

Evie looked at her expectantly.

"Have you not reprimanded him?"

Orla paused until a family group had passed by.

"Of course, I even went to his house and warned Mrs Byrne that if it continues, I will get the Gardai involved. But she laughed in my face and said that her brother, who is a Sergeant in Tipperary, will pull a string or two. "

"The cunning bitch!" Evie exclaimed.

Orla put her finger in the air.

"However, Fr. Gandon has agreed to help me put a stop to Bill's behaviour."

"I don't understand."

Laughing out loud, Orla replied.

"You don't understand the power struggles of local hurling and football. The parish priest has a big say in who gets onto the Redmills under 16 hurling team. And Bill and his parents are hungry for a place on that team, so the priest intends to say that if he does not stop stealing, he will be banned from hurling and publicly disgraced because of it!"

"Ingenious! However, it does not solve my problem."

"That is where you are wrong. Given your permission, I shall tell the priest that you were provoked into taunting her about Packie's misdeeds because of her wicked tongue. I know that he will agree to threaten Hilary Byrne with a "fire and brimstone" sermon from the high pulpit, about women who delight in gossiping about others in the town. Her name will come immediately to everyone's mind so she will do his bidding."

Evie wiped a tear from her eye.

"It's perfect but how can you be sure that the P.P. will agree with your plan?"

"Suffice it to say that I regularly oblige him by locating books, articles, etc from other libraries for his perusal. Might I suggest that you put two ten-shilling notes in an envelope and leave it at the front desk in the library marked for my attention. I will say that you are offering it to the two young people as a way of expressing your regret at the whole incidence. My bet is that Mrs Byrne will donate one note to the priest and the other one to the library as recompense for the missing books."

"Brilliant! I will drop in the money but that won't satisfy the family of Molly Feeney."

Evie plucked a piece of clover and inhaled the fresh scent while Orla tidied the empty wrappings from the sandwiches.

"Evelyn, the Feeney parents are illiterate, only the two younger children can read and write, but I will offer them all places with a free tutor as part of a scheme which I hope to arrange in the autumn for adults with reading issues."

Evie fiddled with her wedding ring.

"I owe you for this if there is anything, I can do to re-pay you for your help let me know."

Orla's pale eyes opened wide with delight.

"As a matter of fact, there is something! I would like you to arrange for Mrs Ryder-Lee to give a talk in the library as part of the autumn series of our "Club night" lectures. My budget will not allow me to pay a famous writer like her, but it would be a real coup to get her. Who knows, even the Meath Chronicle and the national newspapers might want to attend it."

"Consider it done. I have my own ways of inveigling her!" Evie said.

Orla winked.

"We are a right pair, it seems we are wasted in this small town, we should both be in politics, strutting our stuff in Dail Eireann."

Evie lit a cigarette and took a puff before exhaling loud-ly.

"You have taken a great weight off my shoulders, thanks so much Orla, my dear, dear friend."

Orla's eyes misted, and she said in a croaky voice.

"Thanks for nothing, your friendship means a lot to me and so I am going to share something with you, which I have never told anyone."

"Rest assured, I will take it to the grave with me." Evie flicked ash into the grass.

"Today is the anniversary of a most traumatic event in my life. You see I gave birth to a little boy when I was just 20 years old, my family had disowned me, and my coward of a boyfriend fled to England, so I was forced to go to a home run by nuns for fallen women like myself."

"I am so sorry."

Evie's voice was low but gentle as she left her hand on her friend's arm.

" It was sheer hell we were treated like slaves doing all the menial labour for them. When my son was born in 1941, the war was raging in Europe. There was no legal adoption then so I agreed that he could go to an American couple who were living in England at the time. I believe that they all returned to America after the war ended."

Evie stubbed her cigarette with the heel of her shoe.

"So, your son is 17 years old, today must be very difficult for you."

Orla rubbed away a tear from her eye.

"Yes, his birthdays are the worst as it all comes flooding back but I don't regret my decision as I could not have provided for him on my own. Two days after the birth I left the convent and my paternal aunt Margaret took me into her home, she was a widow by then and glad of my company as her son had died from tuberculosis. She paid for me to go back and finish my studies, she was a kind, generous woman."

"Did your parents make amends to you for throwing you out?"

Orla sniggered.

"No. My father died suddenly a few months after I was kicked out and my mother blamed his death on me, as she said I had disgraced the family. My two brothers went to Boston soon after my banishment as they could not wait to escape from the stifling atmosphere. "

Evie craned her neck at a heron who was flapping his wings as he landed smoothly on the nearby river Boyne. After a few minutes, she turned to Orla and spoke.

" I am appalled by your family's behaviour but something similar happened in my own family. When my brother Sean made a local girl pregnant, my parents went mad, Daddy gave him a ferocious beating and he ran away that night. I have no idea if he is still alive, the girl was sent away in disgrace to a Mother and Baby Home, where she put her baby up for adoption."

Suddenly, Orla with tears streaming down her face leaned over and whispered.

"Give me a hug, please, I need it."

By the time Monday morning came around, Evie had a big black eye. She had refused to eat meals with Kevin since he struck her, and left food prepared for him in the oven while taking her own meals in the bedroom. After much deliberation, she phoned Iris to inform her that she would remain at home for a few days at her own expense, following a fall from a step ladder. However, Iris kindly offered to send over Brendan with a typewriter and other requirements and so Evie worked from home for that week. He duly collected completed files every morning, while also bringing her new work for the forthcoming day.

It was exactly what she needed, time and space to be alone with her thoughts so that she could work out what should be done about Kevin and his latest outburst. Meanwhile, he had begun to take his main meal at midday in Royal Redmills Hotel, on the pretext that he needed to eat well to build himself up after the fire. In the evenings, he tended to his cattle and walked the fields before retiring early to bed where he fell asleep listening to music on the radio. Evie too took a walk through the back lanes and into the forest every evening before going to bed with a book by J.R.R. Tolkien, a Christmas present from Val, it had been sitting on top of a pile of books waiting to be read. Now, she decided was the perfect time to delve into Tolkien's world because it allowed her to escape for a while from her own grim marriage.

Chapter Eight

Evie sat in the front room of Dr Macey's old rambling house, on the following Saturday afternoon. A smell of wax polish and leather lingered in the air and reminded her of a convent. After what seemed like an interminable wait he padded into the room in slippers and with a bundle of papers under his arm. He seemed preoccupied and barely glanced at her as he made his way to the far side where an impressive mahogany desk and matching chair stood in the huge bay window.

"I am so sorry for taking up your time on a Saturday afternoon but as I was not actually sick, I did not want to go to your surgery during the week, you see …. I am here to talk to you about … Kevin."

He looked up.

"I guessed that was the story when my housekeeper told me you rang and requested a private appointment for this afternoon."

She smiled hesitantly.

"I don't know where to begin."

He opened a large black leather-bound notebook and removed the top from a silver fountain pen. Then holding it at an odd angle in the air he asked somewhat testily.

"Is he not doing what I recommended?"

"Rest assured that he is following your instructions and taking his medication but it's something else.

"She pointed to her black eye which was still clearly visible.

He screwed up his eyes.

"Come over and sit in this chair, I must take a good look at it."

Leaning over her, he put a monocle into his right eye and studied the bruising. The scent of whiskey lingered on his breath and she was beginning to regret coming to see him.

"Right, you may relax."

He removed the eyepiece and sat down.

"Put it this way, it won't kill you! I have seen worse bruises than yours. Amateur golfers are often hit by balls."

Evie felt like walking out, but she said in a firm voice. "

"You don't understand, it was Kevin who gave me this black eye when he hit me with his fist last Saturday."

She had expected him to express shock or sympathy, but he remained controlled.

"I see, now that is a different story. Again, let me tell you that it is not the first time that a wife has sat here in front of me with a shiner!"

Evie protested.

"But it was wrong of him to hit me."

He leaned over to the window-sill and pulled hard on the tassel of a blind to block out the bright sunshine.

"I presume you had a row can you tell me what it was about?"

Suddenly, the phone on his desk jingled and he lifted the receiver and gave a few monosyllabic responses.

Evie's heart sank as it dawned on her that he was on Kevin's side. Then it all came back to her, just before his wife died from leukaemia about 8 years earlier, their dog had eaten poison in a neighbour's field but Kevin had miraculously saved the life of the canine. After his wife's demise, the doctor mollycoddled the red setter for the rest of his days because the animal reminded him of his beloved. And Kevin became a hero in his eyes.

"Mrs Moore, you look as if you are a million miles away!"

She felt her face redden.

"My apologies, I did not realize that you had finished your phone call."

"Now, the cause of the row? Money or conjugal rights?"

She hated his coldness and his usage of the legal term in place of lovemaking.

"Money, but I would prefer not to go into the details."

"Ah, it's always one or the other that causes disharmony. My dear lady, my advice to you is to forget about it as I assume that he has never hit you before."

She paused.

"No, he has not hit me but …."

She was about to say that Kevin had often bruised her upper arm, but he stood up and walked to the mantelpiece where there was a plastic skull.

He took it in his hands and pointed it at her.

"Just imagine that this is your husband's skull and that a heavy beam hit it in the course of a fire. Well, that is what happened to Kevin, he has a head injury, not a severe one but still, a head injury and people with such injuries do strange things while they are recovering."

She stammered. "But .. but… "

He pulled a face in a dismissive fashion.

"Forgive him, he cannot be held responsible for his actions. Now, is there anything else?"

She felt rejected, her time was up and there was nothing more she could say.

"How much do I owe you?"

"Absolutely nothing, Kevin is a gifted vet, and I am delighted to be able to help his pretty wife. You are a lucky woman to have such a brave husband, imagine risking his own life to save an old woman from certain death. No doubt the good people of Redmills will honour him in due course."

She sighed.

"Thank you but I really don't think that Kevin would like a fuss."

He checked his large gold wristwatch impatiently.

"Now, just be proud that you are his woman,"

His words sickened her, she realized that he viewed her not as a separate individual but as an appendage of Kevin.

She heard herself say.

"Thank you but please don't tell him about my visit."

He put the top back on his fountain pen as he replied. "My lips are sealed."

"Thank you."

She took her handbag and walked with her head bowed from the room.

Outside, she located her bike and pedalled furiously down the winding avenue to the main street, almost colliding with the butcher's boy who was delivering the weekly order.

On returning home, she found Kevin lying on the couch coughing like someone in the grip of the flu. She thought of Dr Macey's words and decided to be kind to him at least at a surface level. She did not see any purpose to continue taking her food in the bedroom.

"Here, drink this it will help." She handed him a glass of water.

He swallowed hard.

"I am sorry about giving you the black eye, I don't feel like myself since the fire."

She straightened her shoulders.

"That fire must have been awful."

That's right appease him like a fool.

The nymph in her head seemed to sneer while he got into full flow.

"Words cannot describe that fire! Look, I have just had a phone call from my mother, she was alarmed when I told her about carrying Mrs Goff from the burning cottage, but I think I managed to allay her fears."

Evie drummed the top of the glass cabinet with her fingers.

"Did you mention about the beam hitting you?"

"No way! Are you mad! If I had told her, she would be on the next boat home from Hollyhead. And neither you nor I want that."

She looked at him quizzically.

"Evie, you know well that we never agreed since she married that upstart of an English shopkeeper, only a year after my poor father died."

She gave a cynical laugh.

"You were 14 years old when that happened, don't you think it's time to let it go?"

He sat up straight.

"Never! If she had cared about her two boys, she would not have dumped us in a boarding school and followed him to Manchester."

Evie was tidying away all the newspapers on the coffee table when she stopped abruptly.

Inwardly, she was raking over everything he said.

He acts the bully in our marriage because he distrusts women and feels that his own mother failed him.

"Look Kevin, she got a second chance at happiness and took it, who can blame her for that. And you visited her in England during holidays from school."

"It wasn't our home it was theirs, all full of pricey furniture and showy curtains. Not to mention his two princesses from his first marriage, totally spoiled."

She shrugged.

"Gordon is not short of money he has a big hardware store."

"To hell with the bollocks!" Kevin said as he put on his shoes.

Evie suppressed a response, at least they were back on speaking terms, to appease him she said.

"I hear that Mrs Goff was discharged from hospital this morning, without your intervention she would be in her grave."

"Yes, they are moving into a little house belonging to the Browns near the mill, Kieran told me it will be rent-free."

"They deserve it. Now, I must tackle this mountain of ironing."

She headed for the kitchen.

Go on admit it. You cannot stand being alone with him for more than five minutes.

She started to hum softly to herself as she took out the ironing board because it drowned out the voice in her head.

On Monday, she got a warm welcome from Iris when she returned to Richmond House.

"It's so good to have you back and thanks for all the work you sent over with Brendan."

Evie's face relaxed into a broad smile.

"It kept me out of mischief."

She eyed Evie suspiciously and then moved closer, scrutinising the bruising which had now faded to a faint shadow, thanks in part to some careful make-up techniques.

"My dear Evelyn you would tell me if there was anything wrong."

Evie, who was sitting behind her desk put down the box of paper clips that she had in her hand.

"I don't understand what you mean."

Iris plonked her rear end on the edge of a stool.

"I had a friend who used to appear every so often with strange bruises and marks, a high society lady I may add but she always excused them away, it was only after she died from cancer that her niece found a diary where she recorded all the abuse that she had endured in her marriage."

Evie shifted in her chair.

"How sad, why did she not leave him?"

"Indeed! Only she could have answered that one. Perhaps she was too loyal, too proud, too foolish, or simply could not bear to lose her lavish lifestyle."

"Was she long married to him?" Evie heard herself ask.

"12 or 13 years, it was his second marriage and her first."

"What a terrible life!"

Evie took the silver letter opener and slid it into the flap of a big white envelope.

Iris watched her from under her eyelashes.

"Well, I have said my piece. If you ever need help Evie or just want to talk, remember I am happy to oblige."

"Thank you, Iris. I am fine." Evie said calmly, but her head was reeling as a voice from there questioned her.

Why did you cover for him?

Iris departed for Dublin with her chauffeur at 4 pm. Once the black Zephyr car disappeared down the drive, Evie lifted the phone and rang Robert's number.

Eventually, after three or four attempts he answered the phone and they chatted for a few minutes, keeping the conversation casual. They agreed to meet in the Phoenix Hotel on the following Saturday at midday. When she replaced the receiver, her hand was shaking, and she chided herself for behaving like a schoolgirl.

Later, on the way home, she stopped for a few minutes by the old bridge over the river and watched as five boys rowed a boat downstream. She felt totally confused about Kevin, some days she hated him with a vengeance while at other moments she wondered if she still had some feelings for him, but she had never understood love properly because she had to admit that she had always confused a sense of security and being needed with love.

If your parents had not both died young would you have married Him?

Startled, by the approach of someone, she listened to the tapping of a walking stick on the stony surface of the road, as it came closer.

"Mrs Moore, do give my regards to your husband, so brave and so gentle when attending to the sickest of animals."

She turned around quickly to see a man with a ruddy complexion, lifting his hat to her.

The face looked familiar, but she could not put a name to it.

"Thank you," she said in a stiff tone.

Quickly, she jumped on her bike and cycled for home. She had no intention of listening to some old culchie extolling the virtues of her husband.

Kevin Moore, you might be everyone's hero but I have seen your two faces.

Chapter Nine

At the AGM of the Redmills Drama Society in the town hall on the following Monday, all eyes were on Evie because of her brave husband. Tom Mc Connell opened his address by asking Evie to convey the best wishes of every member of the Drama circle to her husband.

On behalf of the members, Tom presented her with a vintage bottle of brandy and a box of the finest cigars to be given to Kevin.

"I think it is true to say that everyone here has seen at first hand the kindness and dedication of this man called Kevin Moore, initially as a vet and now as a neighbour and civic-minded member of our community. Given that he is still suffering from his injuries we decided not to make a fuss but instead present this small token of our affection to you, to be passed on to your dear husband."

Stepping up onto the stage to accept the gift she blinked rapidly as she shook hands with him and then looked down at the animated faces sitting in rows in front of her. She took a few moments to compose her thoughts before speaking, while a hush fell on the assembled group. There were at least 60 people present that night including the patrons and casual supporters of RDS (Redmills Drama Society) who usually attended the AGM. The Catholic curate and the parish priest were in the front row along with Dr Macey, the Garda Sergeant, and the Church of Ireland Minister the Very Reverend Charles Campbell. While the following three rows comprised members of the local business community who gave generously to the Society.

Clearing her throat, she began.

"Reverend Fathers, Ladies and gentlemen. I am very moved by your thoughtfulness and generosity and I know that Kevin will be too. May I convey his thanks to each one of you for this gift? Kevin is indeed a great vet and a good neighbour."

She paused, glanced at Dr Macey, who was staring back at her with an inscrutable countenance and then continued.

"And of course, a good husband."

A ripple of laughter and a few whistles followed. When the noise died down, she went on.

"I think it true to say that anyone would have done what he did if they heard a neighbour in trouble. Thank you all once again."

Suddenly a flashbulb, then a second and a third one startled her as the photographer from the local paper captured the scene for posterity.

Applause followed while she returned to her seat beside Helen Jones, with a smile on her face which did not reach her eyes. In truth, her head was reeling from this unexpected outpouring of public affection for Kevin and it only served to compound her own guilty feelings about how she was treating him since the fire.

You must make allowances for someone with any kind of head injury

The sentence seemed to swim around and around in her head for the rest of the evening as she barely took in what the other speakers were saying. The chairman reappointed the same committee with just one exception and then went on to outline the current state of the Drama Society's finances which needed an injection of cash before the players could commence rehearsals for their latest production.

Helen nudged her at one point and whispered.

"Don't forget we would love you to take a bigger part this year."

Remember that Kevin will not approve of his wife taking a bigger role and displaying herself.

The voice in her head issued a warning.

She leaned closer to Helen.

"I don't think so, not with - Kevin still feeling off colour."

Helen mouthed into her ear.

"Sorry, for being so thoughtless."

She nodded, the last thing she needed was more abuse from Kevin over an inconsequential part in some drama production. Tom had indicated that he was considering one of Brendan Behan's less controversial plays, amended

of course for the sensitive ears of a small town like Redmills.

The following morning, she rose early and cooked a
large omelette for Kevin. At 8.am there was still no sign of
him, so she called him several times and eventually he came
straight to the breakfast table, in his pyjamas.

"How are you feeling today?"

She left the plate of food in front of him.

He rubbed the stubble on his chin with his right hand.

"Rotten, my head is pounding but those pills make me
sleep."

"I am sorry to hear that, Kevin do you not think that
you should take a few days off work to give your body a
chance to heal?"

"For God's sake woman, I am needed at work, it is a
busy practise and stretches into parts of Westmeath. Andrew
cannot afford to pay me and put a locum in my place too!"

She buttered a slice of toast and then licked her finger.

"The Drama Society had a presentation for you last
night in absentia, in honour of your bravery. Everyone was
there for the A. G.M. even a photographer, so they gave
me a bottle of vintage brandy and a box of cigars for you."

She pointed to the top of the press where she had left
them the previous night.

He looked puzzled.

"Why not ask me to attend if it was about me?"

"Tom said that as you are still recovering from injuries
sustained in the fire that they decided not to make a fuss,

it is just a token of their regard for you. And you are not actually a member of the Drama Society."

For a few minutes, silence fell on the room, then he coughed loudly, and she fiddled with the cutlery on her plate where eggs lay.

The next thing she saw was a salt cellar hurtling past her before it crashed on the floor.

"Goddam you! You must have told them about my headaches."

"I swear to you Kevin that I did not tell anyone, I did not spread the word."

She stood up, intending to refill the teapot with boiling water but he jumped up and seized her by her ponytail which she had hurriedly tied while preparing the breakfast.

"Don't lie to me, I know that you wanted the limelight for yourself and told them not to invite me last night."

She tried to loosen his grip, but he tightened it and pushed back her head as he stared into her face, reminding her of a dog with a bone.

"Let go of my ponytail."

"Tell the truth, you told them that I was not up to the presentation!"

"On my parents' graves I swear to you that I did not do so, perhaps it was Dr Macey."

His grip loosened and she pulled away from him.

"Oh, that old fool! He cannot even cure my cough let alone my headache. If I had a horse or bullock with these symptoms, I would have got to the bottom of it all weeks ago."

She decided to go along with him.

"I know, he is getting old and I suspect will retire in a year or two."

He returned to the table and held out his cup.

"Give me another cup of tea."

She refilled the teapot and poured tea into two fresh cups.

"There we go."

Then she placed one in front of him.

His tone had softened as he patted her hand.

"Evelyn, I am sorry for losing my temper, all these headaches and bouts of coughing, it is enough to send a man to an early grave."

She looked into his eyes and saw a flash of the old, familiar Kevin that she had fallen for when they first met.

"Everything will be all right in time, you work too hard. I am so proud of you and indeed so is the whole town."

She left her hand on his shoulder.

"Put yourself first for a change, not the animals or Andrew's practice."

He pulled her onto his knee and kissed her, gently at first.

She found her lips responding to his and then he put his hand on her breast roughly and she drew back.

"Oh Kevin, you know that I have to be at work shortly, and I am still in my nightdress."

"All the better, less clothes to take off."

He said hoarsely as he began to undo the buttons.

She protested and drew back.

"Please Kevin I don't want to make love now, I have to go."

He laughed loudly.

"We know you don't mean that. You are just too prudish to admit that you like some rumpy bumpy."

She pushed him in the ribs and shouted.

"Get the hell away from me, when I say no, I mean no."

He grabbed her by the waist and planted sticky kisses on her cheek.

She heard herself saying.

"Stop."

She could not match his strength when he forced her back against the wall.

Suddenly, the ringing of the phone echoed throughout the house.

Distracted for a moment, she managed to push him away and escape from his clutches.

"A man can't get any relief."

He kicked the skirting board before heading for the phone in the hallway.

She walked to the kitchen and mechanically filled the sink with dirty dishes.

He stood framed in the doorway, shouting.

"Some fucker on the phone trying to sell me veterinary products, he read about me and the fire in the paper."

"Hmm – that's an opportunist."

She did not turn around but kept stacking delft on the draining board.

"You are so smug! But trying to get my conjugal rights from you is like poking a dead fish."

For several seconds all she could hear was the sound of pigeons cooing in the trees, suddenly a great tidal wave of anger hit her.

"You treat me like a piece of meat."

He guffawed.

"It's time you got rid of your pathetic romantic notions about marriage, did you seriously think it was about giving you boxes of chocolates with pictures of idyllic English cottages and a squeeze or two of your tits. I am doing nothing wrong you are my wife."

A silent tear slid down her face.

"You are a brute!"

She watched as his mouth fell open and then he shuffled down the hallway, but she heard him mutter.

"You are not the only woman in the world!"

"You bastard!"

He gave a deep cynical laugh.

Two hours later, at the very moment that Evie had finished applying make-up for her days work at Richmond House, Iris burst into the office. She had a pencil and notebook poised in her hand.

"Evelyn, you are exactly 75 minutes late."

In a hushed voice, Evie said.

"It's Kevin since the fire he is permanently angry with me and he has constant headaches and fits of coughing. I am so sorry Iris I will make up for the lost time this evening and work late."

Iris sat back in a swivel chair and pointed at her to take a seat at the window.

"Now tell me, I have a sixth sense for marital matters. All has not been well between you and that man for some time."

Suddenly, tears flowed, despite her best efforts to hide her worries and Iris handed her some tissues.

"Take it slowly."

"He shouts at me over the slightest thing, and he thinks nothing of hurting me."

"Hurting you?" Iris sat up straight.

"Yes. I lied to you about my black eye, he hit me with his fist over an argument I had with Mrs Byrne, who runs the newsagents shop."

"I knew it! I knew that you were covering for him."

Iris took two cigarettes from a packet. Then she gave one to Evie and placed the second in a long slim holder while Evie fiddled with the silver lighter on the desk and after a few seconds, lit them.

"I am sorry to burden you with my domestic problems."

"Don't be ridiculous! I want to help. Was he ever abusive before the fire?"

Evie hesitated.

Iris held the expensive cigarette holder at an angle between her two fingers as she declared.

"Anything you say to me here in this room stays in this room."

"Yes, from time to time but not as frequently as in recent weeks, maybe just a few times a year." Evie conceded.

"Give me an example of something before the fire."

"Well, just before I took my week's leave he bruised my arm in an argument because he insisted on going down to his brother in Cork for some fishing while I had to while away the time in Dublin with Val my friend."

Iris shook her head in dismay

"It's appalling behaviour, especially from someone who should know better. Tell me, how is he in the bedroom?"

Evie's shoulders shook for a few moments before she whispered.

"He -is very rough -and insists on his conjugal rights but - Dr Macy says that I must give in to Kevin and all his demands … yet every time -I feel violated as if I have been attacked by some stranger, he is totally self-centred ."

Iris exploded.

"These bloody men and their needs! It's like a conspiracy, as if women were put on this earth purely to satisfy the sexual demands of men. Are we still in the stone age when men just took what they wanted from women without a thought for their feelings or needs?"

Evie rocked back and forth, now, and then taking a puff from her cigarette.

"Most days I hate him and then I try to imagine leaving him, and it seems like a huge hurdle – as you know my parents are dead and my brother disappeared at 17 years of age."

Iris stubbed out her cigarette.

"Don't worry about your brother after all these years, you must prioritise your own well- being and needs. You will feel better for getting Kevin's abuse off your chest and sharing it with me. I want to help if I can and day or night feel free to contact me if you are in danger."

Evie dried her eyes with a fresh tissue.

"Thank you so much."

"Now, you must freshen up and I will send for some of cook's delicious fruitcake with strong coffee and a little cognac on the side."

"Thank you so much for everything."

Evie picked up her face- powder compact and lipstick.

Iris gave her one of her generous smiles that were famous for lighting up a whole room.

"One last thing my dear Evelyn, please mind yourself through all of this."

Evie fiddled with the tube of lipstick.

"Do you think that he needs a psychiatrist or a specialist in actual head injuries?"

"I have no idea, but he needs help. Now, let me lift this phone and get some sustenance from the kitchen. And in the circumstances, there is no need for you to work late in lieu of time missed."

Evie took a few deep breaths.

"Iris you are so kind to me and so thoughtful, I appreciate your help with such a delicate matter, already I don't feel so bad now that I have shared it with you."

"Not at all, I am happy that you were able to trust me. Just don't tell any of my fan club members that I am a big softie as my readers like to see me as one of those inaccessible writers who live in their own cossetted world."

Evie laughed.

"Yes, I know they like to see you as some type of movie star, exuding glamour, money and an air of mystery."

Iris put her finger to her lips, playfully.

"Shush! Don't destroy my image!"

Chapter Ten

Evie launched herself into her work with gusto for the remainder of the week, hoping to impress Iris with her work ethic despite all the problems with Kevin. And it worked, Iris was so pleased that the mountain of paperwork on the spare desk had been cleared that she readily agreed to give a talk to Orla's group in the Library.

On Thursday, in Wilson's restaurant hidden away from the main street, Evie and Orla met for lunch. They chose the set menu, lamb cutlets with cabbage and potatoes but the food was disappointing and so they ordered a large dessert of apple pie and cream followed by coffee to wash away the lingering taste of grease. Nevertheless, both women were in great form because they exchanged good news with each other. Orla's face glowed as she recounted how her plans to silence Mrs Byrne and the Feeney family had gone like clockwork.

"Don't worry Evelyn, you won't have any more trouble from Hilary Byrne or her co-conspirators. Fr. Gandon saw to that!"

"Thank you so much," Evie said.

"By the way, I got the money you left at the desk and it too has found a home. Mrs Byrne agreed to give ten shillings to the library and ten shillings towards the upkeep of the church."

Evie threw her head back and laughed loudly.

"I have good news for you too. Mrs Ryder-Lee will give a free talk in your library on the first Wednesday in November, but you must ensure that all your literary acquaintances attend as well as a few politicians. She will have my guts for garters if no one of note turns up, of course, I will inform all the newspapers."

"Consider it done! And thank you too. It is a major coup to get such a prestigious writer. It will put Redmills on the map and hopefully will help me to get a grant from Meath County Council to expand the collection of books and services I can offer. I will make sure that some of the county councillors are in attendance."

"Fingers crossed," Evie replied.

"I also intend to write to Jack Lynch, Minister for Education and request that a representative from his Department graces us with his presence. I mentioned to you before about my plans to start up a literacy scheme where voluntary tutors will be assigned to individuals to teach them basic reading and writing. I never cease to be shocked by the numbers who have left school without skills you and I take for granted."

"Certainly, there are many people locally in that position. I have heard Kevin talking about farmers who can read but cannot write and vice versa. Orla, count me in on your scheme, I would be happy to help out one evening a week."

"Perfect. I will keep you informed," Orla said as she stubbed out her cigarette.

No sooner had Evie arrived home from work that evening to prepare dinner, than the back door swung open and Kevin entered, looking dishevelled and weary.

"I had to go back to the doctor today for stronger painkillers, my head was bursting by the time I had finished in Kennelly's farm."

Evie felt like a weight had been lifted from her shoulders.

"I am glad that you went. Are the new tablets starting to work?"

His facial muscles relaxed.

"Put it this way, I feel human again. He is sending me back to the hospital on Monday for chest x-rays because of the wheezy cough. However, if these tablets don't help long term with the pain, I will have to see a specialist in Dublin. I am off work until Tuesday, I broke the news to Andrew, but he was fine about it."

She took a deep breath.

"That's all positive. Mrs Ryder-Lee asked me to pass on "her regards" to you."

He stared at her through eyes like slits and for a few moments, she thought that he was about to erupt in anger.

I must not let it slip that I discussed his mood swings with Iris.

"Did you discuss my health with that old bitch?"

Her heart pounded.

"No, I did not but I resent you calling her an old bitch."

He coughed up phlegm which he wiped away with a handkerchief and then he pointed a finger in her direction.

"Who told her about me?"

She grabbed the two newspapers that she had purchased on her way home and held them up triumphantly.

"Well, the Meath Chronicle and the Redmills Champion have a piece about you on the front page, both also mention that you are recovering from a blow to the head as well as smoke inhalation."

"Give me those papers." He snapped them from her and read through them quickly."

"Evelyn, they also printed a photograph of you, you remind me of a doe caught in headlights."

She leaned across his shoulder.

"I know, I was shocked that they decided to make a presentation to me on your behalf at the Drama Society."

He snorted.

"Well, at least my mugshot isn't splayed across the paper. I am sick of everyone fussing about my health, I just want things to go back to normal."

"And they will."

She patted his arm and then began to fold the newspapers which he had dropped onto the chair.

"I rue the day I ever went near that inferno and carried out that old biddy."

"Ah Kevin, you don't mean that!"

"I bloody well do! Mrs Goff is sitting in her new rent-free home enjoying the life of Reilly while I drag my weary bones around."

"Trust me, you will recover if you follow all the medical advice."

"Hmm. You sound like my boss, Andrew gave me the same lecture, now at least that old twit of a doctor is trying his best to help me."

She fixed her keen hazel eyes on him.

"The whole community accepts that your act was a very heroic one and so every person you meet is just trying to help you in their own inimitable way."

He wheezed loudly for a few seconds before exclaiming sarcastically.

"Evelyn Moore, soothsayer and diplomat!"

"You know I am just speaking the truth," she observed.

He rubbed his temple.

"Evie can you make me a strong whiskey, I just want to forget about all my problems."

She hesitated.

"Should you be mixing alcohol with tablets?"

"Let me be the judge of that, I know what I am doing. Put a double measure into the glass and plenty of sugar with cloves."

"Right, coming up! I will have your favourite dinner in about an hour, floury spuds, turnip and fried steak."

A sneering whisper inside her said.

Licking his boots now!

"Nice! That should fill out my skinny carcass."

He remarked, as he padded into the sitting room to rest.

She watched from the corner of her eye and when she saw his bent shoulders her conscience nagged her.

The man is clearly ill.

On Saturday morning, she rose early and prepared food to keep him going while she was in Dublin. She insisted on bringing him breakfast and he ate it propped up in bed with several pillows.

Later, when she went to collect the tray, he was smiling.

"Thanks, Evelyn, that was very tasty, there is nothing like scrambled eggs and toast, I will get up later and check on the cattle."

"No problem. It is great to see you taking it easy for a change, you really do need a few days rest in bed."

He shrugged.

"Well, I have plenty of reading to keep me going. Andrew gave me a pile of Veterinary journals from England to peruse while I am off work. Eradicating Bovine TB is a big challenge, we need more money poured into this area of research."

"You will have to write to the Minister for Agriculture and see what happens."

She said glibly as she picked up his shirt from the floor. She was aware that he was studying her dark green suit and her high- necked green blouse.

"How come you are all dressed up in your best business attire?"

She moved to open the curtains.

Be careful! Keep your tone casual and don't overexplain.

"Do you remember that parcel I got from Dublin from a friend of Mrs Ryder Lee?"

He smirked as he rearranged his pillows.

"The idiot that has to get you to type out his own notes before he can read them?"

"Yes. Well, he wants to meet with me in Dublin today to discuss the whole project, he is planning two books, one on his case notes in Africa and the other on his travels across Kenya. I am getting the 9.50 train to Kingsbridge. I booked a hackney he should be here in thirty minutes."

She stooped to get the breakfast tray from the floor where he had left it and then headed for the door.

"The lucky git! I would love a trip across the African plains, imagine all the wildlife."

His eyes had a faraway look.

She paused and decided to humour him.

"Someday, maybe we could go on a safari when we retire."

He exhaled.

"Keep on dreaming!"

Changing the subject, she said,

"I have plenty of food prepared for you, you will just need to warm it up in the electric cooker."

"Good, thanks, Evelyn. Do you know that I was in a farmer's house yesterday where they still have not been connected to the main supply of electricity?"

She pursed her lips.

"But surely there are hundreds of homes scattered across the countryside in similar circumstances, not every household was able to avail themselves of the Rural Electrification Scheme."

He threw back his head.

"Of course, that is true but this farmer in question has plenty of good land and livestock not to mention his money, piled up in a bank."

"He cannot take it with him when he dies."

Inside her, an elated voice was murmuring.

He suspects nothing about your trip to Dublin.

He said softly.

"Evie, I am sorry if I have been rough with you recently, I was not feeling well but this new medication is giving me hope."

She gave him her best smile.

"That is great news, now have a good rest, I must hurry."

Get out of this room now before he demands sex, be wary of his soft voice.

She escaped from the room almost falling over a pair of mucky shoes that he had left in the hallway.

"Bring a raincoat! It looks like there is a lot of rain on the way," he called to her.

"Yes, thanks for the reminder."

She shouted back as she went down the stairs. A sense of excitement was making her feel like a young girl again, now that she had a whole day with Robert in Dublin ahead of her.

She rushed through the wash-up and then filled a briefcase with a bundle of freshly typed notes for Robert. She also managed to squeeze in a crisp white linen blouse with delicate frills on the short sleeves and a v neckline. Once she was on the train, she would swap this in the toilets for the dark drab blouse which she was wearing, she hated the spinsterish appearance which it gave her when combined with the suit. However, she had been wary of wearing the pretty white one with the revealing neckline in front of Kevin lest he grew suspicious.

When the black hackney arrived, she took a final look in the mirror and applied thick black mascara, which Iris had gifted her, from New York.

Then gathering her handbag and briefcase, she rushed outside, allowing the door to bang in her wake. Her heart was thumping loudly.

Acting like a teenager, afraid that your parents will see you wearing a blouse which reveals too much cleavage.

When the driver opened the car door, she gave him a big smile which revealed nothing of her inner turmoil.

"Perfect timing! Thank you."

"Yes, I try my best. The weather forecast is good you have picked the right day for a trip to the city,"

He revved the engine.

" I love the city," she replied.

Then she sank back into the leather seat and she felt her worries dissipate as the car reached the gateway and turned onto the main road.

Chapter Eleven

Robert was waiting for her on the platform when she alighted from the train.

At first, she did not recognise him dressed in grey well-pressed trousers with a navy jacket and a blue shirt, he looked like some distinguished diplomat.

"Evelyn, how are you?"

In the crowds rushing past, she had walked by him without a second glance.

Turning around, she saw those unmistakable blue eyes twinkling at her.

"Robert! I thought we had agreed to meet in the Phoenix."

He nodded.

"You are right but they have a wedding reception there in the early afternoon and preparations are in full swing so I thought that I would meet you here instead."

He kissed her on both cheeks in the French manner of "la bise."

Immediately, the spicy scent of aftershave filled her nostrils.

"What a good idea! Who wants to get caught up in the minutiae of someone else's wedding?"

He smiled sardonically.

"Indeed, enough to have endured one's own wedding!"

They both laughed.

"You look lovely Evelyn."

"Thank you, Robert, you don't look so bad yourself!"

She eyed his grey-black hair and sky- blue eyes. Then she noticed that he was growing a moustache and she teased him.

"Am I right in saying that you are growing a Ronnie?"

"Indeed, I am hoping it might take the attention away from my head of grey hair because my facial hair is still black."

"Vanity, Vanity!" She exclaimed.

He winked at her.

"I think that we should head outside, it is so stuffy in here with all these passengers milling around."

"Good, the train was packed, there is a replay match in Croke Park at 3.30 between two minor hurling teams from Meath and Cavan."

He rolled his eyes.

"There is nothing like youth! Please allow me to carry your briefcase, my car is just parked outside. I am hoping that you might agree to take a drive out to Dun Laoghaire with me."

Her heartfelt fluttery and she hesitated.

What is he suggesting!

Then in a tremulous voice, she said.

"I typed up some of your notes and I have a few ideas about your proposed book, but I will need to get the 5.35 train home."

Throwing his shoulders back he chortled.

"Don't worry I am not suggesting anything untoward! I am proposing that we chat about my stuff over a nice lunch in the Royal Marine Hotel and afterwards we can take a walk along the pier before I drop you back here."

How foolish, thinking that he wanted to seduce you like some Regency heroine.

"What a lovely idea!"

She was trying hard to hide the emotion in her voice.

He left his hand on her shoulder and smiled.

"Right, that's agreed, follow me."

Outside, the sun was shining in a cloudless blue sky. Soon, they had left the congestion of the city centre behind, and as they sped along the main artery to Dun Laoghaire in Robert's cream coloured Volkswagen beetle car, he pressed a button which released the "soft top".

When the sea air rushed in and Evie turned up the collar of her jacket, Robert shouted above the noise of the wind.

"Are you ok?"

She held back tendrils of hair with her hand which were blowing into her face and shouted at the top of her voice.

"Never better! I did not realize that this car is a convertible!"

"It suits you, you look just like a movie star."

She did not hear him as she closed her eyes and allowed her mind to wander, while the wind played with her hair.

This is living not just walking on eggshells all the time with Kevin.

In the hotel foyer, people were standing around in small groups chatting. A large number of priests in flowing black cassocks with three-peaked birettas were queuing to enter the conference hall while a handful of obese American tourists, bedecked in gaudy slacks and Aran jumpers were waiting to board a bus for some sightseeing in Wicklow.

"Hell is other people,"

Robert whispered as they made for a snug corner of the big lounge where two armchairs and a table were perched near a bay window.

"What a panoramic view of the harbour!"

Evie feasted her eyes on the boats before taking a seat.

"Yes. I think we won't bother with the dining room at all, we can have the food served here."

Robert looked around at their fellow diners who were all engrossed in conversation.

Evie agreed as she took off her jacket.

"I don't want a full lunch."

A smartly dressed waiter appeared and took their order of smoked salmon on brown bread with salad and a large pot of coffee. They decided to concentrate on Robert's business first and leave the afternoon free to go for a walk along the pier. His eyes lit up as he flicked through the thirty pages of typed notes which she presented to him.

"You will see that I am working on a dual system. Pages relating to medical matters have a green asterisk at the top while those pertaining to travel, or your musings have a yellow asterisk." Evie explained.

"Simple but ingenious! I found several more notebooks filled with scribblings from my African days which need to be managed by your capable hands."

He gave her a wry smile.

"No worries at all, post them on to me in batches. And many thanks for your generous cheque, there really was no need."

"I cannot expect you to work for nothing. Now that order has been put on these early notes, I am fired up about writing a book or two. Indeed, I think that I should scrap the stuff which I wrote last year and start from scratch."

"Good idea! Given, that I am fresh to all your notes and observations, I can see clearly that you have the makings of two totally different books or perhaps even three."

"Three!" He repeated incredulously.

"Yes. Medical, travel, and a book of musings."

"Musings? I am not sure what you mean."

Well, do you have any photographs from your years in Africa?"

"Yes, I bought an expensive camera while I was on holiday in South Africa, but I am not sure how many photos are good enough to publish."

"Don't worry about that, from my time with Mrs Ryder-Lee I have learned that anything is possible with a good imagination."

He coughed.

"Sorry but I have a hopeless imagination, I blame it on the fact that my family for generations have all been in medicine."

"It doesn't really matter about the photos as you can always pay a good illustrator to brighten up pages in the third book with wildlife scenes. My boss has published two illustrated books on the botanical world."

"Really, but I think of her as a novelist."

Evie fiddled with a delicate gold chain at her neck.

"Iris, as I call her, has many strings to her bow. She studied art and botanical illustration in London before deciding that she wanted to be a writer."

"That woman is multi-talented," he remarked.

Then the waiter appeared with all their requirements balanced on a tray. When he had departed, she poured the coffee into two white cups edged with the logo of the hotel in gold letters.

"Good food and good company."

Robert observed as he tucked into a large open smoked salmon sandwich.

Two hours later, after he had paid the bill along with a generous tip, they left the shade of the hotel and went out into the bright sunshine.

Suddenly he planted a kiss on her lips.

"I have been wanting to do that all morning."

She looked deep into his eyes.

"Why don't you do it again?"

His kiss this time was a lingering one which made her want even more but they were right in the middle of the footpath, and they had to stop when a frosty woman with a walking stick approached and waved it at them.

"You are causing an obstruction in a public place! Disgraceful behaviour."

They both laughed when she shuffled off.

At his invitation, she held his arm as they made a pathway through the crowds on the pier. Whole families, couples, children, and mischievous dogs competed for space while they enjoyed the Indian summer. At the far end, hidden from the hurly-burly of icecream sellers, jugglers and three-card-trick men, they found a bench in the shade of a large rock.

Nearby, two men were observing the seascape through binoculars and in the distance the mail boat was ploughing its way through deep dark green water to Hollyhead. While a flotilla of small boats was bobbing about on the horizon.

"This is like heaven."

Evie sighed loudly as seagulls wheeled overhead.

"Your mood has changed, have you something on your mind?" He ventured.

"It's nothing."

She nervously tightened the green slides helping to hold her hair in a bun.

"Come now, tell me."

She looked for a moment into his face and then turned towards the sea again to hide a tear that had escaped from her left eye.

"Look, it's a long story, Kevin was injured when he rescued an old woman from a blazing cottage. He has been pushing me to the limits of endurance ever since."

"Perhaps I can help in some way, after all, I am a medical doctor despite my appalling note keeping!"

His attempt at a joke failed as her face remained solemn.

She frowned.

"It is good to talk with someone who has no connection with either Redmills or Kevin because down there he has been canonised but to tell the truth, he is like the devil when he goes into one of his rages."

He reached across and held her hand.

"Let it all out in your own time, I am a good listener."

For a couple of minutes, the tears flowed while he remained silent and just stroked her hand. Then she dried her face and began at the night of the fire.

When she had finished, she gave a desolate smile.

"Now you know!"

Her mind was still racing as she had left out whole chunks about Kevin's sexual demands.

He let go of her hand and stood up to have a better view of the sea, but she realized when he turned back to face her that he was deep in thought.

"Evelyn, I am just appalled by his behaviour, but I am not really surprised."

Her mouth fell open with shock.

"I don't understand."

"Well, that day on the train when I noticed the bruising on your arm with the finger marks, I guessed that he had done it to you despite the cock and bull story you told me about him saving you from a bullock. You see I have heard every excuse under the sun about domestic abuse. It is also the reason that I did not keep my word and send you on the name of my colleague who works in gynaecology – now is not the time for you to be seeking tests for childlessness."

She turned crimson in the face.

"I am sorry for the lies."

"Don't be sorry, be concerned about yourself. Some men are abusive to their partners anyway even without sustaining a head injury. Now, not for one minute am I condoning their behaviour, because both in Africa and In Ireland I have seen horrific injuries inflicted on wives by their husbands and boyfriends."

"Most days I feel that I am the only one suffering in this way."

"Domestic violence is quite common, but it is all swept under the carpet by the women themselves who are afraid not only of further violence but of losing their children, home, and financial security."

"I felt ashamed that it was happening to me and now this awful head injury has made it ten times worse."

"Yes, the head injury has compounded the aggression but what we need is a change in the law to protect women and to look after their physical and mental welfare."

She raised her eyebrows.

"It's a man's world and it is so hard to swim against that current. Doctors, priests, all favour husbands."

"I agree. My colleague, Eoin told me about two heart-wrenching cases recently. The former involved collusion between a husband and the local priest who were successful in having his wife committed to a mental institution on the grounds of insanity. The latter case involved a woman sustaining serious back injuries after being flung down a set of stairs by her errant husband, yet despite the case going to court it was thrown out as his legal team brought in a line of fake witnesses to say she had been drinking heavily on the night in question."

She exhaled slowly.

"Those are dreadful stories. Sometimes, I thank God that I have no children to witness his shocking behaviour."

"Evie, forgive my probing questions but I only want to help. Has he raped you?"

For a few minutes, only the distant shouts of children mingling with the cries of sea birds could be heard.

Then she said quietly.

"Yes, although I never thought of it as rape before … he has always been savage in the bedroom but since the fire, it is worse - I tried to mention it to his doctor - he said that given Kevin has a head injury, I must meet all his needs."

He tut-tutted and put his arms around her shoulders.

"Nonsense, you must be careful, think of your own safety. He needs to see a specialist in neurotrauma."

She rummaged for a packet of cigarettes in her handbag and offered one to him which he declined. However, he lit her cigarette with a gold lighter from his pocket.

She took a few puffs and then spoke.

"I cannot believe that I have told you about the intimate details of my marriage, but you are a medical doctor. I know that he must see a specialist. Now, his own doctor is helping him to accept this fact."

"It is imperative that Kevin gets the right treatment."

He fiddled with a gold cufflink in the shape of a lion that had come loose.

"That is so beautiful. Allow me to help you with it."

When it was secured, he said.

"Look Evelyn, I know it was difficult for you to talk about the sexual aspects of your relationship with Kevin but at least now that you have opened up about all the abuse, you have discovered that there are others like you. This will give you strength to do something about it."

"What do you mean?" She asked.

"The decision must be yours, perhaps you will seek further help for your marriage. Perhaps you will decide to leave him. The important point is that you are aware of choices, you do not need to stay in an abusive relationship and just endure the suffering until something awful happens."

She threw the butt of her cigarette on the ground and stamped out the last glow from it with her foot.

"Thank you, you have been most helpful. I am tired of pussy-footing around him."

On their way back along the pier, she held his arm and his face glowed as he talked about his love of the sea. Suddenly, they were aware of a flashbulb and then another as a roving photographer took their photos.

"Move in closer together, you make such a handsome couple."

A tall photographer with the gift of the gab persuaded them to pose for three more.

Evie laughed at the contorted faces that Robert was pulling at the camera but eventually he gave in, put his arm around her and smiled.

"Perfecto!" The photographer aped a Spanish accent.

When he had taken Robert's name and address, and promised to post on the photos, he stole a quick look at Evie's gold wedding band.

"I meant it when I said that you and your lovely wife make a beautiful couple - so photogenic."

Robert handed him a stack of half-crowns, while he exchanged a wink with Evie.

"Go along now and find a few more fools to photograph before I change my mind about that tip."

The man smirked.

"Thank you so much, sir."

They left him to gather his equipment while they strode off hand in hand but as they reached the car, Robert's face grew serious.

"Evelyn, I want to say one last thing before we head for the train station."

She gave him a look of apprehension.

"Ok."

"I am giving you my home phone number again just in case you have mislaid it. Carry it with you at all times and if you ever need urgent help call me."

"Thank you, you are so kind."

"Also, as you go deeper into my notes you will see that I have written about trips I took with a woman called Karen, a freelance writer and poet."

She waved her hand dismissively in the air.

"That is none of my business, no need to say any more."

"Oh, I think there is! You see we lived together for almost two years … she is American and had been divorced for several years at that time, so she wanted us to marry but I did not wish to commit to her. After all, I got married too young and I value my freedom."

She bit her lip.

"I still fail to see why you want to tell me all this."

He grimaced.

" I am making heavy weather out of it I know. Since I returned to Ireland well-meaning men and women, in my wider circle tend to see me as a lovesick widower. And they try to match-make by seating eligible ladies beside me at dinner parties."

For a few minutes, there was silence.

Does he think that you are pursuing him?

Then she cleared her throat and spoke in a matter-of-fact voice.

"That must be so annoying for you. Anyone should know that an attractive man like you can find a new wife if he wants one."

"Exactly! "

"Anyway, to get back to basics, the whole point in me telling you all this is so that you will not be afraid to seek temporary refuge in my home if you ever need it, because quite simply I will not pounce on you like a prowling lion."

A smile of amusement crossed her face.

"Now, I understand why you told me about your love life in Africa. Thank you for your offer of help, I shall bear it in mind."

He looked at her closely.

"Good. I really enjoy your company and I find you very attractive, but I am aware that you have a marriage to sort out, and I do not want to come between a husband and wife."

Her heart seemed to tick loudly.

"Thank you, Robert."

He inclined his head slightly which made him seem like a puppy appealing for attention.

"Of course, you are a godsend in terms of my book proposals and preparation for publishing, and I am looking forward to working with you for a long time to come, but I have to confess that I am drawn... "

She walked around to his side of the car and put a finger on his lips.

"Shh... I know how you feel .... despite all my problems. I was so delighted when you sent me those flowers although I put them on my parents grave because hell would have opened if Kevin saw them."

" I just had to send them even though I knew you could not take them home."

They hugged for a moment and then he kissed her passionately on the lips and she returned his kisses.

Minutes later, she drew back and exclaimed.

" So much for clearing the air!"

He stroked her cheek.

"Easier said than done!"

She could not resist kissing him again, but he said.

"Let me get you back to Kingsbridge in time, we don't want that husband of yours kicking off because you have missed the last direct train to Redmills for today."

An expression like a dark cloud covered her face as she got into the passenger seat.

"Robert, you are right, I cannot miss that train. Thank you for a wonderful day.

"Thank you, my lovely Eve-lyn!"

His voice was full of emotion as he reversed out of the parking space quickly. She secretly admired his spotless fingernails which were well-manicured in marked contrast to Kevin who always seemed to have dirt under his nails and weather-worn hands.

Chapter Twelve

The following Monday afternoon was so humid that they flung open every window in the office wing at Richmond House. Still, there was not a puff of air and little rivulets of sweat slid down Evie's face and chest. Mrs Higgins arrived with an old noisy fan and placed it in the centre of the office but even that seemed to have little or no effect on the sticky conditions.

It was a great relief when the Art Deco clock announced 4pm with light tinkles.

"Anyone for some chilled lemonade and a slice of Victoria sandwich cake?"

Cook bustled in with a tray and left it on a side table.

"Thank you, Mrs Butler, why don't you take an hour off and rest outside in the shade," Iris said.

"Right, if you say so."

When she had gone Iris shook her head in exasperation.

"That woman, she always has to play the martyr, I shall put her in my next novel."

Evie laughed and then chose a slice of cake.

"I will be as fat as a fool if I continue to eat like this."

"Never mind, you have a lovely figure. Now pour as much lemonade as you like, it will cool you down," Iris directed.

Then they both moved to the bay window and sat on the large window seat.

Eating in silence, they gazed out at the broad expanse of fields where horses grazed and now and again swished flies away with their long tails.

Abruptly, the shrill ringing of the phone disturbed their peace and made Iris jump.

"It never stops! Finish your slice of Victoria sponge, they can always ring back."

Iris directed, as she probed the last few crumbs on her plate with a small silver fork.

Evie stood up automatically.

"Are you sure? I don't mind!"

"Look here you have spent the last 50 minutes taking shorthand dictation from me, your brain needs a rest."

"Thanks, Iris, it is such a lovely scene."

She sat down again and resumed eating her cake.

Iris feasted her eyes on a grey mare at the edge of the horizon.

" I have been around horses all my life. I think what I find most calming about them is their ability to put their heads down and just get on with the business of chomping grass."

Evie wiped a tear from her eye.

Animals are wonderful, I still miss my darling dog Leo he was so loyal and so funny."

"That shooting was a dreadful business! Remind me why that idiot shot him."

Iris brushed off cake crumbs from her pale pink dress.

"Oh, it was lambing season and some dogs from the town came out and worried his sheep. So, he just went around the whole locality early one morning and shot every dog that was not tied up."

" The brute!" Iris exclaimed.

"The worst part was that Leo always slept in the hall at night in a big basket, and Kevin had only let him out a few minutes earlier. As you know Kevin is kind to all animals domesticated, wild or otherwise."

Iris shooed a big bumblebee out the window with her napkin.

"Yes, I know. It's such a pity that you won't get another dog."

Evie shook her head.

"No. It's still too raw, that was only last February. Somehow, I could not bear another dog around the place at present, it would seem like disrespect to poor Leo's memory. I cried for days as you know."

Iris patted her hand.

"It was a savage thing to do to an innocent dog no wonder you are still grieving him."

"Do you know that Kevin actually shed tears too when he saw what Delaney had done?"

"Really!" Iris rolled her eyes.

"He has refused to go anywhere near their farm since and his boss Andrew backs him up. So Jackser has to travel miles to get a vet when one of his animals is sick."

Iris guffawed.

"That will teach him."

Evie emptied the last of the lemonade into her glass and then swallowed it in one mouthful.

"Now, I have a few letters to type, I wonder if Brendan is free to drive into the post office with them?"

"He is helping out in the garden with some pruning, but I will send him in to you."

"Thank you, they are replies to letters from your fan club in Austen, Texas."

Iris stood up and headed for the hallway.

"We have to keep the fans happy, after all, they are our bread and butter!"

At that moment, the phone rang again, and Evie hurried over to answer it while Iris stopped and listened.

"Good Afternoon, Richmond House."

A short pause and then she replied.

"Yes, Kevin is my husband, has something happened?"

This time a longer pause while Iris moved closer.

"Ok, Yes. Which ward is he in?"

Iris frowned as she tried hard to hear what the caller was saying.

Eventually, after another few minutes when Evie put down the phone, Iris asked.

"What has happened?"

" Kevin had an appointment for chest x-rays today at 2pm in the hospital. However, the humidity has made him very wheezy, so they decided to admit him because he needs more tests in the morning. If you ask me it's good news, now he will have to do what they say."

Iris's face brightened.

"Yes, I think it has worked out for the best."

Evie sat down and twirled an eraser on her desk.

"That woman on the phone is the ward sister, and she said that Mr Gibney the consultant intends to have him checked out thoroughly."

" Look here, you can go home now and type those letters in the morning."

"Are you sure?" Evie asked.

"Yes. You will need to go home, before going to the hospital, to get pyjamas and fresh clothes for Kevin and you want to make the most of the visiting hour."

"True. I promise that I will come in earlier in the morning and do them."

Iris fixed her with her keen eyes.

"One last thing before I leave, as we have said before you need to learn how to drive. It is different for me I am much older, but you are a young woman and it really is important that you master that skill."

Evie stayed silent for a few minutes and then spoke.

"You are right, but Kevin is totally against the idea and since the fire, I did not want to stir things by going on about driving lessons."

Iris wagged a finger in the air.

"Now Evelyn, you must think of yourself and your needs, not his! Men should never have the upper hand, marriage is a union, a partnership, not a dictatorship."

Evie removed the loose sheets of paper from her typewriter and put a grey cover over it.

"I know. Thank you for everything."

Two hours later she arrived at the semi-private ward which Kevin was sharing with three other patients. He was sitting up in bed with a few pillows to support him, chatting to the man in the nearest bed. His face lit up when he saw Evie, but she noticed the black shadows under his eyes.

"Aha! Here comes my lovely wife! I am so glad to see you."

She bent down to give him a kiss on the cheek and he took her hand in his.

Her first thought was how rough they felt in comparison with Robert's soft and hydrated hands.

"Kevin, I got such a shock when the ward sister phoned. How are you feeling now?"

He released her hand and pointed at a chair.

"Not bad, pull up that chair."

When she was seated, he introduced her to the patient on his right.

"Larry, this is my better half, my wife Evelyn, I could not carry on without her."

"Evelyn, this is Larry, he is a sales representative for one of the whiskey companies, but like my own case the humidity proved too much for him and he ended up in this prison."

He laughed at his own joke just as a line of visitors filed into the ward and then dispersed, each to their own loved one's bedside.

Evie was pleased to see that Larry's wife, who had just arrived wanted some privacy and had drawn the curtain around his bed. She was not in a mood to tolerate Kevin playing the role of adoring husband to perfection.

It was difficult to have any type of meaningful talk with him as a succession of nurses and wards-maids interrupted. The former to check his temperature and blood pressure and the latter to take his order for breakfast and dinner the following day. He even flirted with the young nurse who arrived with medicated lozenges for his sore throat.

The most irritating part of all was that every one of them made a point of telling her how fortunate she was to have such a courageous husband.

And each time she answered.

"Indeed, he is a real hero."

While Kevin looked at her intently, her inner voice said.

He is like the cat who got the cream, with all the females fussing around him.

When a sharp bell to signal the end of visiting sounded, he started to cough, and she poured him a large glass of water from the jug on his bedside locker.

He swallowed it and then grinned like a schoolboy at her.

"You will miss me tonight Evie, all alone in that big bed of yours!"

She ignored the jibe

"I will call in on my way home to the hall, the drama rehearsals are starting tonight. Helen and Tom both feel that I should take on a bigger part this year. It's one of Brendan Behan's plays which Tom is adapting."

She leaned down to give him a parting kiss.

He gave a surreptitious glance around the ward and then took her hand roughly in his. Before she knew what was happening, he put it under the bedclothes and squeezed it painfully.

She winced silently in pain.

Then, still clutching her hand he whispered in her ear.

"If you dare to take any part in that play you will be sorry. That jackass Behan only writes about prostitutes and drunks."

She managed to withdraw her hand while he made a great show of kissing her on the lips.

Get out of here before the hypocrite does something else.

"Goodbye, I will phone tomorrow afternoon to see if they are keeping you for a second night. All the other visitors have gone."

"Yes, my darling you do that."

He beamed at her.

Just outside the door of the ward, she paused to check on her right hand which was still sore like she had caught it in something.

Then to her disgust, she heard Keven saying in a loud voice.

"Did you see my woman putting her hand under the blanket? She misses me in more ways than one!"

"You must be one of those randy vets!"

Larry exclaimed as the man in the bed near the window gave a loud wolf whistle.

She ran down the length of the corridor and took the back stairs to the main exit.

Outside, she waited under the nearest tree and counted ten until she felt calmer. Then she collected her bike and rode straight home.

A tiny voice inside her urged caution.

Don't go against him.

Next morning, on her way to work earlier than normal she met Nick, the postman. He gave her a letter from Val and one for Kevin with an English postmark, in the familiar handwriting of his mother. She could not wait to read Val's letter and further up the street, got off her bike and leaned against the wall of the church while her eyes scanned the two pages.

The bell was ringing for early mass and she saw a woman in a plaid coat with a black mantilla approaching.

"Mrs Moore, I heard that your good husband is in hospital, how is he?"

Evie forced a smile.

"Thank you, Mrs Rogers, for asking about Kevin. He will be fine."

"The poor soul I will light a candle for him now."

"Thank you, you are so kind."

"The whole town is praying that he will have a speedy recovery. Look after him."

Evie nodded as the woman crossed herself and hurried into the church

She never ceased to be amazed at how quickly news travelled in Redmills, and it filled her with anger that they all thought Kevin was akin to some saint.

She bent her head while her eyes returned to the letter. It emerged that Val had some leave to use up before the winter and wanted to spend a few days in Redmills if it suited.

Hurriedly, she folded the letter and put it in her handbag, because she noticed Annie and Mary Kenny approaching. The sisters liked to boast that they had not missed a daily mass in 10 years but still gossiped about everyone else's business.

She hopped onto her bicycle and peddled furiously with her eyes downcast, pretending not to notice their arms waving frantically as they tried to stop her.

She could not tolerate any more praise for Kevin from nosey auld ones. In recent weeks she had begun to skip Sunday mass because of all the enquiries she received about his state of health from mass-goers.

I will write to Val and invite her down for a few days, forcing Kevin to be on his best behaviour.

Chapter Thirteen

Two days later, at 6 o'clock in the evening, Evie cycled to the stark red brick hospital dating from Victorian times. She sneezed as she walked up the heavily polished old stairway, and then she felt a tug at her sleeve. Turning around she saw a fair-haired nurse from Kevin's ward with a badge on her chest displaying the name, *Sharon Casey*.

"Mrs Moore, I am surprised to see you here!"

Evie stopped in her tracks.

"What do you mean?"

"They moved Kevin to St. Matthew's Hospital in Dublin this afternoon, there was a free bed on Mr Marmion's ward. He specialises in head injuries of all kinds."

"Why did no one ring me to let me know?"

The nurse shrugged.

"Apologies about your wasted journey, but it was all hands on deck, this afternoon. A bus carrying 20 children collided with a car on a bad bend near Tara and they were brought here."

"I am sorry to hear that news, will they be ok?"

"Yes, there are no life-threatening injuries, it's mostly shock and some broken bones."

"I am relieved to hear it. Also, I am pleased about Kevin's move to Dublin too as he needs a full assessment."

"It's for the best. He is a model patient, not to mention his bravery."

Evie feigned a big smile.

"Thank you, Sharon. When do you think they will discharge him?"

"That depends on the tests and their results. Probably, a few days."

"Right, Thanks again."

Running through Evie's mind was a sense of relief that she would get a total break from him.

"You can use the phone in the hall to ring St Matthews and check if he has settled. Maureen on the switchboard will put you through to an outside line." Sharon suggested.

"Thank you, you are so thoughtful."

Evie left her hand on the young woman's shoulder.

"Perfect. Now I must run."

The nurse replied as her eyes focused on a patient in her nightgown who was perilously close to falling down the stairs.

A woman with a strong Donegal accent answered when she phoned the hospital in Dublin. In an officious tone, she informed Evie that she could not speak directly with Kevin. His medical chart showed that he had been lightly sedated following a bumpy journey in the ambulance from Redmills to Dublin and was sleeping.

On her way home, she called into the library where Orla was holding a training session for voluntary tutors on her new "literacy scheme."

At the end of the evening, Orla assigned a student to each of the ten participants.

She left Evie until last, by then the others had gone.

"Evelyn, I have decided to match the most difficult case, Patsy Mc Ginley, son of Biddy, with you if that is ok?"

Evie hesitated.

"I can't say that I know them."

Orla looked up into her face.

"You do know her, she was married to Paddy Mc Ginley, the poor tinker who drowned in the Boyne, about nine years ago. She had three children with Paddy and then after his death, she got involved with Dessie Duggan, an eccentric bachelor who lived at the edge of the new forest near the tinker's camp.

"Now, I remember. She had a child with Duggan and was disowned by all the tinkers, but he stood by her and they lived together in his tiny stone cottage until his death."

Orla sighed.

"Dessie Duggan was not the brightest, but he was a kind old fellow, and he took her in. They had a second son and when Dessie died, he left the cottage on one rocky acre to her. She still lives there with the five children, mercifully there was no living relative left on his side to contest the will."

A look of sadness covered Evie's face.

"She has a beautiful shire horse and Kevin keeps an eye on the animal free of charge as he cannot abide neglect, but he calls her Biddy Duggan."

Orla gave a soft giggle.

"It was Fr. Gandon who convinced Dessie to make an honest woman of her just before he died. Anyway, he also persuaded her that the children need to learn to read and write."

"Fair play to him, so she has five children altogether."

"Yes, the eldest lad is 14, and said to be quite a smart boy, he works as a casual labourer with different farmers, but he seldom went to school."

Evie's dark eyebrows rose.

"That is shocking, but I know that the tinkers have different customs and beliefs than ours."

Orla grinned.

"I used your name as a carrot to entice her, you see she was reluctant to commit to our plan because she was afraid that some harridan would be in charge. And then I recalled that Fr. Gandon had mentioned Kevin cared for her horse, so once I mentioned your name she agreed that you can go to her house to teach Patsy."

Evie made a face.

"You are a wily woman!"

Orla laughed.

"An innocent Dubliner like myself has to wise up among all these cute country mugs and superstitious itinerants. I believe that all the shelves of books here scare her, the poor soul!"

Evie's mind was working feverishly.

At least Kevin won't object to my participation in the scheme as he already knows Biddy.

Winking at Orla she said.

"Right, that's settled, when do I start.

"Thursday evening around seven."

"Biddy is nervous, but I know that you will put her at her ease. She thinks of your husband as some sort of God so be warned, he will be a hard act to follow."

Orla said with a wry grin.

"Nothing new there, the whole town has canonised him."

"Is everything, all right?" Orla asked.

"Well, he has been transferred to a hospital in Dublin for tests, and I don't want to ask Mrs Ryder-Lee for more time off. Four American academics are arriving on Friday for the weekend. And there is a lot of preparation to be done, she is taking them on a tour of Dublin including places mentioned in Ulysses."

Orla removed her glasses and rubbed her eyes.

"That's very bad timing."

"So, it will be Saturday before I am able to visit him."

Orla said firmly.

"Look you can't be expected to bi-locate. He will be fine, I can drive you up on Saturday afternoon once the library closes, if that helps."

Tears appeared at the corners of Evie's eyes.

"That would be a big help. Thank you, Orla, you are like my guardian angel."

"Steady on Evelyn, one saint in your circle is enough!"

When Thursday evening arrived, Evie cycled over to Biddy Duggan's cottage. There was an unseasonal chill in the air for mid-September and she was glad to see smoke curling from the chimney. A few white and brown hens along with a cockerel were scratching in the dirt near the rusty iron gate while a large ginger tom cat sat on a windowsill observing her.

She left her bike against the stone wall and approached the half-door of the cottage.

A woman with several front teeth missing and crinkled skin stuck her head out.

"Are you his wife?"

"Yes, my name is Evelyn Moore, I am here to help Patsy."

The tinker woman removed the latch from the lower part of the door and exclaimed.

"The blessings of God on you, come inside, my name is Biddy Duggan."

Evie felt the callused skin of Biddy as they shook hands.

Inside the small cottage, a turf fire was blazing in the main room.

"Sit down, I sent all the young ones outside to play except Patsy as I want him to learn."

Biddy pointed at two wooden stools and a table.

"I'm off out now I can't be bothered with book learning. There's my young man."

Suddenly, a tall lad with auburn hair and perfect snow-white teeth emerged from a room at the far side of the chimney breast.

"Are you my teacher?"

He took a seat opposite her.

"I am not a school-teacher but I hope to teach you to read and write, you can call me Mrs Moore. I take it that you are Patsy?"

He smiled and said in a low voice.

"I would like that."

Over an hour went by as he listened intently to all that she taught him. When the natural light faded, Patsy lit a Tilley lamp as there was no electricity in the cottage. She had brought two picture books with her as well as a poster displaying the full alphabet. To her surprise, he already knew the entire alphabet and was able to read simple words.

"Don't tell me Ma that I can read a bit, or she won't allow you to keep on helping me. I found old books belonging to my stepfather Dessie and I tried to teach myself."

"That's great news but don't worry your secret is safe with me. It means that your progress will be much faster than someone starting from scratch."

His face coloured.

"You are kind like your man, he is good to our mare Queenie and looks after her for nothing."

"Next week you must show me Queenie."

"I will to be sure and I will have all my homework done for you."

His grey eyes sparkled.

"That's it for tonight, it is getting late."

She tidied her books into a leather bag.

"Mrs would you like me to cycle as far as the main road with you, this back road is dark and full of potholes, but I know every one of them."

"Thank you, Patsy, I would appreciate your help."

He whistled a tune as she followed him outside. Then he rode ahead of her indicating with his right hand when to slow down and when to swerve right or left to avoid mini craters full of water. Just before they reached the main road, he stopped and pointed up a narrow laneway.

"That's where Fishy lives."

Evie brought her bicycle to a halt suddenly.

"Who is Fishy?"

Patsy laughed.

"Some say that she has a cure for everything under the sun, but others call her a witch."

Evie was intrigued.

"What's her name?"

"Her real name is Mrs Dolphin."

"Yes, I have heard of her, it is said that she can cure many ailments with various concoctions which she makes from herbs."

Patsy leaned in closer.

"Don't tell Ma that I told you, but she cured the ring-worm on my face about two years ago and she helped my sister get rid of warts. They come from all over to buy her bottles."

She nodded.

"I am glad she is able to help so many people."

His eyes opened wide.

"Might she be a real witch?"

Evie shook her head emphatically.

"No, witches only exist in children's storybooks, she has learned from past generations how to use certain plants to heal people, even mainstream medicine uses plants to help heal."

He looked up at her in awe.

"That's what I like about you Mrs apart from the reading and writing, you know a lot about everything. Someday I want to be like you."

She chuckled.

"I am no genius but once you master writing and reading you can read books until the cows come home."

His voice sounded shaky as he answered.

"Thanks, Mrs now I will leave you here as Ma will be waiting for me."

She adjusted the flashlamp on the front of her bike. "Goodnight Patsy."

"Goodnight Mrs."

By the time she reached home, she was tired but happy. She had enjoyed teaching Patsy because it took her mind off her own worries. He was a fine young boy and she felt sure that in a short time he would be able to master both reading and writing.

Then she twiddled the dials on the radio until she found her favourite BBC station. Soon the sound of Elvis Presley's extraordinary voice filled the house while she poured a glass of brandy and tapped her foot to the beat *of Jailhouse Rock.*

It felt so good to be able to just do as she wanted without humouring her husband and trying to anticipate the smallest sign which might indicate that his mood had changed.

Chapter Fourteen

Saturday afternoon brought heavy rainfall which caused traffic congestion in the city centre. At the gate of the hospital, a rag-and-bone man was trapped underneath his cart which had turned over, while desperate pedestrians tried to free him and his horse.

Orla left Evie outside the sinister grey building and promised to return at 4pm. She took the stairs two at a time to Kevin's ward and offered a silent prayer.

I am 15 minutes late for visiting hour, please don't let him make a scene.

She spotted him sitting by his bedside in his dressing gown, there was just one other patient in the ward, and he had three visitors around his bed.

He saw her and grinned.

"I thought that something had happened to you."

"Sorry, Kevin, there is a road accident just outside and traffic is delayed."

He stood up and hugged her.

"Evelyn, it is so good to see you, I missed you so much."

She looked into his eyes.

"It was so frustrating that they would not allow me to speak to you on the phone. I rang every morning and evening to be updated about your progress. Did they tell you?"

"Yes, they did. Now sit down in that spare chair and relax, you look frazzled."

She smiled at him as she removed her raincoat and pulled over a chair beside him.

He is in a good mood.

"Tell me, how is your headache and your cough?" She asked.

He smoothed back his hair with his hand.

Since yesterday, the coughing has stopped, thanks to a mixture of drugs which they are pumping into me."

"And your headaches, have they done all the tests yet?

"They are waiting for the results, so far so good, the consultant will be making his rounds on Monday morning, but I have to admit that he is right about getting plenty of rest as it is giving my body a chance to heal."

Her face lit up.

"I am so glad that you are here, by the sound of it they know what they are doing."

He patted her hand.

"Well, this place specialises in all kinds of trauma to the head. Frankie, over in that bed, is a farmer from Kildare, he sustained a head injury about three weeks ago when a bull pinned him against a wall."

Evie twisted her wedding ring.

"That's terrible, will he recover?"

"Yes, there is a deep wound on the side of his head which has to be managed carefully and he gets severe headaches far worse than mine, but we get on like a house on fire."

Evie smiled.

"I will have to pardon your pun!"

He gave a boyish grin.

"Oh, the fire reference! Yes, we talk about horses all day long, he breeds them for hunting and when we tire of that, Frankie takes out the cards and we play card games."

Already there is a big change in his temperament.

"It's great that you have so much in common."

He sipped water from a glass beside him and then agreed.

"You are right, a man could go mad here, all alone in a grim ward."

She took out a stack of newspapers along with bottles of orange and a tin of biscuits.

"You are spoiling me! Did you get this week's *Farmer's Journal?*"

"Yes, local, national, and farming newspapers here, along with two letters from your mother. I brought a writing pad, envelopes and a pen as you can write a long letter to her."

"Ok, I cannot say that I don't have time now."

She told him about her time teaching Patsy Mc Ginley and he leered at her when she mentioned Biddy, his mother."

"Be careful around that one! She knows how to look after herself."

"But you treat Queenie her horse without any charge!"

"Indeed, I do because you know I love horses, but she is cunning."

His expression had hardened.

"She seemed all right to me, but I only met her for a few minutes."

"You know the first time I went to her cottage it was shortly after her auld fellow's death and the poor mare had laminitis. I explained to her that the treatment was slow and that it would be costly."

Evie saw a flicker in his eyes which she recognised but could not name.

"What did Biddy say?"

He gave a throaty laugh.

"She told me that she could not afford to pay my fees but that she would do anything to make sure the mare got the necessary treatment. And she offered to let me poke her."

For a few seconds, Evie felt a rush of blood to the head.

The creep is trying to shock you.

She looked at him aware that he was waiting for a reaction.

"What do you want me to say?"

He rubbed the stubble on his chin with his fingers.

"Well, don't you care about the choice I made?"

She looked across at the other patient, who was still deep in conversation with his relatives.

"Look here Kevin, I did not travel all the way to Dublin just to listen to you playing games with me."

He ignored the barb.

"Put it this way, if some tasty horsey woman from one of the local stud farms had made me the offer I might not have refused."

"Keep on dreaming!" She retorted.

There was silence between them for a couple of minutes and then a mature nurse appeared to take his blood pressure.

"Ah! Florrie Nightingale!" He exclaimed as she did her work.

When she was finished, she leaned closer to Evie.

"Your husband is a very naughty man he tries to shock the young nurses with his randy stories about grooms and jockeys."

"Boys will be boys!" Evie replied as if she hadn't a care in the world.

"Right, that's me finished."

The nurse gave Kevin a friendly tap on the shoulder and left the ward.

"My friend Orla drove me here today, but it might be more difficult to visit tomorrow as the buses and trains will be packed with supporters up for the replay of the big match in Croke Park."

He rubbed the stubble on his chin.

"Don't even try to visit me tomorrow, it will be like the gates of hell opening when all those match goers crowd onto public transport. Andrew left a message for me at reception, he will be in the city tomorrow and intends to visit."

She could feel waves of relief washing over her body.

"Are you sure?" She asked sweetly.

"Positive. I hope to be home by the end of the week at worst, but there is no need for you to worry about coming in to see me. I had a chat this morning with matron, I said that I need to speak with you daily by phone as I pretended that you are keeping an eye on a couple of sick bullocks for me. She agreed that I can wait by the desk at ten o clock every morning for you to ring."

"Good, so we can actually have a conversation."

However, in her head a voice warned.

He has even managed to circumvent the rules of the strictest hospital in the country.

"By the way all your bullocks are fine, I met the Goffs, both mother and son, in town last week on the main street and Kieran checks on them every day."

"They paid me a visit during the week before I was transferred here."

"Mrs Goff has recovered well," Evie remarked.

"She was all over me like a rash. Hugging me and telling everyone in the hospital that I saved her life. She even brought me a large box of cigars and a bottle of "Mountain Dew" but I gave them to the men on the ward the day I was leaving."

"Quite right! I don't think that this hospital would allow you to sip from a bottle of illicit alcohol."

He threw his head back and chortled.

"The matron here rules with an iron hand, while my powers of persuasion worked on her with the phone calls. I don't think they would extend to drink!"

She collected her things and then kissed him on the cheek.

"I will walk to the main door with you."

He said as he tightened the belt on his dressing gown.

The porter was ringing a large bell when they went downstairs. Visitors began to stream out of various wards and private rooms, while inside the main door a young girl sobbed her heart out as she studied her boyfriend, who had a grey countenance and a racking cough.

"That poor chap had a malignant brain tumour removed last year," Kevin whispered.

She shivered.

"That's so tragic. "

He drew her close.

"My little woman, you cannot take the troubles of the world upon those petite shoulders!"

She wiped away tears from her eyes.

"I know. Kevin, you take care, and I shall phone you every morning."

"You, too! Goodbye Evelyn and safe journey home."

"Goodbye, Kevin."

He kissed her and then they went their separate ways.

While she waited in the car park for Orla, a voice inside her head berated her.

Those tears were not for that sick young man, you were crying for yourself.

On Sunday afternoon Evie was just about to go for a long walk when a black Ford car came up the driveway.

Opening the door, she could hardly believe her own eyes when Val emerged from the front passenger seat carrying a week-end case. Then the driver waved at Val, turned the car around and headed for the main road.

"This is a lovely surprise! I am delighted to see you, Val."

"Hello Evie, I hope it is not too much of a shock to see me arriving on your doorstep out of the blue!"

They embraced.

"Come on inside, it really is great to have you here, I am in dire need of company."

Val gave a cheeky smile.

"Good, I can be an impetuous hussy at times. I am on leave now for a week and when I heard Dr Irwin saying that he was driving to Kells today to visit his sister, I asked him for a lift. I can get the train back to Dublin on Wednesday morning."

"That's the best news I have heard in weeks. I told you in my letter about Kevin's health problems following his rescue of Mrs Goff."

Val nodded and left her case at the hallstand. Then following Evie into the sitting room, she sat on a chair near the window.

" I take it Kevin is still in the local hospital, I must visit him tomorrow."

Evie remained standing.

"Sorry, I meant to ring you, he was moved last Wednesday to St. Matthews Hospital in Dublin and is in the care of a specialist."

"That's good news."

She studied Evie's face.

"I suppose so, I visited him yesterday, he was in good form as his medication has been changed again and he is undergoing a series of tests. Now, I will make something quick for you to eat."

"No Evie, we stopped on the way here, I treated the doctor to a four-course meal in that hotel outside Redmills on the Dublin road, just to thank him."

What about a whiskey and soda?" Evie asked.

A big smile spread across Val's face.

"Why not?"

They chatted for a couple of hours until the Angelus bell rang out on the Radio. Then, giggling like two adolescents they took a hackney ride to the Central Cinema in Redmills where the movie *Singing in the Rain* was showing. Afterwards, with images of Gene Kelly and Debbie Reynolds still in their minds, they agreed to finish off the evening with a drink in Butlers Bar nearby.

Every head turned to have a good look at them as they walked through the smoke-filled pub, to the small room with the word "Snug" in black letters on the door.

"It is abominable that women are relegated to a separate room from men," Val said loudly.

On the bar stools at the counter, a row of men sat guzzling pints of Guinness. Then, one of them shook his fist at the two women.

Evie whispered.

"Ignore him, he just wants to have us thrown out. Some men are such idiots that they believe a woman's place is in the home night and day looking after their husband's needs."

Val exploded into laughter.

"Don't tell me that we have travelled back in time to some medieval tavern where the only women who appear are wenches."

Just then, Evie realized that an eerie silence had descended on the whole place, the customers were still eavesdropping on their conversation. She closed the door of the snug and sat down beside Val on a worn settee which was covered in a red fabric.

"Why not order two black rums with some blackcurrant cordial?"

Val suggested and then rang a brass bell. When the publican appeared to take the order, she teased him by offering to carry down her own tray of drinks from the bar, but he answered in an icy tone.

"Ladies are not allowed in the bar. Mrs Moore can you tell your friend that we adhere to rules in the country even if they flout them in the city."

Evie sighed.

"Can you please just get us the drinks?"

He waddled off, mumbling to himself while Val took out a packet of Carroll's cigarettes and passed one to Evie. They had just finished lighting them when he returned with the order and put the glasses noisily down on the table.

Val slowly counted out coins into his hand and added a tip.

He grunted and left the room. Then the two friends shook with laughter as Val explained that she had given him a bent halfpenny.

"He can buy a gobstopper with it to shut his mouth!" Evie declared.

Suddenly, the door opened and a man with bloodshot eyes and a bald head entered.

He was holding a pint glass half-filled with porter in his right hand.

He gave Evie a look that reminded her of a cross dog who was about to bite.

"Mrs Moore, you should be ashamed of yourself, drinking like a fish and your poor husband lying above in a hospital in Dublin."

Speechless she looked up at him while Val said.

"Don't stoop to his level, say nothing."

He moved in closer.

"You are just two Dublin wans, out drinking in a pub late at night, waiting to see what you can snare!"

Evie said in a controlled voice.

"How dare you! Go back to the bog-hole you call a house."

He lifted his arm and threw the contents of his glass onto her white lace blouse with the blue trimmings.

"Look at Mrs High and Mighty now." He shouted.

She quickly put on her cardigan as she could feel his eyes on her bust, and she feared that her blouse had become see-through with the black stain spreading across it.

Val who was by then apoplectic with rage jumped up and gave him a sharp slap on the jaw.

A group of his supporters had gathered in the doorway, and they shouted for the publican who rushed in with his arms swinging.

"Mrs Moore, you and your friend have five minutes to gather your belongings and leave, otherwise I will send for the Gardai."

Clearing his throat, he pointed a finger in the direction of the bald-headed man.

"Barney Reagan, get the fuck out of my pub too, the women were minding their own business until you went in to pick a fight."

A ripple of laughter ran through the group.

A voice from the shadows said.

"Billy Conway bet a full pound note that no one would have the cheek to go into the snug and insult the vet's wife. That's what started all this bedlam."

Butler exploded in a paroxysm of rage.

"You shower of eejits, this is not a betting shop, I could lose my license over your tomfoolery."

Val exchanged a glance with Evie as they stood up because there was no direct route to the door without pushing past the crowd of sleazy men.

Then the publican roared at the top of his voice.

"Any customer who does not return to their seat immediately will be barred for life."

In a flash, they all went back to their original places at the bar while Evie left the premises by the side door and Val hurried out onto the street through the front door.

Outside they hugged each other for a few moments, as both were shaking.

"What in God's name just happened there?" Val asked.

"I have no idea, but it seemed as if that drunken mob would have hurled glasses at us if it was allowed to continue any longer," Evie said.

Then they hurried down the street until they reached the grey door where Michael Rogers, the hackney man lived.

He opened it after the third knock.

"Michael, can you please drive us home?"

He smiled.

"Just give me a minute while I get organized."

"Thank you so much, Michael."

"No problem at all Mrs Moore, that's my job."

He went inside in search of his keys while Val blew her nose hard.

"Sorry Evie, for causing such a scene, if I had not come to stay with you this would never have happened."

"Nonsense! They are just a crowd of drunken jackasses! I treasure our friendship, and nothing will ever change that."

Chapter Fifteen

Val left early on Wednesday morning. It was with a heavy heart that Evie waved from the platform to her friend when the train pulled out of the station bound for Dublin. Val's presence had been like a tonic and without Kevin in the house, she had been able to relax fully. Since his hospitalisation, she had come to recognise that a lot of her time since the start of their marriage, had been spent trying to pre-empt one of his dark moods or outbursts. By contrast, Val was easy going and it had been an extra bonus each evening to return from work to find a hot meal prepared for her.

From the railway station, she went directly to the office. Iris was in Dublin, hosting a lunch in the Shelbourne Hotel for her American visitors before they departed for New York. She phoned Kevin, who said that he had developed a cold with catarrh, and he complained vociferously that it had been caused by a draught from an open window in the ward.

"If I don't get out of this place soon I will discharge myself," he shouted down the phone.

She had tried to calm him, but she had to let him go when he got a fit of coughing and needed some water.

Later, she rang the matron, who explained what had happened.

"Mrs Moore, the consultant, changed Kevin's medication on Monday and he seems to be experiencing side effects from the new tablets. While his headaches have gone, he is drowsy and a little agitated as he wants to go home. Now, Mr Marmion is doing his rounds in the wards as I speak."

Evie's jaws tensed.

"Do you mean to say that Kevin does not have a new infection?"

The matron cleared her throat and spoke slowly into the phone.

"Mrs Moore, there is no need to worry at all. May I suggest that you meet with Mr Marmion."

Evie's grip on the phone relaxed.

"Ok. I shall meet him on Friday as I will need to give my employer notice that I am taking a day's leave."

There was a delay and Evie could hear her rustling through papers.

Then the matron spoke.

"That is fine, I shall ring his secretary and tell her to put you in for an 11.30 appointment. His rooms are here on the ground floor."

"Thank you and good day to you," Evie said.

Then opening the French doors in the reception room, she lit a cigarette and gazed outside, where a wild rabbit was nibbling at the grass in the weak sunshine.

She had to get to the bottom of this latest development before they sent Kevin home to her in a worse state than ever.

On Friday, at precisely 11.30 am Mr Marmion, a man of small stature with horn-rimmed glasses and snow-white hair emerged from his office and beckoned to Evie.

"Mrs Moore, please follow me, my name is Mr Marmion."

He took a seat behind a large desk and she sat opposite him.

He rummaged through a stack of files until he located a fat one bulging with papers, which he opened.

"Mrs Moore, all the tests on your husband have come back clear. I believe that in time he will make a full recovery and I intend to discharge him tomorrow."

For a few moments, she thought that the room was spinning but after taking a few deep breaths she felt better.

"I don't understand, he was agitated yesterday when I phoned."

"What do you expect? His body is adjusting to new pain killers. He has been a terrific patient and who could blame him if he wants to get out of here."

She shook her head.

"He is still coughing and suffers from dry throats."

He leaned forward in his chair.

"Yes, he is a heavy smoker and I have advised him to cut back or better still cut out the cigarettes altogether. New research is emerging that links tobacco smoke to cancer and a whole host of other diseases."

For a minute, his myopic eyes peered at her.

She decided to have one last attempt at keeping Kevin in hospital.

"Since the fire, he has been aggressive towards me."

"Aggressive! In what way?" He demanded.

Her voice trembled.

"He lost his temper with me and struck me on the face, and he forced himself on me."

"All at the same time?" He said incredulously.

"No, I am talking about two different days."

He looked over the top of his glasses in a sneering fashion.

"Mrs Moore, I am a very busy consultant, whatever do you mean by saying he forced himself on you."

Her heart pounded.

"He insisted on making love to me against my will."

"Mrs Moore, your husband has a head injury and suffers from the after-effects of smoke inhalation, all sustained while rescuing a poor old lady from a burning building. Of course, he will be moody and demanding until he recovers, you must allow for psychological as well as physical injuries."

"But he gave me a black eye one evening and another time during sex he …" Her voice trailed off.

He looked out the window for a couple of seconds and then he smiled humourlessly.

"Kevin is a typical veterinary surgeon, I played rugby with several of them during my college days. They don't dress things up in frills like other professionals, they spend their days with animals and farmers."

"So, it is acceptable to rape your wife whenever you wish because you are a vet?"

He met her gaze.

"Come now, no one said anything about rape, how ridiculous you ladies are. When you married him, you undertook to satisfy his needs in the bedroom among other duties. In future just take a drink or two when he is in an amorous mood, it will relax you and save a lot of angst."

Her eyes narrowed and she stared at him for a moment, too shocked to speak.

Suddenly, he closed the file and then lifted the receiver of a black phone with his right hand.

"Good day, Mrs Moore, I have a string of other cases waiting with valid concerns unlike yours."

She got up, shakily.

Stand up to this creep, he sees all females as second -class citizens.

"You have been of no help to me whatsoever, my journey here was wasted not to mention the fact that I took a whole day off work!"

"Kevin is a rough diamond, as well as a hero, cherish him."

He pointed the tip of his black fountain pen at her.

She hurried from the room and down the long corridor until she reached a door with *Ladies Lavatory* marked on it. Once inside she locked the door and banged the walls with her fists until she felt better.

When she entered Kevin's ward at 2 pm, he was sitting by his bedside talking with two men.

"Here comes my lovely wife!"

The two older men both in dressing gowns nodded at Evie and then returned to their own ward further down the corridor.

She kissed him on the forehead.

"Kevin, you look great! I see that your friend's bed is empty has he been discharged?"

"Yes, he went on Wednesday and I am free to go tomorrow morning."

He grinned at his own joke.

"You make it sound like you are in Mountjoy Prison."

She said as she drew up a chair at the side of the bed.

He waved his hands in the air.

"I heard that you were meeting with Marmion this morning, how did you find him?"

Her inner voice prompted.

Keep it simple, be matter of fact.

"Fine, he said that you will make a full recovery in time, but he has advised you to give up smoking, it is exacerbating your cough."

He rapped the end of the bed.

"Fuck him! He is full of his own importance but he knows how to charge top prices."

"It's great news that you are coming home tomorrow," she said gently.

Back to placating him already.

"Yes, I am on my own now in this ward and I hate it."

"By the way, there is no need to hire a hackney, Mrs Ryder-Lee has offered to have Brendan drive you home, once you are discharged."

He smirked.

"At least the old dame is good for something!"

"Don't be like that! She has a kind nature and has offered to allow Brendan help me with driving lessons, but I just haven't had the time to take up her offer yet."

"I - don't know if that's a good idea, for a start her flashy automobile is as big as a bus and even if you do learn to drive, you certainly won't be getting your hands on my Land Rover."

She could feel her face reddening.

"Why not?"

"'Tis a funny thing but I don't think women make good drivers."

"Rubbish, next you will be telling me that women should not have been given the vote," she replied.

A light knock on the door and a nurse with strawberry blonde hair and chocolate brown eyes entered.

"Ah, Mrs Moore, my name is Pauline, I have been looking after Kevin, have you heard that he is going home tomorrow."

"You are looking after me well, I cannot complain about the nursing care."

He said winking at the nurse.

"Yes, good news - indeed." Evie tried to sound enthusiastic.

Look at the way his face lights up when he is talking to her.

"Now Kevin, I just have to check your temperature and blood pressure and then I shall leave you to talk in peace with your good wife."

Evie moved to the window for a few moments.

When the nurse had finished her duties, she smoothed out creases in the counterpanes on the empty beds. A few minutes later she turned to study Evie who had returned to her position near Kevin.

"This man has been all alone since Wednesday but some of the lads from the other wards visit him, he has kept both patients and staff amused with his stories from the countryside, everything from injured racehorses to amorous bulls."

"And I have plenty more stories to tell if you have the time."

He sat back into the chair and spread his legs.

"Do you hear that cheek!" The nurse left the ward with a big smile on her face.

They are flirting right in front of my eyes.

The remainder of the visiting time flew by as a succession of staff came and went from the ward. First, a cleaner to remove dust which had been spotted earlier on the windowsill by the eagle-eyed matron doing her rounds. Then a girl from the catering staff who wanted to check Kevin's order for breakfast the following day and finally a young priest who informed Kevin, that he had a mass in the small oratory attached to the hospital every morning.

"This place is as busy as Kingsbridge Station."

Evie observed when they were finally alone.

"So that chauffeur fellow you call Brendan will bring me home tomorrow."

"Yes, unless you want me to come here too."

"No, I don't want a fuss."

"Great! I shall phone Brendan and tell him to be here around midday."

He nodded.

"I am looking forward to travelling in style! The other patients will think that I am a moneyed landowner from Meath if they catch sight of that fancy automobile."

"Yes, it just glides along like some sleek bird!"

Then the shrill sound of the bell echoed throughout the hospital and she kissed him quickly on the forehead.

"Goodbye Kevin, I am looking forward to having you home."

"Are you really?"

He rolled his eyes.

While her conscience said.

Liar, liar.

Then he walked to the door of the ward and watched her disappear down the stairs.

About twenty minutes later she reached the bus stop which served the train station. Suddenly, she realized that her pale blue silk scarf which had been a present from Iris was missing. She remembered draping it over the back of the chair while she had been sitting in the ward.

You must go back to the ward.

She ran back to the hospital and this time slipped in a side entrance and took the lift to the first floor. Outside the door to Kevin's ward, she paused for a few moments catching her breath. Then she opened the door quietly as she knew patients usually had a nap at this time.

She saw Kevin and the blonde nurse looking out the bay window. He had one arm around her waist while the other was hovering near her left breast. They were so absorbed in their own world that they were oblivious to her presence. She closed the door slowly, feeling as if an electric shock had just gone through her body.

I need to get my scarf, pretend I saw nothing.

She drummed her knuckles against the door. For a few minutes, there was no reply and then the door was opened by the nurse.

"Mrs Moore, visiting time is long over, you should not be here, Matron will be furious if she sees you."

Evie pushed past her. From the corner of her eye, she saw Kevin sitting in his chair nonchalantly flicking through a newspaper.

"What the hell has happened? He asked.

For a moment she hesitated, trying to control the urge to confront them about what she had just seen.

Don't attack them now.

"I left my silk scarf here, I came back to collect it, it is an expensive one."

The nurse stood like a sentinel at the door.

"Take it and go. I should be reporting you for pushing me, but I will overlook it."

Evie took her scarf and put it into her handbag. When she was out of earshot of Kevin she whispered to the nurse.

"I saw you, trying to get a thrill from other people's husbands, I should report you."

She saw shock register in the eyes of the young woman, but she hurried off down the corridor, suppressing the desire to laugh out loud.

Chapter Sixteen

By the following Wednesday, Evie was pleased to see that there was a marked improvement in Kevin. He was so happy to be back tending to sick animals that he whistled as he left the house in the mornings. And his headaches had gone, thanks to his new medication. Even the fact that they made him drowsy in the evenings suited her as he invariably went to bed early after a hot meal. She had been dreading an angry outburst about her involvement in Orla's literacy programme but to her astonishment on Tuesday morning he praised her.

"Good work Evelyn, in my travels around the county I still encounter farmers who go to great lengths to hide their illitcracy from me. In future, I can suggest that they join the library's scheme."

She smiled at him.

"You do that. By the way, don't worry about food on Thursday evening when I am teaching young Patsy, your dinner will be in the oven."

Do you hear yourself – sucking up to him?

For a moment he looked nonplussed.

"Oh, I forgot to tell you that I am going to a card night on Thursday, some of the lads in Kensley Stud

Farm are into poker and they have invited me to join them."

"Kensley Stud Farm! Is that the one near Maynooth?" Evie wrinkled her nose.

"Yes. They start their card games around nine at night and sometimes it can go on until the early hours of the morning but at least it's different from working with animals. "

"I am delighted for you since the fire you were just going from bed to work. It will do you good."

He studied her for a moment and then he changed the subject.

"I should be cutting back on the fags, that know-all doctor in Dublin reckons that my cough is related to tobacco smoke."

"Yes."

He pulled a face as he walked past her.

"Baby steps Evelyn, I am trying."

On Friday morning the postman delivered a parcel from Robert just as she was on her way to work. Curiosity overcame her and she unlocked the door and went back indoors to unwrap it. There were several more notebooks from his time in Africa as well as a lovely card showing a still life painting of fruit and flowers in autumnal colours.

Opening the card, she was delighted to find the following lines.

To Evelyn.

"It seems a long time
since I heard from you
but I am a patient man.
Robert."

She knew that he was being ultra-cautious lest Kevin read it. Smiling, she hid it at the bottom of her handbag and put the notebooks in the filing cabinet. Then humming to herself she locked up and cycled to work. Later, when Iris went to The National Library to do some research, she typed Robert a long letter, telling him everything that had happened since they last met. She was grateful that he had given her plenty of time to work out where she wanted their friendship to go and as her fingers slipped lightly over the keys of the typewriter she was in no doubt.

You saw Kevin with that nurse on Saturday so have some fun yourself.

She signed the letter, which ran to three long pages, with a blue fountain pen and added an "X". Hopefully, he would have it by Monday's second post at the latest as she had suggested that she would meet him on the following Saturday under Clery's clock at midday, unless he phoned her in the meantime.

That evening, she had just finished making a white sauce to serve with baked cod and chips when Kevin arrived home red-faced.

He just grunted when she greeted him and went straight upstairs to the bathroom to wash.

Then as the clock in the hallway slowly ticked away several minutes, she tried to keep the dinner hot. Her heart seemed to beat faster when she heard him emerge from the bathroom and bang the door into his own bedroom. Eventually, he appeared in fresh clothes but with a sour face.

Appease him. You knew the good humour would not last.

"Kevin would you like water or something stronger with your dinner?"

He took his place at the table.

"A glass of milk will do I hope that fucking dinner is not burned."

"No. I think that you will enjoy it."

He sucked in air and then exhaled loudly as she served the food, then she sat down opposite him. In the background, a male voice on Radio Eireann announced that he was about to present a concert from Vienna which had been recorded.

To the strains of Mendelssohn's music they ate their meal, she did not dare to look at him directly, she could sense that a storm was brewing.

Once he had cleared his plate he enquired about dessert.

"Just a few minutes and I will heat up the custard to go with some apple pie."

She made her way to the cooker.

A moment later he grabbed her by her hair which was in a loose ponytail and pulled her over to the back door.

"Kevin, stop." She pleaded.

Then, poking a finger into her face he held her with his left hand.

"I was called out to a hill farm today, to put down a poor horse who had fallen into a deep dyke, if that wasn't bad enough when it was all over the farmer's wife invited me in for a cuppa …"

He paused while she tried to wriggle away from him.

"Please Kevin let me go."

He tightened his grip.

"Anyway, who happened to call while I was having the tea and scones only their next-door neighbour, a man called Eamonn Cooke. He proceeded to tell me all about the night you and that slut from Dublin went into Butler's Bar and made a disgrace of yourselves."

"I am sorry, but it was not our fault, the men had a bet on to see who would start a row with us by firing insults in our faces."

His hands moved to her shoulders and he shook her vigorously. Then pushing her against the wall he continued.

"Don't blame drunks in a pub for having a go at you. If you had any respect for yourselves, you would not have entered a kip like that at all."

"We were at the cinema next door we just wanted a quiet drink in the snug."

"I was told that you were both very drunk and were asked to leave."

She protested.

"We had just had a drink brought to us, there was no time to get drunk!"

"You stupid cow! This is the second time recently that you caused trouble in public."

She saw him eye her breasts and for one awful moment, she thought that he was about to rip her blouse.

She put her free hand across her bosom in a protective manner. Then he mocked her.

"If you thought that I would bother with your tits you can forget it."

Instead, he stamped on her foot and then shouted into her ear.

"If there is a third incidence you won't get off so lightly."

She bit on her top lip as she tried to extract her foot.

He laughed in her face.

"You are pathetic!"

Then he opened the door and pushed her outside.

"Learn to act like a lady not a whore!"

She shouted back at him.

"I thought people were deemed innocent until proven guilty, but you would not even listen to my side of the story."

He walked past her as the sound of a car crunching up the driveway took his attention. She hurried back inside and shut the door, she did not want anyone to see her in such a dishevelled state. Then a big black Ford Prefect came to a stop near the window, it had a Dublin registration and as she peered out through the net curtains, she saw Kevin's mother alight from it.

An alarm went off in her head.

Get into the bath before she sees you in this state.

She raced to the bathroom and stripped frantically while the bath was filling up. She could hear voices in the hallway but then they died away. After soaking for twenty minutes, she rinsed her hair and wrapped a huge bath towel around her body as she walked across the landing to her room.

Her mother-law was standing at the foot of the stairs craning her neck.

"Evelyn, I thought that you were going to stay immersed in that bath all night."

"Esther, how good to see you! Sorry about the bath but I was gardening earlier, and you know how clay goes everywhere."

Why not just tell her that her beloved son is a bully.

"Hurry up and come down, Kevin has just been called out to some emergency with a cow calving."

"Give me five minutes."

She saw the older woman shake her head with exasperation and then return to the kitchen.

When she went downstairs, she found Esther standing at the cooker frying rashers.

"Take a seat, I will finish that."

Evie said as grease erupted from the pan and hit her on the wrist.

"Thank you, I had a very early start this morning and my varicose veins are hurting."

Esther's wrinkled face looked sharper than ever.

They chatted for a few moments about the rough seas on the crossing between Hollyhead and Dublin. Then Esther complained bitterly that she had not kept her informed about Kevin's medical problem. Evie was so tired of listening to her whiny voice that she turned around and snapped.

"Kevin is a stubborn man he did not want me troubling you with his problems. I just went along with his wishes."

Esther stubbed out her cigarette in a ceramic ashtray when Evie left a plate of food in front of her.

"I don't believe that he is stubborn, instead of praising his courage you are assassinating his character."

Evie sat down at the table and poured the tea.

Count ten before you speak.

"Look here, we all know that your relationship with Kevin has not been ideal, he likes to tell you his own news."

"What are you on about?."

Evie remained calm.

"I was merely trying to explain why I did not fill you in."

Esther ran a manicured hand through her shiny grey curls.

"What you think does not matter, I am his mother and the minute I got his letter and found out that he was in a Dublin hospital, I decided to visit and see with my own eyes."

"Well, he is doing well now."

Evie buttered bread like her life depended on it while Esther glared at her.

"He is working far too late! He should have his feet up at this hour."

"But he enjoys working, he loves animals," Evie observed.

Triumphantly, Esther retorted.

"He is just like his father, so kind and loving."

Evie wanted to shout in her face and tell her the truth about her son. Instead, she fiddled with her wedding ring.

Suddenly, Esther's voice broke the silence.

"You look so pale, with all that loose hair around your face, you are not expecting, are you?"

"Expecting what?"

"You know well what I mean, are you in the family way?"

Evie rounded on her mother-in-law.

"How dare you! Every time you visit you ask that same question. And my answer remains the same, your darling white-headed boy refuses to have any medical investigations relating to our childlessness."

Esther's voice was as cold as ice.

"I have told you several times that the fault for your childlessness lies with you, the men in our family have always been virile. You have only to look at Kevin to know that he is a real man."

Evie made a derisive noise in her throat.

"Tell me, how do you know a real man? Does he have bigger private parts than others?"

Esther left down her knife and fork.

"Don't be so crude! You think that you are very clever just because you went to some fancy commercial college after your Leaving Certificate, but I see through you."

Evie made a face.

"I don't intend to waste any more time arguing with you. We both know that all we have in common is Kevin, so we can either insult each other until he returns or else tolerate each other."

Esther relented.

"Look here, I would just love to have a grandchild and given that my other son is a man of the cloth I have pinned my hopes on you and Kevin."

Evie gulped down a mouthful of tea as Esther reached for her bag on the floor. She took out a paper bag and shoved a box into her hands.

Evie opened it, to reveal 4 hand-painted egg cups in blue pottery depicting wildlife from the English countryside.

"Thank you, Esther, they are lovely."

"When I saw them, I thought of Kevin as I know how much he loves a boiled egg."

You are incorrigible, everything is about you and your son.

They spent the remainder of the meal chatting about the surgery that Esther's husband had undergone for cataracts.

Then Esther asked.

"Can you please show me to my room, I am tired."

"Certainly, just give me ten minutes to make the bed. It is the blue room near the head of the stairs."

By the time the bed was prepared, Esther had wandered through the other rooms, running her finger along furniture to check for dust. And when Evie called her, she swept in like a Prima Donna.

"I see that nothing has changed, it is several months since I visited, and you still have separate bedrooms. No wonder you are childless."

Evie moved closer to her and said in an overly sweet voice.

"Sleep well, I know that the sea crossing can be tiring especially for people of an advanced age."

Then she hurried out while her mother-in-law bit her shiny red nail with exasperation.

Chapter Seventeen

When Evie informed her mother-in-law the following morning that she would be late home due to her participation in the Literacy Programme, Esther rolled her eyes.

"It will give me a chance to have some precious time alone with my son."

Evie ignored the barb as she stacked her cup, saucer, and plate on top of the other dirty dishes in the sink.

"Son, I will make your favourite meal, colcannon, followed by apple pie with cloves. It's obvious from your trees weighted down with apples, that you don't get many apple tarts here."

He leaned across and patted her hand.

"Thanks, Ma, no one can cook like you not even the finest chefs in Dublin."

Esther giggled like a young teenager while Evie replaced the lid on the sugar bowl with a bang.

"Kevin, I thought that you were going over to Kensley to play poker tonight."

He turned on the charm for his mother.

"That was before my darling mother came all the way from England to see me, I can play poker any night.

I would not miss this evening alone with her for all the world."

You two-faced bowsie and all the times you complain about your mother behind her back.

Esther waved a hand in the air.

"Thanks, Kevin, you are so appreciative."

Evie felt like throwing up at the whole charade.

"I have to be in early for work this morning. Mrs Ryder-Lee has invited some important literary people for afternoon tea."

Esther brushed crumbs off the table

"Off you go then! I can tidy up."

"Thank you."

Esther made a conspiratorial face at her son, as Evie pretended not to notice.

After work, despite the light rain, she cycled at top speed until she reached the Lisheen road. Instead of riding directly to Patsy McGinley's home she dismounted from her bike and studied her watch, she still had at least half an hour to spare before she was due there. Then checking to make sure that there was no one approaching in either direction she opened the rusty gate which marked the lane up to Mrs Dolphin's cottage and got back on her bike. Soon the outline of it appeared and she gasped when she saw the freshly thatched roof and whitewashed walls with matching red door and window frames. She had expected a shack, but it was obvious that this woman was running a successful practice.

A few light taps on the knocker and a tall, thin woman in her late sixties opened the door.

"Yes, Can I help you?"

Evie gave a nervous smile.

"I hope so may I come inside I am not sure what I want."

A huge smile spread across her clear skin.

"Certainly, follow me, what is your name?"

"Evelyn Brown."

Evie concealed her second name as there was a possibility that this woman had heard of Kevin or even read about his part in rescuing Mrs Goff in one of the local papers."

"Sit down and tell me what ails you."

The woman led the way into a small room which reminded Evie of an old -fashioned chemist's shop, from her childhood. Along the four walls were shelves, some filled with books and notebooks and others with dark green bottles and jars.

She took a seat near the small window while the older woman sat at a desk and proceeded to write in a notebook.

"I- I have bruises on my arm, shoulders and foot, I would like to know if you can give me any ointment to speed up the healing process?"

The woman left down her pen and looked directly into Evie's eyes.

"You can call me Mai all my friends do. Did some man give you these bruises?"

Evie hesitated for a few moments.

"No, I got them when I fell from my bicycle."

A cold piercing stare and then in a matter-of-fact voice.

"Look here Evelyn, either tell the truth or leave, I am too long in this business not to know when a woman is covering for their spouse."

Evie's face turned scarlet.

"I am sorry, you are correct, my husband pushed me and then…"

"Ok. let me see them, take off that cardigan and blouse and your stockings."

Evie removed her clothes.

"Turn around and let me see."

Mai took out a huge magnifying glass and studied the bruising for a few minutes.

"I am guessing that this happened yesterday. They are fresh bruises, your poor foot looks very sore."

"Yes, that is true."

"Right. Put on your clothes and I will be back in a few minutes. I have the perfect treatment for those ugly bruises."

She hurried from the room while Evie sat on the edge of her chair, smoking a cigarette.

Eventually, after several minutes the woman returned and sat down.

"Apply this ointment four times a day for seven days and I guarantee you that your skin will be as clear as a newborn baby's. I am using a plant that grows wild in shady places and woodland called *Polygonatum multiflorum*."

Evie stubbed out her cigarette.

"Thank you, may I ask where you learned all about herbs?"

Mai gave a cynical laugh.

"If that is a veiled way of asking if I am a witch, the answer is no. I studied herbalism in London under a Russian doctor who believed in combining the best of herbal medicine with orthodox medicine. I learned so much from him, but he died during the Blitz on London along with my husband who was a psychiatrist."

Evie took a puff from her cigarette and exhaled slowly.

"I am so sorry to hear about your double loss."

Mai touched the diamond ring on her finger.

"I was heartbroken our son Paul had just finished university, so I decided to come to Ireland and start a new life. My parents were Irish, hence the name Dolphin, my husband's Russian name might not have gone down so well with the Irish."

Evie agreed.

"Dolphin is a great name and I even heard someone refer to you as "fishy."

"Really!" Mai threw back her head and laughed.

"Paul is an architect and lives in Dublin, he married an Irish woman, they have five children. I am just a regular grandmother and the opposite of a witch despite the rumours, but I take it all lightly."

Evie nodded. "It is a real pleasure to meet you. How much do I owe you?"

"I take into account each individual's circumstances and charge accordingly."

"Well, to be honest, we are both working."

" I appreciate your honesty. Then the fee is one pound for the first consultation and if you think that my treatment is not working you can come back to me and I shall review your progress. May I say that I can help also with marital problems if you wish to talk to me at any stage. I have provided a listening ear to many a troubled wife."

Evie handed her the money.

"Thank you, I shall bear that in mind."

"Take my card, I got the phone installed here as it can be a lonely place in winter, but I have some good friends who come to visit."

"Thanks again for everything."

Evie followed Mai to the front door.

"My pleasure, I suspect you need a friend who will not judge, you know where I am if you need me."

They shook hands and then Evie cycled slowly down the lane. Somehow, she felt lighter as if all her worries about Kevin had been taken from her shoulders.

Patsy was waiting outside when she arrived.

"Mrs- I thought that you were not coming this evening," he said sheepishly.

"Sorry that I am late, but something came up."

"I did all my homework and I tried to read a book I found in the shed belonging to my stepfather, it's about horses but some of the words are too hard."

"Don't worry in a few weeks you will fly through that book, you are a smart lad."

"Thanks."

He opened the door into the cottage.

"I will be back in a minute I want to close in the hens for the night before the fox gets them in this rain."

A smell of woodsmoke filled the main room. Biddy along with her four other children were around the table, sorting through tin cans filled with blackberries, which they had just picked.

"I hope that I am not disturbing the work," Evie said.

"We are picking out the best of the crop for you, you can take home a can."

Biddy wiped her purple-stained fingers on her crossover apron.

"Thank you, you are very kind," Evie replied.

They made no attempt to move so she took a seat on a rickety stool near the fire.

Biddy nodded in her direction and spoke to the tallest child, a girl of eight or nine years.

"Molly, make a sup of tae for the woman, and she about to show your big brother how to read."

The child hurried off to get a teapot from the press.

"Do you know that my auld relations, all tinkers, would not let you pick blackberries after St. Michaels day the 29th of September." Biddy declared.

Evie pulled a face.

"Yes, I have heard of that superstition but it seems silly - today is October 9th and those blackberries are still perfect."

"God's truth they are fine, but my mother told me that the saint kicked the devil out of heaven on that date and so the demon cursed all the blackberries in the hedges. Did you know that?"

Evie had heard the tale many times, but she decided to humour the tinker woman.

"No, that's something I never heard before."

Biddy clasped her hands together.

"You see us tinkers are not stupid we know a lot about the countryside."

"I am well aware of that Biddy."

When Patsy returned, Biddy beckoned to her family.

"Get inside, we can't be in the way while the scholar is learning."

They scampered off, their faces and fingers covered in purple stains, except for Molly who brought a cup of strong black tea.

Evie took out a tin of Lemon's toffees from her bag.

"Share these."

The little girl's eyes opened wide with delight.

"Ta very much, ma only buys us bull's eye sweets or gobstoppers."

Evie laughed as she skipped off to show the others.

Patsy tut-tutted at the tea.

"You could trot a horse on that tae."

"No, it's fine, it will keep my brain alert."

"Sorry about the mess and the noise, look at that table, I will clear a corner where you can leave your books."

While he was stacking dishes into a basin she spoke.

"Patsy, the evenings are closing in and the weather is worsening so I was wondering if you would come to my house from next week, I don't like cycling home in the dark."

His eyes grew moist and he pulled up a chair beside her.

"Will Mr Moore mind if I go to your place? People look down on us because my mother was a tinker and so was my father."

Evie had to take a couple of deep breaths before she replied as his candour was touching.

"No way! I thought that you got on well with him, does he not heal Queenie when she is sick."

He rubbed his nose.

"Yep, he does, and he has a way of looking into her eyes that calms her down, but he is different than you."

Evie allayed his fears.

"Naturally, he is different, he is a man."

Patsy smiled.

"Right so, I will go to your house next week, I don't mind the dark at all. And if you want any work done, I can help out on Sundays when I get a day off from my own job."

"I will bear that in mind Patsy."

She took out a stack of flashcards with different words marked on them in various colours.

He sat down beside her.

"Don't forget Mrs that you have to see Queenie before you leave, I plaited her tail this evening. She's a beauty, I bet that she would win a prize at the Horse Fair in Ballinasloe if I brought her there."

"Be sure to remind me later, now it's time to get down to work," Evie said firmly.

On Saturday morning, Kevin drove Evie and his mother to the local train station.

He wiped away a tear as he hugged his mother tightly before she boarded the train.

Evie watched with an air of detachment. She was relieved that her mother-in-law was leaving, she was tired of Kevin's fawning behaviour. Not only was he all over his mother but he had gone out of his way to be demonstrative of his affection towards his wife.

It had taken every ounce of her willpower to refrain from shouting at him the previous evening after he had kissed her passionately on the lips and declared.

"I love you, Evelyn."

Instead, she had managed a dry response.

"Ditto."

While Esther, who had looked on silently closed her lips tightly.

Once on the train, Evie walked through carriage after carriage until she found an empty one, then she took a window seat facing Esther. While the train chugged along through the outskirts of Redmills, Evie lit a cigarette aware that she was being observed closely.

When the engine picked up speed Esther delivered a verbal blow.

"I don't understand why it is necessary for you to go into Dublin on a Saturday to do work for some globe-trotting doctor. God knows Kevin works his back off with those sick animals and you already have steady employment with that Ryder-Lee woman."

Evie felt a knot in her stomach as she lied.

"It's not about money, this doctor is a friend of my boss and so I feel obliged to help him out as he intends to write two books about his years in Africa. I type his hand-written notes, there are boxes of them but he pays me well."

She pointed towards her briefcase on the spare seat.

Esther lifted an eyebrow.

"Small wonder that you cannot conceive, running around like a spinning top, you should be at home like other women looking after your man."

"Look here, I like to be independent and have my own money."

Esther turned her head away and glared out the window while Evie, who was excited at the thought of seeing Robert pretended to read *The Redmills Champion.*

In Kingsbridge station, they parted company. Once Esther boarded an express train to Cork to visit her son, Evie took a city bus to O'Connell Street.

Robert was standing patiently under the clock at Clerys department store. He saw her as she was crossing the street towards him and he waved excitedly reminding her of a small boy.

His moustache is fully grown, and he looks more distinguished than ever.

He moved to the edge of the pavement and waited while she weaved her way through double-decker buses, cars, and horse-drawn vehicles. Once she reached him, he took her into his arms without a word and they kissed passionately.

"Get out of the fucking way, you toffee-nosed fornicators."

A hawker pushing an old pram filled with knick-knacks, shouted as she tried to negotiate a pathway between them and the other pedestrians. They stopped and looked around to see the source of the profanities. Then, they both laughed as Robert took out a pocketful of silver coins and handed them to her.

She gave a toothless grin.

"Musha, thanks sir, I did not mean what I said. I hope you and your fine lady have a long, happy life."

Robert winked at Evie and then turned to the woman.

"Move along now and don't be so quick to condemn other people, have you not learned anything from the Bible?"

She dropped her head and gave one mighty shove to the pram as she moved off.

"She went like a scalded cat," Evie remarked, as he put an arm around her waist.

"It's so good to see you. You remind me of an African violet, beautiful and mysterious."

Go on flirt with him, he is gorgeous.

"And you remind me of Clark Gable in Gone with the Wind, sporting that tash."

"Fancy that!"

He smirked as they walked towards the Gresham hotel at the top of the street.

Chapter Eighteen

"How about a walk in Phoenix Park?" Robert suggested as they left the hotel following a three-course meal. Evie studied the gathering storm clouds for a minute.

"I would love a walk but just have a look at that sullen black sky."

He laughed heartily as he unlocked the door to his car.

"Don't worry I won't let down the soft top on the roof today if that's worrying you."

Five minutes later, he parked near the entrance to Dublin Zoo and they set off for a walk along a pathway that wound its way into the centre of the vast park.

Robert's tone changed.

"The whole concept of a zoo sickens me, all those poor animals from sunnier climes imprisoned in cages until they die. Lions, tigers, and elephants should be free to roam the plains of Africa."

Evie tightened her grip on his hand.

"I know it's horrendous, I cannot bear to think of their suffering. Kevin as you know is a vet, when he was a student, he campaigned for better conditions for them."

"And did he succeed?"

"Just a few token changes were implemented but he reckons that in time large animals will be kept in mini reserves rather than behind bars and concrete walls."

"I hope so. It was wonderful to go on safari in Africa and see herds of elephants in the wild."

"Watch out!"

A branch from a horse chestnut tree suddenly snapped and fell to the ground, missing Robert by inches. On closer inspection, they realized that three young boys had climbed the tree and were shaking the branches vigorously.

"What are you doing up there?"

"Mister, we are just collecting conkers but a lot of them are still on the tree."

A boy with a strong Dublin accent shouted.

Robert laughed.

"Enjoy yourselves. Would anyone like a few coins to buy chips?"

Three heads quickly peered out from the foliage and then climbed down to the ground.

Evie noted their dirty faces, threadbare jumpers, and short trousers which revealed scratched, skinny legs.

She rummaged in her handbag and gave them coppers, while Robert handed a few shillings to the tallest boy.

His eyes were like saucers.

"Thanks, sir."

While another boy of seven or eight added.

"Thanks, Mrs."

"Where do you live?" Robert enquired.

The smallest child answered.

"The flats in Gardiner Street, me Ma sells apples and oranges in Moore Street because me Da went off to England, I have seven sisters."

Evie shook her head. "I hope you are all attending school."

A chorus of voices said.

"We are."

Robert took a ten-shilling note from his pocket and gave it to the middle boy who was covered in freckles.

"Give this note to your mother and tell her to buy meat for tomorrow's dinner."

The child took it and put it into his shoe.

"Nobody will steal it from me now."

"Good, now off you go to the chip shop and treat yourselves."

Robert's eyes twinkled and in a second the boys had disappeared.

"You are so generous Robert!"

He turned to her.

"About ten years ago I had patients in those flats, most families still exist in crippling poverty, as soon as the boys reach 15 or 16 years of age, they take the boat to England, if they are lucky enough to have the fare for the crossing."

She kissed him on the cheek.

"I know, in Redmills, not a week goes by without at least six or seven young people emigrating – there is no work for them in this country."

His shoulders shook with disgust.

"When you think of the time, energy, and money that is wasted by the government on banning writers like Brendan Behan and J.D Salinger, while all around us there is abject poverty, it makes my blood boil."

"You should go into politics you would do a better job than the crowd in Dail Eireann."

He winked and drew her closer, while they enjoyed a lingering kiss under a huge sycamore tree. When drops of rain began to fall, they stopped.

"Luckily, I brought this umbrella."

He opened a large black one as she rested her head on his shoulder.

"I love listening to rain falling."

"And I love being here with you under a sprawling tree in a downpour," he declared.

When the shower cleared, they headed for the Victorian flower gardens with a large ornamental lake. Suddenly, out of nowhere a herd of fallow deer crossed the road a few yards ahead of them and disappeared into a copse of trees.

"I would love to paint them, they are wild and free," Evie said wistfully.

He stopped and looked into her eyes.

"How has Kevin been treating you, since his discharge from St. Matthews?"

"There is an improvement in his health but he has mood swings if things don't go his way,"

"My offer still stands, if you ever need to get away from him, you can stay at my house."

Change the subject before you reveal how he attacked you over the episode in Butler's bar.

" I know thank you. Robert, do you mind if we don't continue this subject?"

His eyes widened and then he replied.

"Whatever you wish, Lyn."

It was a term of endearment which he had used only once before, and she loved it.

"Thanks, Robert, I mean Bobby," She said with an air of mischief.

He grinned.

"It's the first time anyone has ever called me Bobby, you know that there are two Irish American brothers rising to prominence in the USA, John F. and his brother Bobby."

"You must be a mind-reader, I was just reading about the Kennedy family last night in the Irish Press. I guess that's where I got that name!"

He turned to her.

"Evelyn Moore, I think that I am falling for you despite my best efforts to keep our relationship at a platonic level."

Her eyes grew teary and she hesitated before answering.

"I know, I wish that I was not entangled in such a complex web with that man known as my husband."

They walked on in silence for a few minutes, a boy ran by them in hot pursuit of his brother who was brandishing a catapult.

"Oh, I have enjoyed every minute of this afternoon," she whispered.

He put his arm around her waist and planted a kiss on her nose.

Then he said, "I have a surprise for you in the car."

Her eyes lit up like those of a child.

"Tell me please."

"Do you remember the photographs that we had taken in Dun Laoghaire?"

"I do."

"Well, I got them a few weeks ago but I was wary of sending them to you by post so now when we are apart, we can at least look at photos."

"That's brilliant. Sometimes, when I try to recall your face I wonder if our meeting was just a dream," Evie said.

"Well, no longer! You look stunning in the photos he really captured your beauty."

"You old smooth talker!" She exclaimed with a laugh.

It was well past eight O'clock when she finally reached home. She found a hastily scribbled note from Kevin explaining that he had gone to Kensley Stud Farm to play card games and that he would stay over for the night because he was not on call that Sunday.

She kicked off her high heels, lit a fire in the big grate in the sitting room and poured herself a double brandy.

Then as the music of Buddy Holly emanated from the radio, she tore open the big brown envelope containing the black and white photographs. The first large one captured Robert with his arm around her while making a mischievous face at the camera. And the second one, equally large, showed him planting a kiss on her cheek. There were also two pocket-sized versions of the same photos.

For several minutes she studied them, examining Robert's handsome face and his eyes which seemed to speak to her. She also noted her own radiant expression that the camera had captured.

Then she ran her finger along Robert's image.

"You really are the image of Clarke Gable," She exclaimed before kissing it.

Later, when she went to bed, she took the photos with her and placed them under her pillow. In the morning she would lock the big ones away in her filing cabinet while the small ones would fit under the lining of her red handbag.

Her dreams that night were about her schooldays, a red-faced nun was caning her for kissing a young teenager with Robert's beautiful blue eyes.

Next morning, she hid the photos as planned and then cycled to second mass in Redmills.

It was a typical autumnal morning the trees were decked out in shades of brown and ochre and a mist was just lifting to reveal a blue sky. It had been weeks since she had attended mass, but it was better to go and occupy her mind than wait at home for Kevin to appear. The church was full, but she found a seat at the back where a pillar obscured her view. A long meandering sermon from Fr. Gandon on the evils of what he termed fornication and extra-marital sex, almost sent her to sleep.

You would swear he was able to read your mind and your longing for Robert last night.

The Angelus bell rang loud and clear by the time the mass was finally over. She hurried outside into the sunshine with her head down, hoping to avoid queries about Kevin's health from inquisitive mass goers. Then she heard someone calling her name and turned around to see that the priest had come directly from the altar and was waving at her.

"Mrs Moore, how good to see you! You have not been here for a while."

She ignored his comment.

"Fr. Gandon, how nice to see you."

"Come into the vestry with me for a few minutes."

"Ok, But I have people calling later." She lied.

He made a pathway through the crowds as people greeted them both. One woman in a camel haired coat pulled Evie's sleeve.

"Mrs Moore, how is that brave man of yours?"

"Fine." She muttered.

Suddenly, the priest spoke in a sharp voice.

"Some other time Miss Kenny. Leave us in peace."

Once inside, he closed the heavy door and urged her to take a seat as he sat behind a big oak table.

"Mrs Moore, where is your husband today?"

She twisted her ring nervously

"He went to play cards with some friends last night and is coming home later."

He eyed her suspiciously.

"A parishioner who teaches in a National school out in the country came to me recently. She had a story about your husband."

"My husband!" Her face turned red with shock.

"Yes. One of the pupils told her that she saw the vet with her mother. It appears that they were kissing, and the child was upset. Her mother was recently widowed."

Evie felt like the blood was slowly draining from her body, but she said.

"Why tell me, why not confront him? And are you sure it was Kevin?"

"Come now Mrs Moore, I am trying to nip this in the bud before it goes too far. Yes, it was Kevin, the child is twelve years old and gave a perfect description of him."

Seething with rage, she banged her fist on the table.

"What do you expect me to do about it?"

The priest hesitated.

"Calm down, I just wondered if he has lain with you recently in an intimate way, I thought that since the accident you might be asking him to abstain because of his headaches and all the treatment in hospitals."

Shaking her head, she exclaimed.

"My boss always says that fact is stranger than fiction! Just because my husband is carrying on with a widow you turn the blame back on me!"

"Now, now don't take this the wrong way." He loosened his priestly dog collar.

She stood up.

"I am leaving don't blame me because Kevin cannot keep it in his trousers!"

"There is no need to be so coarse, Mrs Moore, I am trying to help your marriage."

"Keep your nose out of my marriage."

She opened the door and rushed outside, allowing it to bang in her wake.

Chapter Nineteen

The trees looked stunning on that October afternoon, bedecked in every hue of brown, red, purple, and yellow. Evie cycled slowly, trying to calm her nerves by concentrating on the blaze of colours. In desperation, following Fr. Gandon's revelation she had rushed home and phoned Mai Dolphin, who had agreed to see her.

When she arrived at the pretty cottage, she found Mai apple-picking in an old orchard at the back.

"Come and join me, it will do you good."

She called, while Evie propped her bike against the stone wall.

"I am so grateful that you agreed to see me, I felt that I would explode if I did not get it all off my chest," Evie explained.

"Here, take a basket and fill it with windfalls, I am nearly finished, then we can go inside and have some herbal tea. "

Evie exchanged a wan smile with her.

It was well past 4 o'clock when they went inside the cosy kitchen where a kettle was boiling on the range. Mai made two large mugs of camomile tea and presented one to Evie along with a chunky slice of caraway cake.

"Now, start at the beginning and tell me everything."

She drew up a chair and faced Evie across the table.

Evie massaged her forehead.

"Do you know that I already feel better, thanks to your calming presence."

"Good, you need to feel safe here if we are to make progress."

"Also, your ointment was miraculous, there is only the slightest hint of bruising left on my foot and arms."

"I am glad, I started out studying philosophy and mathematics and then as the years went by, I became interested in psychology and later herbalism. After my husband's death, I decided to give back to others some of what I had learned along the way."

Evie lowered her voice.

"Before I go any further, I need to tell you my correct name, it is Evelyn Moore."

Mai waved her hand in the air.

" Don't worry, women who are being abused and bullied within the so-called safety of their family homes are often ashamed to reveal their true identity because they feel they are in some way to blame."

As the minutes turned into an hour, Evie talked while Mai listened, only now and then interjecting. Finally, when a large ginger tabby cat awoke and jumped from his basket onto the windowsill, Mai stood up and let him outside.

"Ginger, off you go, you lazy boy!"

Evie laughed, "I think he has heard enough!"

Mai smiled.

"Perhaps."

They sat in silence for a while, then Mai spoke.

"Now that I have heard the full story, you must give yourself plenty of time to think about those questions which I raised including leaving him. Then we shall meet again when you feel ready, I don't expect answers, that is not what this exercise is about, instead, I want you to face up to reality."

Evie fidgeted with her cigarette packet while Mai continued.

"But in the meantime, if you intend to stay in that poisonous atmosphere, you need to find ways to mind yourself."

"I - I think that I will lock my bedroom door in future, I am sick of being forced to have sex."

Mai shrugged.

"It will not be easy, but you must try to take back some of your power, he enjoys placing you in the role of victim. Do you intend to confront him with Fr. Gandon's tale?"

Evie picked at the pink polish on her thumbnail.

"I need time to think about all that. My head is reeling but talking with you has been so helpful."

"I hope so."

Evie took out her purse, but Mai put her hands together as if she were praying.

"No need for money today, I don't work on Sundays."

"But you have just spent the whole afternoon listening to my woes," Evie knitted her brows.

"And I feel privileged that you shared them with me so keep your money this time. My own dear Aunt Lily suffered at the hands of her husband, and I felt guilty when she died that we had not done enough to help her."

"Did she die recently?"

"I was in my twenties when she passed, but she had suffered for years at the hands of a drunken husband."

"I am sorry," Evie said.

"My dream is that someday there will be places of refuge where women can go to get away from dangerous husbands."

Evie wiped a tear from her eye.

"That sounds great, for many years I convinced myself that it is all my fault, he chips away at my self-confidence."

Mai's eyes focused on hers.

"Remember that if you need to get away from him you can stay here for a while."

"You are the kindest person I have ever met," Evie said.

"Let me give you a big hug."

Mai extended her long arms and they embraced.

Later, Evie had just unlocked the door when Kevin arrived home, worse for wear.

Resting his bottom on the edge of the table, he related how he had won over fifty pounds at the card games.

"It was like taking sweets from a baby, I had forgotten the thrill of winning," he remarked.

"You were always lucky at cards."

She placed the kettle to boil on the electric ring of the cooker.

"I don't want anything, I had a big meal in Navan on the way home."

"Navan! I would have thought that was miles out of your way."

"Not really, I left Tommy Finlay home, his van is in for repairs."

"Right."

She proceeded to make a sandwich for herself with ham and hard-boiled eggs.

"Where did you spend the day?" His voice was low, but his eyes scanned her body from head to toe.

"I went to second Mass …" She paused.

Be careful I am so tired.

"And where did you go then?"

For a moment she felt her stomach knotting as she lied.

"I cycled to the Harvest Fair in Dunsany with Orla."

He sniggered.

"I cannot imagine that dried up prune taking any interest in a fair."

"Well, she enjoyed it, all the stalls and the sheepdog trials."

"You cannot be serious! Are you winding me up?"

Keep the lies going before he breaks you down.

"Yes, she even guessed the weight of a large fruit cake and won it."

"Well, fuck me!" He pushed back his fringe from his face.

"Yes, she was delighted."

"Now, I am off to bed, I didn't get much sleep last night, I slept on a mattress."

"Ok, don't forget to take your tablets."

He took out his wallet from a back pocket and extracted a pile of pound-notes, then leaving them beside her he said.

"Evie, buy yourself some nice jumper during the week, you have been through a lot with me since the fire."

There was a strong smell of whiskey from his breath, but she continued cutting crusts off the sandwiches, without looking up.

"Ah! Thank you, Kevin."

He took a piece of ham and picked at it.

"You are welcome, as they say easy come easy go. Good night! I could sleep standing up like an old horse."

"You look drained, get some rest."

On Monday afternoon, Iris made an announcement.

"Before the winter arrives, I want you to start driving lessons with Brendan, he is taking you out at 2pm today for an hour."

"This is a surprise, you are very thoughtful Iris, thank you."

"I am a woman of my word, you should be driving for the last few years, cycling around in all kinds of weather."

"I know, I promise that I will do my best."

A small voice reminded her.

He won't like this news so don't tell him.

"You can practise here on the estate for some weeks, heaven knows there are enough lanes and then the main driveway as well."

"That's great, I will make up the lost hour by taking work home."

Iris smiled. "No need to do that just jot down a list of places in Dublin, which might appeal to readers in Scotland, I have a radio interview in Edinburg shortly."

Evie tided a stack of stamped addressed blue envelopes.

"Certainly. By the way, I will buy a small car once I am confident."

"Good, you can fit in at least one hour every week or maybe two if I don't need Brendan. I am too old to learn, my eyes as you know are not the best."

"Once I get my car, I can run messages for you instead of Brendan, leaving him more time to help in the garden."

Iris gave a tinkly laugh.

"Indeed, you see there is method in my madness."

Just then, Brendan arrived.

"Evelyn, your carriage awaits!" He nodded at Iris.

"Brendan, take good care now of Evelyn and be patient, you men are always wanting in that department."

"Not me!" He replied with a boyish grin.

To her surprise, she enjoyed the lesson, Brendan was a gentle teacher and by the time it was over, she was able to move the car forward in low gears as well as reverse it.

"It feels empowering to sit behind the wheel and actually drive!"

Evie remarked later to Iris, who was all ears about her experience.

"Keep up this enthusiasm and I might even be persuaded to try some driving lessons."

Iris then inhaled tobacco smoke through a long cigarette holder.

"Yes, it's easier than I had imagined," Evie glowed with confidence.

Suddenly, Iris's mood changed.

"Are you going to tell your husband?"

"No. Not until Brendan is satisfied to let me drive on my own on a public road. Then I will arrive home some evening with my own car, done and dusted!"

"I like your style! It will be too late for him to object."

Iris moved to the ashtray and flicked ashes.

Evie rubbed her hands together.

"The man has no idea about what's ahead of him!"

An inner voice teased her.

At last, you have come to realise that your marriage is like a chess game.

Chapter Twenty

"Is this monkey suit too big?"

Kevin paraded into the kitchen in a jet black dress suit.

She glanced up from the ironing board.

"No, I think it's a perfect fit.

"Ok. I see you have a new frock -"

Stand up to him never apologise for spending your own money.

"It's actually called a ball gown."

"I would say that cost more than a week's wages," he inclined his head.

"I put that money you gave me from your card playing towards the cost, I got it in a sale."

If he knew the real price, he would hit the roof.

Evie continued to gently iron creases from a delicate grey stole, borrowed from Iris.

He fiddled with a cufflink on his shirt.

"Speaking about cards, I am going away tomorrow, and I should be back early on Monday."

She frowned but did not look up.

"Where?"

"To Galway, there is a big tournament there, a few of the lads are going."

She heard a buzzing in her ear like a siren.

Don't bother answering him.

He cleared his throat.

"What the hell are you doing with that iron? I will be leaving in ten minutes, hurry up!"

When he had gone into the sitting room, she left down the iron and muttered under her breath.

"Fucking bastard."

The twelfth Redmills Harvest Ball was bigger and better than ever. It was a clear moonlight night in late October and as the crowds took to the floor to dance, the hotel management flung open all the doors. The cool air rushed inside dispelling the overpowering smell of powdery perfume, mixed with sweat and tobacco smoke. All the well-heeled members of the business and farming community were in attendance determined to enjoy themselves to the music of the famous showband know as Clipper Carlton. Kevin was in his element as local dignitaries and couples commended him for his courageous actions.

At the end of the night, the newly elected Lord Mayor presented him with a Waterford glass bowl and decanter on behalf of the local community.

In his inimitable gravelly voice, while camera bulbs flashed, the Mayor said.

"Kevin Moore, our very own hero, this is to honour your valiant efforts in carrying Mrs Goff from a blazing inferno and saving her life."

To which Kevin duly replied.

"I only did what anyone here present would do if they found themselves in similar circumstances."

Thunderous applause broke out while Kevin was captured for posterity with a broad smile as he accepted the crystal. Evie, standing beside Andrew and Elizabeth in the front row had a painted smile on her face.

The same sentence buzzed around in her brain like an irritating fly.

This publicity will just make him more arrogant than ever.

It was after four am when they finally reached home. On the short journey from the Redmills Arms Hotel, Kevin's driving had been erratic as the numerous brandies which he had consumed, dulled his brain. At a bad bend in the road just outside the town, they narrowly missed colliding with a man who was driving his cattle to the fair in Trim.

Once inside the house, he removed his dickie-bow and flung it on the table.

Slurring his words, he said.

"I – thought -only harl-ots wore purple."

Gathering up the folds of her long gown she ignored him and hurried to her bedroom. Then with her heart racing, she locked herself inside, she had been preparing for this moment all night.

Her breath was laboured as his fists pounded against the door.

"Let - me -in, I want -to show you how much I love -you."

In a calm voice, she replied,

"Go to bed Kevin, you are drunk."

No response.

Suddenly, a hoarse cough, followed by a string of curses as he retreated to the bathroom for a glass of water.

She stood by the window for a long time and studied the ghostly shades of light and dark in the sky. For a few seconds, it occurred to her that she was in some sort of parallel universe. *Am I dead and condemned to do my purgatory here with HIM?*

Then pinching her arm, she dismissed the idea, while her head thumped from too many gin and tonics. Exhausted, she lay down on the bed and in a few seconds, she fell into a deep sleep.

Several hours later when she awoke the house was shrouded in silence. From the evergreens came the raucous cawing of crows.

Her satin dress was scrunched around her breasts and she was naked from the waist down.

Sitting bolt upright in bed, her heart sank when she saw that the door was wide open.

He found a spare key and violated me while I slept.

She listened for a few minutes but could not detect his presence.

Jumping from the bed she slammed the door and stepped out of the dress.

She felt dirty, like a soiled piece of linen.

Grabbing a housecoat, she ran across the landing and allowed the bath to fill while she rummaged for Dettol in a tall slim press.

When she found it, behind jars of bubble bath and shaving cream her trembling fingers struggled to open it. Then using the cap as a measurement, she emptied the pungent antiseptic into the hot water.

For at least half an hour she remained in the bath while the whole room steamed up. Eventually, emerging from the tub she towelled her body dry.

There was still no sound from downstairs. Padding into his bedroom in her fluffy slippers the empty top drawer of his dressing-table revealed to her that his toilet bag was missing along with his electric shaver.

He has gone like a thief in the night.

Then it dawned on her that she had no idea of the time. She hurried to her bedroom and checked her wrist-watch.

The hands showed 4:20 pm.

She ran like a madwoman down the stairs.

A hasty note on the kitchen table informed her that he would be home early on Monday morning.

She took a box of *Friendly* matches and walked to the sink.

Then she grabbed his note and lit it, in seconds it was just a heap of ashes.

You selfish pig.

On Sunday afternoon, she had arranged with Brendan to take an extra driving lesson as Iris was in London for a holiday.

"I cannot believe that you have made such progress in a few weeks."

Brendan said after she had driven slowly around the estate several times and brought the car to a smooth stop in front of the conservatory.

She made light of her efforts.

"I have been keeping track of the lessons and in total, I have had eight, so it is about time that I mastered basic driving skills."

Brendan readjusted the mirror.

"Still, this is a big car and not the best for a beginner, but you are a natural driver."

"You are too kind, the real test will come when I go out onto public roads."

The tiny imp in her head was pushing her.

Ask him about a locksmith.

"Brendan, do you know of a trustworthy locksmith who would change a lock today?"

He eyed her for a minute and then laughed.

"You Dubliners! Do you think that he will fit locks and then send someone in to steal from you?"

Her face reddened.

"Maybe, but there is also another reason which I know you will keep to yourself."

She spoke slowly to make the lie sound convincing.

"Of course, I respect you."

"Since the fire, Kevin is inclined to sleep-walk so I thought about changing the lock on our bedroom door as I am worried that he might go out onto the road some night in his sleep." Brendan ran his fingers along his bald head.

"Don't worry Evelyn, your secret is safe with me. Poor Kevin. I will drive over to my cousin Mattie on my way home, he will sort you out."

"Thank you so much, Kevin would be annoyed if he knew I told you about his little problem. He is away until tomorrow morning, but I need the lock sorted as soon as possible. I will make it worth his while."

"Consider it done. He will call this evening to your house he has a big family, and the extra money will be useful.

"I really appreciate this favour, thank you."

Evie opened the door and stepped out of the car.

"Any time Evelyn, you are welcome."

Brendan replied, then he walked around to her side of the car and left a gentle hand on her shoulder.

"If you don't mind me saying so you look a bit pale."

She gave a deep throaty laugh.

"Don't mind me, I just drank too much at the Harvest Ball on Friday night and I still feel tired."

"Ah! That explains it. I have no sympathy for you!" He chuckled loudly.

Thanks again Brendan, I am looking forward to meeting your cousin."

He winked. "No bother!"

As she cycled home, she remonstrated with herself for telling lies to Brendan but then another voice said.

This is about self-preservation, you could not tell him that your own husband violates you while you sleep.

Chapter Twenty - One

"Yesterday, Andrew's brother died suddenly in Hull, leaving me with double the work to cover this week,"

Kevin said, as he paced the kitchen impatiently while she fried eggs and sausages. He had returned from Galway only twenty minutes earlier and after a mad rush to the bathroom where he washed and shaved, he had demanded food.

Ignoring her lack of interest, he continued talking.

"The practice is too big, I will have to ring around for someone to cover Andrew's workload."

"Good idea," Evie replied, but inside her mind was in turmoil.

I cannot confront him now, about his assault on me on Friday night, he is like a bat out of hell.

When she placed the food in front of him, he banged the end of his fork on the table.

"The work of a vet never ends I should have chosen an easier profession."

She felt anger well up inside her.

"For heaven's sake, you have just come back after a weekend away."

"One full weekend off per month is not enough and don't get me started about every second Sunday off, it is in name only because there is always some emergency."

Drying her hands, she said.

"I have to hurry, or I will be late for work."

"Is there any more tea? He asked.

"Get it yourself, there is plenty in the pot." She replied.

He shouted some comment as she hurried down the hall to collect her bags, but she left by the front door and headed for town. At the post office, she spent ten shillings on stamps for a parcel containing 90 pages of typing to Robert, along with a note to say that she would be travelling to Dublin on Friday evening and staying for two nights at the Phoenix Hotel.

Keeping the tone of the letter humorous, she had not given any reason for her trip to the city as lines imprinted on her mind from a woman's magazine guided her.

"Cultivate an air of mystery when interested in a man."

Brendan was waiting outside her office when she arrived at Richmond House.

"Well, did Mattie do that job for you?"

Unlocking the door, she nodded as he followed her inside.

Then in a breezy voice, she said,

"Thanks so much for your help. No more sleep-walking for Kevin."

Yet a warning bell went off in her head.

You haven't told your husband that you changed the lock, wait until he finds out!

"No problem Evelyn. Now that Mrs Ryder-Lee is away I could give you some extra driving lessons this week maybe from 1-2 pm each day."

"Well, if you're sure you're not going to cause hell with the other staff."

He blew his nose loudly.

"No, I will be working like a trooper in the garden all week and as it's our official lunch hour, they can't say much."

"Right, that's settled. Maybe, I could venture onto the main road and do a few miles in the real world."

His face glowed.

"By the time the boss returns, you will be able to drive into the village with the post."

"Brendan, do you know where I could buy a reliable second-hand car?"

He leaned on the desk with his two hands.

"I know one car dealer in Dublin who sells older models of the Ford Prefect, I think it would be a good choice for you and he sells clean cars."

"Clean cars?" She looked surprised.

Throwing back his head he guffawed.

"By clean, I mean that they have not been tampered with, no dodgy parts or shoddy mechanical work."

"Oh, I see! Please ring him and see what he has in stock."

His eyes narrowed.

"Evelyn does your husband know that you are interested in buying a car, some men are funny when it comes to their wives driving."

She hesitated.

"Well, I haven't told him yet."

There was the warning bell again inside her.

But I cannot allow fear of Kevin to stop me now.

For a few awkward minutes, only the high-pitched screech of a peacock on the lawn filled the room.

In a gentle voice, he continued.

"I am awfully sorry to ask that question, it's none of my business except that I don't want him saying that I enticed you to buy a car."

She studied his face for a few minutes.

"Is there something that you are not telling me?"

His cheeks had reddened.

"Evelyn, don't mind me I am just an old fellow, I will be 64 years old in January."

"Come now Brendan, have you heard something about Kevin?"

"Well, just that he frightened the daylights out of poor Maisie Larkin a few weeks back."

She swallowed hard as her blood seemed to freeze in her veins.

"Why?"

"Your husband was driving along when he came across Maisie and her donkey, bringing home turf from the bog. It seems she gave the ass a belt of an ashplant and your husband got out of the jeep, grabbed the stick, and threatened her with a similar blow on the back while shouting curses at her."

At least, it's not another story about his philandering.

"Look Brendan, my husband is passionate about animals and he sees a lot of animal abuse, so I suppose he acted in the heat of the moment. I am not condoning his behaviour but maybe it will stop that woman beating her poor donkey again. I was shocked myself when I first moved to Meath at the harsh treatment of donkeys."

"Look, I don't like it either and I know your man is great with animals but apparently he insulted Maisie by saying that she was nothing but a frustrated spinster who needed a good rub of the relic from some auld man."

She stumbled over her words

"I am not responsible for his coarse tongue."

Brendan stood up straight.

"Look here I did not mean to tell you, but you did question me."

She smiled faintly at him.

"Yes, indeed I did. Let's forget about it, Kevin, I am sorry."

"No bother. See you at 1 o'clock." He winked at her and left the room.

With her mind racing, she lit a cigarette and inhaled slowly.

She hated hearing all these sordid tales about her husband.

Someday I want to be free of him.

On Friday evening as soon as the clock in the courtyard chimed five times, she locked up and Brendan drove her to the train station. She caught the 5.35 to Kingsbridge, every carriage was crammed. She had forgotten that it was Halloween and young boys from St Ciaran's boarding school were returning home for the weekend. A youth with a naggin of rum peeping from his pocket gave her his seat. When the last glimpse of Redmills disappeared through the trees, she sat back and closed her eyes. Everything was going to plan, Kevin had been so busy all week juggling Andrew's work along with his own that there had been no time to quarrel. On Thursday morning as he was leaving the house, she had told him about spending the weekend in Dublin, just as she had hoped he immediately assumed that she would be staying with Val. She replayed their conversation in her head.

"The sooner that useless whore goes back to London with her yellow-faced man the better."

She had retorted.

"Don't blame Val, you swanned off last Saturday for two whole days and nights. Besides, I have stocked up on all your favourite food, so you won't starve."

Giving a sly chuckle that he made no attempt to suppress, he then added.

"I did and I enjoyed every minute of it."

Suddenly, she heard a voice and opened her eyes.

"Tickets please, tickets please!"

An official was standing in front of her.

When he was finished, she sighed and returned to day-dreaming.

Following her lunchtime driving lesson, Brendan had announced that there was no reason why she could not drive solo to the village in future.

"All you need now is plenty of practise and then you can buy your own car," he said proudly.

The very thought of it filled her with excitement and empowered her.

Inclining her head towards the window she listened to the clickety-clack of the rail joints as the wheels rolled over them.

My first step towards escaping from Kevin's clutches is in sight.

As the train reached Black Bush station, she was asleep.

Robert was waiting for her at Kingsbridge. This time she spotted him from a distance despite the crowds milling around. The truth was that she carried around the two smaller photos which he had given her and not a day went by when she did not study his features.

"What a sight for sore eyes!"

He wrapped his long arms around her.

Dressed in a sharp grey suit, white shirt, and a purple tie with matching handkerchief, he looked distinguished. And she felt a longing to hold him.

He is gorgeous.

"Oh it's so good to see you," she responded.

He returned her hesitant kiss with gusto.

A feeling of euphoria enveloped her as he took her case and they jostled through the crowds waiting for trains to the four provinces. She was wearing a red suit from Switzers, which she had bought for a book signing in Hodges Figgis the previous year. It was the exact shade of Hawthorn berries and when combined with her neat bun gave her an air of sophistication.

"You look divine."

He called across to her as a man pushing a trolley loaded with cases separated them.

"And you Mr Gable are looking mighty fine yourself."

She countered with an American drawl.

A matronly woman with a dowdy coat and a lilting Cork accent tapped her on the shoulder.

"Is that Clarke Gable?"

Evie stopped in her tracks and continued speaking in an American accent

"Yes. Do not approach him, he is a busy man."

But her advice went unheeded. The woman elbowed her way through the boisterous schoolboys and approached Robert.

"Mr Gable, I saw you in *Gone with the Wind,* please give me your autograph."

She fumbled in her handbag and took out a fountain pen and the only piece of paper which she could find, a crumpled-up prayer card to a lesser-known saint of the early church.

"I beg your pardon?"

Robert glanced at Evie who was in hot pursuit of the woman.

"Mr Gable, this lady wishes to have your autograph," Evie explained.

He hesitated.

"I don't do autographs but for you, I shall make an exception."

He proceeded to scrawl the words, Clark Gable, across the back of the card while Evie had to bite hard on her lip to prevent herself from laughing.

"Now, my pretty lady!" He handed it back to her.

She gasped.

"Oh, thank you! I will tell all my friends they will be so jealous."

Robert shook his head as she hurried off.

"Is that woman three sheets to the wind?"

Evie shook with laughter.

"The smell of sherry from her breath would knock you."

They withdrew hurriedly from the station and walked to the car park while Evie mocked him about his efforts to emulate an American accent.

When they were seated in the car Robert's face grew serious.

"Are you really going to spend two nights all alone in a bed at the Phoenix Hotel?"

She caught the longing in his eyes.

"Only if I have no better offer!" She replied.

"Good." He said as he leaned across and left a hand on her knee.

Suddenly, she pulled him towards her.

"Kiss me like we were sixteen again."

"You won't have to ask twice."

He looked into her eyes before gently kissing her soft lips.

Intimacy with Robert was totally different from anything she had ever experienced. He was so loving and generous that the actual sex act with him seemed to be just a natural follow-on to their lovemaking. When she got married, she had been a virgin, due to inhibitions and fear of pregnancy instilled in her by the nuns who had taught her. In the early years of their marriage, she had convinced herself that Robert's total selfishness and rush to climax had been due to his sexual inexperience. However, having finally expressed this opinion to Val who had had several partners, she realized that he had no desire to change his ways and was happy just having his own needs met.

Now, thanks to the patience and loving kindness of Robert, she had discovered that her fears of never being able to enjoy a normal loving relationship with a man, following years of brutality from Kevin had been groundless. And after their first act of sexual intercourse, he had held her close for a long time and stroked her hair, while she nuzzled into his hairy chest and dozed.

The time seemed to fly by in Robert's neat but eccentric home where shelves groaned under the weight of books on every topic under the sun. Mementoes from his years in Africa competed for space with photographs of his two sons, taken from childhood through to their graduations. Only one grainy image of his deceased wife, a petite woman with sad eyes, was on display, it captured her telling a bedtime story to the boys.

On the second night, after dinner, they lay on the rug in front of a big, roaring fire and made love. In the glow of post-coital intimacy, Robert opened a bottle of brandy and they shared accounts of their respective marriages until dawn broke and they desired each other again. Later, they fell into bed exhausted and slept through until late afternoon when Evie awoke with a start and realized that the last train for Redmills would be departing in just over one hour.

For the next twenty-five minutes, she washed, dressed, and packed her case like one possessed while Robert checked every room to see if she had omitted any of her belongings.

The gate to platform four was about to close when they arrived but Evie hurried through and climbed onto the nearest carriage as Robert called after her.

"Take care my gorgeous Lyn."

It was his pet name for her, and it always made her feel special.

She took the first vacant seat and pushed down the window as if her life depended on it.

The train was just pulling out when she shouted above the noise of the engine.

"You too, my handsome Mr Gable."

She could see him laughing as he gave her a thumbs up sign to acknowledge that he had heard.

Inside the carriage, two young girls tried to suppress their giggles by covering their mouths. While their grandmother pointed a finger at Evie and rebuked her.

"Have you no respect for yourself?"

Evie gave her a disdainful look.

"Mind your own business."

But the older woman was not easily silenced.

"Shouting like a fishwife through a window, you are a disgrace to womanhood."

The two girls were now deathly silent as the train slipped through the outskirts of the city and headed for open countryside.

Evie frowned.

You old harridan.

Next, she slowly took out a cigarette, lit it and then blew coils of smoke in the direction of the grandmother, who conceded defeat and moved to another carriage hastily followed by her two charges.

The imp was back in her mind

Don't end up like that stupid woman so constrained by convention that she cannot bear to see anyone having fun.

Chapter Twenty - Two

When she reached home the house was silent and in total darkness. Flicking on the light switch she gasped when she saw the kitchen in total disarray. Two heavy, burnt saucepans filled the sink, and the table was strewn with the remains of several meals. Stale slices of bread were juxtaposed with tea-stained cups and encrusted plates revealing globules of bacon fat and a frying pan with congealed grease. While the floor was strewn with crumbs, particles of dried mud and cigarette butts.

This is revenge because I took the weekend off.

It was the same throughout the house. In the bathroom, a large ring of dirt clung to the rim of the bath and several wet towels were strewn across the floor along with his soiled underwear and muddy socks. Worst of all was the sitting room where the latest editions of the newspapers were abandoned on the floor beside an ugly stain of coal on the green flecked carpet. Approaching his bedroom cautiously she peered in through the half-open door and realized that he was asleep in bed although it was not yet nine pm.

Let sleeping dogs lie!

She closed the door gently and returned to the kitchen where she set to work with the radio playing soft music in the background.

She was just nearing the end of the clean-up when the stairs creaked.

Her jaw muscles tensed, and her throat seemed dry.

He is coming.

He breezed into the room, in fresh slacks with a cream shirt and new jumper, leaving a smell of his cloying aftershave in his wake.

She studied him from the corner of her eye.

"The wanderer returns! How are you, Evelyn?"

She placed the last cups on the dresser and then faced him directly.

"Fine. Val was asking about your progress."

He sat on the edge of a wooden chair as he tied his laces.

"I hope you told her that my cough has disappeared, and my headaches are few and far between thanks to the miracles of modern medicine."

"Indeed, I did, she was delighted that you are feeling much better."

He stood up and yawned.

"I did not have a spare minute since you left. Thankfully, Andrew is back tomorrow."

"Good. He will probably give you a few days leave in lieu."

An image of Robert's chiselled cheekbones filled her head.

Kevin Moore, if you knew what I did in Dublin, you would not be so smug.

"Andrew rang earlier I am off now until Saturday, he has arranged for a young lad fresh from college to do my work."

She hesitated.

"You look as if you are going out."

He drummed his fingers on the worktop.

"Do you remember me mentioning a friend from my days at university called Charlie Eivers?"

"The fellow who dropped out of college to work on a ranch in Texas."

He smirked.

"Exactly! He read a feature in some daily newspaper about my valiant efforts in rescuing Mrs Goff from the fire, so he rang me, and I am going to visit him in Kildare."

"Tonight?" She said incredulously.

"Yes. His father died last year, and he is back running the farm, a substantial one by any standards. He abandoned his wife in Texas, and so he is delighted with any company."

"Right, don't forget your case"

The words were out before she put any thought into them.

"Don't fuss, I have already put a few things into a bag, but I needed 40 winks before I set out on the journey."

He took a step towards her, but she moved backwards and started to stack up saucepans.

Grinning broadly, he pinched her bottom as she froze.

Then he whispered into her ear.

"Your skin is glowing, how about a quickie?"

Her voice rose, cracking with rage.

"You cannot have me every time you feel like it."

The second the words were out of her mouth she regretted them.

She watched as his face changed to an angry red.

"We will soon see about that."

He grabbed her by the head and hairpins from her bun flew in every direction.

Then as her dark hair fell around her shoulders, he squeezed the base of her neck

"Kevin, please let go you are hurting me."

"If you behaved like a normal wife there would be no need to hurt you!"

He released her but stared coldly into her eyes.

A warning voice sounded deep within her.

Just do as he says before he harms you.

I won't leave here until I get it."

She heard herself saying.

"Ok.

He shoved her in the direction of the stairs and slowly she climbed the steps.

In the bedroom, he opened his belt and pointed at the bed.

Suddenly, she felt his full weight pressing against her, forcing her head back roughly as he pinned her on the bed.

Then to black out what was happening she kept repeating silently to herself.

You must escape from this devil.

On Monday morning, Evie arrived early at the office, she hung her coat on the rack and changed into a navy suit with a white polo neck. Then slipping on high heels she applied lipstick and some eye shadow. Iris arrived moments later, full of joie de vivre after her trip to London.

"Good morning Evie! You must be feeling the cold, wearing that thick polo neck sweater."

Don't tell her that your neck is bruised.

"Yes, the weather is chilly. Did you have a nice time Iris?"

"Wonderful, apart from an indecent proposal from a poet ten years my senior!"

Evie digested this for a moment.

"Really?"

"Yes, he should be neutered."

Smiling, Evie asked.

"Did you get a phone call from your publisher, I told him that you were staying at the Dorchester."

Iris sat on the edge of her own desk.

"Yes, he has asked me to amend a few paragraphs in my latest work, he says they are far too racy for little innocent Ireland and that the book will be banned here if I don't change them."

Evie threw her hands in the air.

"Just when sales of your last two books here have broken all the records."

"I know! So, I shall have to gloss over the sex scenes, as it seems there is no sex yet on this island."

Evie burst out laughing.

"Iris I wish I could paint your expression of disgust."

"Oh, don't bother, between the meddling of the church and the state in matters of conscience, it is a wonder that anyone is allowed to have a private life."

Evie pulled a face, she sensed what was coming next.

"Tell me how is that husband treating you?"

"More or less the same, I spent the weekend in Dublin with a friend, it was like being in a different universe."

Iris lifted an eyebrow.

"If I am not mistaken it sounds like you have found someone to distract you."

Evie looked startled.

"Is it that obvious?"

For a few minutes, there was a tense silence while the older woman searched for a spare cigarette holder. Then she pressed hard on a red embossed lighter and the distinctive smell of her American cigarettes quickly filled the room.

"It's obvious to me because I had one or two affairs during my own marriage, so I know the signs."

Evie lowered her voice.

"Please don't tell anyone!"

"Your secret is safe with me, I am happy to hear that you are trying to distance yourself a little from your husband, that's all."

"Thank you, ultimately I will have to leave him, but I am not ready just yet for all the practicalities of such a decision."

The imp in her brain sneered.

You finally admitted that you must get away from him before he wastes your life.

Iris scrutinised her while the clock ticked away the seconds.

"I know it will not be easy to start all over again when the law still favours the man, especially if there are no children but don't despair, there is a light at the end of the tunnel."

Evie's face brightened.

"Yes, but gradually I hope to make my own way in the world again. My next step is to buy a car and thanks to you for insisting that your chauffeur be my driving instructor."

With a big smile, Iris replied.

"Chauffeur indeed, Brendan is not overburdened with work here so it was the least he could do. He filled me in earlier on your progress. I am delighted, no more cycling in bad weather and having to change into your office clothes on arriving here."

Evie's eyes sparkled with joy.

"I can't wait, I have enough in my savings account to buy a good second-hand car and I have asked Brendan to choose one for me."

"Terrific, now we must get down to work."

Iris decreed as she eyed the pile of letters on her desk waiting to be signed.

The following day Brendan arranged for a salesman to bring a green Ford Anglia to Richmond House. Evie spent all lunch hour driving around the town guided by Brendan who took the passenger seat.

"It's no use trying to deny that I want this car!

When they returned, she parked it near the wing which contained the office.

Brendan rubbed his chin.

"Even though it's a smaller model than I had in mind for you, I think you should take it. It has had just one owner and would not be for sale except that he died suddenly, his wife has no use for a car."

"And the price you mentioned, can you get a few more pounds knocked off?" Evie asked.

Brendan hesitated.

"Are you paying by cash or hire purchase?"

"Cash."

"Right, he will probably knock off another few pounds in that case. Have we a deal?"

"Absolutely!"

He opened the car door.

"Ok Evelyn, I will sort out the details. I think you are doing well the car is in great nick."

Evie felt like a child waiting for Santa Claus.

"Thanks, Brendan, for everything."

"You are very welcome, Evelyn. "

On Thursday afternoon she took possession of the Ford Anglia and Iris generously allowed her to leave work at four pm.

"Drive home safely and enjoy yourself, it's not every day that a woman buys her first car."

Iris walked with Evie to the vehicle and kissed her on both cheeks.

That same evening, when young Patsy Mc Ginley called to the house for his weekly lesson, Evie showed him the car proudly.

"She's a great bus, Mrs."

She laughed.

"But it's neither a bus nor a woman Patsy!"

He grinned cheekily.

"I know but that's the way menfolk like me talk about cars, I listen to them at fairs, do you know that my old grandfather said that back hundreds of years ago we were not called tinkers but "the walking people.""

"Yes, I have heard that the term is a direct translation from an Irish expression."

He kicked all four tyres as she watched.

"If you like, I can wash and polish her for you when she gets dirty."

"Thanks, you are very good."

"Not at all Mrs -sur- you are teaching me book learning for nothing."

"And it is my pleasure to do so you are a smart student. Now, did you get your homework finished this week?"

She enquired as they headed for the house.

"By the hokey I did, and I was able to read most of that book you gave me."

"Then you need a more advanced one this week," she observed.

Before entering the house, she stopped for a few moments and looked back at the car which in the moonlight seemed to take on an eerie presence. Inwardly she chided herself.

Don't be silly it's just a car.

When a chill went through her body, she closed the door and walked to the range where she warmed her hands.

Patsy, who was waiting for her to commence the lesson remarked.

"Beg your pardon Mrs but you look like you have just seen a ghost."

She said dismissively.

"Now Patsy, I don't believe in ghosts. It's just a cold night."

He looked at her from under his red eyelashes.

"Sorry, I have a big mouth as me ma says."

She rubbed her hands together.

"Forget it. Open your copybook and show me the composition you wrote."

While he rummaged in his old saddlebag an inner voice whispered.

God protect me when Kevin finds out that I have bought a car.

Chapter Twenty - Three

"Well, a new motor car for the missus!"

Kevin rushed indoors from the storm, leaving puddles of water on the kitchen floor.

It was Friday evening, and she was frying smoked cod to go with mashed potatoes and peas.

"Yes, it is mine. I was not sure if you would be home for dinner, but I made it anyway."

I cannot believe that he is so calm about the car.

Leaving his wet coat and boots on the floor he took a seat at the table.

"Yeah, I got up at four am this morning and drove straight to work. Then I called to Ray O'Dea's hill farm, so far he has three bullocks down with blackleg."

Evie added more cream to the potatoes as she asked.

"Is that a contagious disease?"

"No, it is infectious, animals ingest bacterial spores while grazing, so he is in big shit."

"Oh, that's awful."

She filled two dinner plates with piping hot food as he glared at her.

"Imagine he knew that my wife had bought a car before I did."

Her heart seemed to almost stop.

Go easy.

She left the plate on the table in front of him and then took a seat at the opposite end.

"Brendan sourced that car for me, I only heard about it on Monday, I would have told you, but you were away at your friend's all week. "

He stacked up peas on his fork and swallowed them greedily before answering.

"When I was leaving his farm, O'Dea shouted into the jeep at me.

"Really?"

Her head was repeating the same two words.

Breathe slowly.

Kevin squeezed tomato sauce onto his fish.

"The fucker made a remark about you."

Evie picked at her mash because her appetite had disappeared.

Kevin stared at her.

"I will tell you exactly what he said."

Rain and wind beat against the window while she scarcely dared to breathe.

Then he mimicked the thick accent of the farmer.

"I suppose you had a good ride in the back seat of the new Anglia with your missus."

She left down her cutlery.

"It's coarse and typical of an old farmer but I don't care, since I moved to Redmills I never cease to be amazed at how quickly gossip travels here."

He nodded.

"That's right about gossip travelling fast so don't have even a minor accident with any of the locals because I don't want my name sullied any further by you, you cute cunt going behind my back like that and arriving home with a car."

She refrained from answering but her palms were sweaty as she wondered what his next move would be.

The shrill ringing of the phone in the hallway made him jump and he hurried to answer it.

She was clearing away the dirty dishes when he returned but his mood had changed.

"Evie, make me a cup of tea with a few biscuits, I have to drive to a farm near Bective, a bloody cow with a twisted gut."

She pulled a face as she measured tea leaves into a pot and poured boiling water on them.

"What a night! It's pouring down."

Her stomach still had knots in it, but she dared to hope that the subject of the car was closed.

He munched on ginger nut biscuits as she filled his teacup.

"Is that too weak?" She enquired?

I am so relieved, it's out in the open that I don't mind playing the dutiful wife.

"No, it will do."

He stretched across the table for the sugar bowl while she was cutting neat slices from a fruit cake. For a few moments, a strong whiff of lily-of-the-valley filled her nostrils.

Anger filled her chest.

Was he with another woman?

She returned to her own place at the end of the table and nibbled on a piece of cake.

He smiled at her.

"I like the cake."

" I made it during the week."

When he had emptied his plate, he said.

"I hate having to go to that prick 's farm, on such a bad night."

"The poor animal must be suffering." Evie ventured.

"Of course, but that old Scrooge was too mean to make the call during the day as he was hoping she would have a miraculous recovery."

"More tea? There is plenty there in the pot."

He removed the tea-cosy and refilled his cup.

"After a few days away, it makes me see things more clearly. I don't intend to be still doing this in ten years from now. I might move closer to the city and concentrate on small animals."

"Right, it's worth considering," she said nonchalantly.

By then I hope to be long gone from this marriage.

He stood up quickly, knocking over a jug of milk.

"Can you not get a smaller jug?" He shouted.

"Sure, next time we can use the small cream jug."

She hated herself at that moment for appeasing him, but she felt it was better than making a bad situation worse by arguing back.

"Get me my grey hat and a spare raincoat."

His cheeks were crimson as he struggled to fit his feet back into the wellingtons.

She rushed upstairs to his room and returned a few minutes later with coat, hat, and an extra pair of wool socks.

"You are a topper!" He said as he buttoned up his coat.

Then she opened the back door and he stood for a couple of minutes as wind hurled in dead leaves onto the mat.

"Evelyn, I am sorry if I am rough at times."

She faked a smile.

"I know."

He hesitated.

"Well, what about an apology from you too for all your selfishness?"

She would choke rather than apologise.

"Drive safely Kevin."

He grabbed her left breast and squeezed it hard.

"Go on say sorry."

"I am sorry for my -."

"For your fucking self-centred behaviour."

"For my self-centred behaviour."

He released his grip but the whispering in her head was back.

There is that smell of lily-of-the-valley again.

"Did you buy a new aftershave?"

It was out before she could stop herself.

He looked quizzically at her.

"What?"

"There is a smell like a woman's perfume."

He shifted his shoulders a little.

"Well, it must be the new soap that Elizabeth brought back from England when she was over for her brother-in-law's funeral. She left a stack of it in the surgery."

Evie peered out into the darkness

"I don't like it, it's too sweet like a cheap perfume from Woolworth's store or one that any old whore would wear."

He eyeballed her.

"What the bollocks are you saying?"

"Just wondering?"

She gave him a thunderous look.

"Evelyn, sometimes, I think that you are sick in the head, imagining all sorts of things, now I have to go before this storm gets any worse."

"Watch out for falling branches."

Her voice dripped with sarcasm, but he made a dash for the jeep as she closed the door.

Later, as she listened to some jazz on the radio, she kept saying to herself.

That smell was too strong to have come from soap, it clearly came from perfume.

On Saturday evening, they attended the bazaar in the town hall. An annual event, the proceeds went towards the poor of the parish and was presided over by Fr. Gandon.

"The great and the pushy of Redmills are here."

Orla whispered to Evie with a mischievous glint in her eye.

When all the seats were taken, people stood along the sidewalls, forcing the priest to make an announcement.

"Ladies and gentlemen, I am now officially closing the doors, for safety reasons I am reliably informed that the hall is full. Thank you for such a wonderful turnout, now let the merriment begin."

The finale of the evening was a Wheel of Fortune where local VIPs were invited to spin the wheel. Sitting in her seat in the second row Evie inwardly fumed when the priest invited Kevin onto the stage.

The hypocrite, after whingeing to me about Kevin making advances to some widow woman.

"Kevin Moore, we all know you as a veterinarian extraordinaire but now I am delighted to name you: Person of the Year because of your outstanding courage in saving the life of Mrs Goff."

She was so annoyed that she did not catch the rest of his speech. To tumultuous applause and the flashing of cameras, Kevin was presented with a generous gift voucher for fishing tackle and a silver cup with his name inscribed on it.

Afterwards, Kevin, along with other VIPs was invited by the committee to Flanagan's public house for a few drinks. Although Evie was invited, she declined and opted instead to go to Orla's house for supper. On the way home, they bought bags of chips which they washed down with a bottle of whiskey. By the time the church clock struck midnight, Evie's reticence had dissipated, due to the alcohol. And she told her friend about Fr Gandon's hypocrisy and Kevin's manipulative ways.

Orla sitting by the fire, studied the flames as she said.

"Your husband is a street angel and a house devil, and by the sounds of it a philanderer to boot."

"I -I am thinking of leaving him but I need to plan for my own future before I just walk out, or I will be left penniless and without a roof over my head," Evie said.

Scowling, Orla got up and refilled their glasses.

"If you ever need a place to stay you are welcome here but do be careful with him as everyone thinks of him as a saint."

Shaking her fist in the air, Evie took her time before answering.

"Some days I hate him so much that the very sight of him disgusts me, but it's great to share it all with someone, thank you Orla. Do you mind if I stay here tonight as I feel tipsy and I don't want to drive home on my own in case, he starts a row?"

"Of course, you can stay overnight but I assumed that you had travelled to the bazaar in Kevin's car."

"No, he had to make a last-minute call to a farm out near the Mill so we travelled in separate cars. Mine is parked just around the corner from here outside the lane that leads to the new hardware shop."

"That's fine, give me a few minutes to make up the bed in the spare room."

Evie stood up and slurred her words.

"Let me help you, I feel like a boarder in some convent school who has just had a midnight feast."

Orla pulled a face in mock horror.

"Here comes Reverend Mother, be quiet!"

Then they both shook with laughter.

They slept late the next day until the shouts of children on the street, fighting over marbles, awoke them. After a light breakfast of poached eggs and toast, she left Orla's home and returned to the spot where she had parked her car the previous evening.

To her horror, someone had slashed the two front tyres and damaged the paintwork with a nail. Furious, she ran back to Matt McTiernan's house, which was next door to his garage, a few streets away.

While she waited with bated breath he thought about her dilemma.

"Obviously, it will be tomorrow before I can get new tyres to fit a Ford Anglia.

But I will tow it down here and then I can assess the damage, it will not be cheap as there is a lot of time involved in bodywork."

"Do your best, I don't want it left for a second night on the street. There's my phone number." Evie handed him a slip of paper.

"You should report it to the Gardai, they will soon get to the bottom of this vandalism."

"Yes, I intend to." Evie declared.

A lingering smell of oil came from his clothes and she noticed his nails which were black from years of probing at engines.

"I know that you don't usually work on Sundays so thank you for helping me."

"No problem at all Mrs Moore, I take it that you are the vet's wife."

She hated being viewed as an appendage to Kevin, but she forced a smile.

"You are correct. Thank you and goodbye."

However, instead of heading for the Garda Barracks, she decided to make her own enquiries about the act of vandalism. She retraced her steps back to her car and noticed a young boy with an unkempt appearance watching her from the laneway. She ran to him and as he tried to pass by, she blocked his way.

"What's your name?" She demanded.

"Shay but I did not touch that car."

Evie reckoned that the child was 9 or 10 years old and she caught him by the wrist.

"Who damaged my motor?"

He looked blankly at her.

"I will give you a shilling if you tell me the truth."

The boy's face reddened.

"I swear that I did not touch it, but I saw two big boys at it."

"Do you know them?"

She loosened her grip slightly.

"No but early this morning, I was on my way to borrow sugar from my Granny's when I noticed them at your car, so I hid behind a tree."

"Go on, tell me what you saw." She urged.

"They cut the tyres and then scraped it, before running off. I followed them as far as the main street but then I lost them as it was raining cats and dogs."

Evie felt as if her chest had been tightened by some force.

"Are you sure that there was no man in a jeep waiting for them?"

He looked at her.

"Won't I get my money from you?"

"Yes, you will." She gritted her teeth.

"I don't know, I told you, the rain was coming down in buckets."

Her heart sank as she let the boy's arm relax.

Then she opened her handbag and drew out a half-a-crown."

"If you promise me something you can have this."

His eyes opened wide.

"I promise."

"You must not tell even your parents that you were talking to me."

"I won't tell a soul, because I am afraid of my auld fellow, he would just beat me and take the money to the pub."

"Good lad."

She handed him the coin.

Quickly, he put it into his pocket and legged it up the street while she leaned against the wall, relieved that it was a Sunday because there was no one around.

She had feared that Kevin had taken his revenge by damaging the car but there was nothing obvious to link him to the act of vandalism on her car.

Shaking all over, she tried to think straight.

Have I become so suspicious of my husband that I blame a random act of vandalism on hi?

She walked to the Royal Hotel and made a call from the phone booth to Mai Dolphin.

On the third ring, Mai lifted the receiver.

"This is Evelyn Moore, I need to see you, but I am stuck in town with no transport."

The modulated voice at the other end reassured her.

"Evelyn, I can pick you up, where exactly are you now?"

"In the old hotel known as the Royal." Evie hesitated.

"I know it, I shall be there in twenty minutes," Mai's voice was full of concern.

"Thank you so much."

Evie felt beads of sweat on her forehead as she put down the phone.

Chapter Twenty - Four

In Mai's kitchen, where red flagstones covered the floor, Evie sat in front of a log fire and watched in silence as flames shot up the chimney. She had little appetite when her host appeared with a bowl of deep green nettle soup and brown scones, but she forced herself to take a spoonful. To her surprise it was delicious, and she finished it all in a few minutes.

"That was wonderful soup, thank you."

Mai laughed.

"I am glad you enjoyed it. I always get the same reaction from people when they see it for the first time but then they are surprised by how tasty it can be."

"Well, full compliments to the chef!" Evie exclaimed.

When the dishes were cleared away Mai pulled up an armchair and sat facing Evie.

"Now, that you have had some sustenance I think it is time you started talking. You looked like you had seen the devil when I picked you up in town."

"I know, it was the shock of having my car vandalised, so soon after buying it. And thanks for accompanying me to the Garda Station, my head was all over the place."

"You are welcome! It was a mean-spirited act and it had to be reported. But I think there was a lot more behind that weary expression I saw on your face."

Mai prodded the fire with a poker while Evie shifted in her chair.

"What horrified me was that I immediately blamed Kevin for it even though I had no proof. I hate the way our marriage has turned out, I am suspicious of him all the time, even about the smell of soap from his hands."

"Have you tried to talk through any of these issues with him?"

"No, it's impossible. He is just so set in his ways and he is always busy."

Mai removed an emerald ring and rubbed it against her sleeve until it sparkled in the firelight.

"Surely, he has days off."

Evie spoke in a low voice.

"Yes, but he allows his days to pile up of late so that he can go and stay with various friends, he has taken to card playing in a big way."

Throwing caution to the wind, Mai said.

"It is a toxic situation, having a husband who is either rushing to work or staying with a friend, it leaves you isolated."

Evie nodded.

"Yes, and if he is at home, he is ruling the roost, making demands on me ."

"You know that you cannot keep procrastinating about the state of your marriage, sooner or later it has to be faced."

Fiddling with her gold charm bracelet, Evie explained.

"I know, that's the reason I bought the car as it will give me independence."

"Yes, I get that but how will it help your troubled marriage?" Mai raised an eyebrow.

"If I leave Kevin, I will have to rent accommodation and I certainly don't want to live in Redmills where I will be regarded as a pariah for leaving St Kevin. So, by owning a car I can rent on the outskirts of Dublin and drive to Richmond House every day, I enjoy working for Mrs Ryder-Lee."

Mai sighed.

"It is great to hear that you are making plans to leave him, and I accept that you need to be prepared before you just walk out."

Evie rubbed her eyes wearily.

"Of course, I shall be pursuing him for money, as I did contribute towards the deposit on our house and the land – it was money I had from the sale of my mother's house."

"It will have to be done through a solicitor as I fear he won't give you a penny. And even then, the law tends to favour the husband in cases where there are no children, and the woman leaves." Mai said.

While Evelyn took out a cigarette and lit it, a log hissed in the hearth. And for a few minutes, they stared into the fire. Then she spoke slowly.

"I know that I will probably never get a halfpenny from him and that scares me. He will just say that I left him on a whim and he such a paragon of virtue."

"Come now, don't think like that. You must stay positive I will help you the man is a brute."

"Thanks so much, you are so wise."

Mai smiled.

"There is one more thing before I drop you home. You seem very anxious and on edge and if you wish I can give you herbs to calm you."

Evie's face changed as relief swept over her.

"That would be great. Some nights I toss and turn for hours as my mind tries to work out the best plan."

"Ok, I shall sort out a few for you."

Mai disappeared into her dispensing room and ten minutes later, returned with two small paper bags. Both had a list of instructions in beautiful handwriting pasted on the outside.

"Firstly, the camomile when stirred into boiling water makes a lovely tea and will relax you at any time but especially at night, Secondly, I am giving you a herb called *ashwagandha*, it can be stirred into hot milk and drank at night time."

"It's a strange name," Evie observed.

"It comes from Ayurvedic medicine, the name actually means *the smell of a horse,* but it has many benefits including helping your body manage stress. It's an ancient herb and grows in India and Africa too."

Evie grinned.

"I hope I don't smell like a horse after consuming it."

Mai grinned.

"It really is a powerful plant and will do wonders for your body. Ultimately, you need to build up your stamina, it should help you cope with what lies ahead."

"Thank you, Mai, I have heard a lot about ayurvedic practises through my friend Val, who has an Indian lover."

"Great! Now, I will drive you home."

Evie hesitated. "How much do I owe you for the herbs and for your time?"

"Five shillings for the herbs and you can put a donation into that blue box, it's for women who are in need of a place of refuge from their husbands."

"Are you sure? What about all the driving you did for me today?"

"Forget it, I am just happy to get every penny towards supporting those battered women who have no option but to stay with violent husbands."

Evie crossed herself without thinking.

"I know that I could be a lot worse off, at least I am educated and that gives me knowledge which is power in a sense."

Kevin was reading the *Sunday Press*, at the table in the kitchen when Evie returned home.

His face had an enigmatic expression.

"Thank goodness! I was beginning to worry about you."

" Mai Dolphin drove me home, I met her by chance on the street, my car was vandalised last night."

He threw a look at her from under his eyebrows.

"The Sergeant rang here about an hour ago, he told me that you had called to the Barracks to report the damage to your car."

"Does he have a suspect?" She asked.

"No, but I had a good chat with him as I look after his uncle's cattle and horses. He promised to do his best to identify the culprits."

The inner imp was goading her.

How convenient that he is a pal of the Sergeant.

She refilled the empty kettle which had been abandoned on the hot stove, then she exploded.

" I know that you paid a couple of boys to do it."

"Do what? You hardly think that I had my wife's car damaged on purpose!"

"I don't know what to think," She retorted.

He pushed the newspaper away.

"Didn't I tell you that you are paranoid!"

She answered in a low voice.

"Time will tell and then we shall see who the devious one is in this house."

He shrugged.

"Think what you like."

"Yes, I intend to."

She was about to leave the room when he said.

"Mai Dolphin, is she the woman who makes all those herbal concoctions?"

She glanced at him and decided to lie.

"Yes, I know her through work, she and Mrs Ryder-Lee are acquaintances and she often calls to the office."

"Mick Doyle got some healing potion from that auld one and swears that his arthritis was cured - then he gave some to his cow who is lame, but in the end, he had to call me to sort out the poor animal."

"You make her sound like some sort of enchantress."

He picked at a spot on his chin.

"Some say that she is a witch ."

She turned her back to him as she threw a shovelful of coal into the fire, hoping he would not guess that she had gone to the woman for treatment.

"Rubbish, she was kind and helped me out."

Where did you go after the Barracks?"

"She encouraged me to report the incident, afterwards I was still upset so she drove me to her home and made a meal for me."

He sprawled his long legs across the floor.

"Look here Evelyn, I am sorry about your car."

She looked around at him.

"What are you saying?"

"Well, the car will save you from cycling in bad weather – it was bad luck that a vandal damaged it so soon after you ac-quired it."

"Um-humm," she said vaguely.

I don't like his tone and the way he dragged out the word acquired.

"If it's any help I will drive you to work in the morning, there is a lot of rain forecast for the week ahead."

"Right, thank you."

"Now, there is a fight on the radio that I want to hear."

He pushed his chair back from the table and hurried to the sitting room.

Once he was gone, she automatically washed all the dirty dishes which he had used while she was away. And then having heated some milk, she poured it into a big mug before carefully measuring out the required amount of ashwagandha. When it was ready, she swallowed it down in a few gulps.

Kevin was shouting obscenities at the live boxing-match on the radio as she tip-toed by the sitting room and up the stairs to her bedroom. Within minutes she was asleep.

Two hours later, the room was filled with moonlight when she awoke with a start to hear Kevin shouting. For a second, she marvelled at how his voice travelled so far from the sitting room. Then it dawned on her that he was banging at her door and cursing because it was locked. She got up quietly and sat on the edge of the bed, but she did not answer when he called her name.

She shivered slightly, although several days had passed since she got the lock changed, he had not noticed.

He will explode – when he discovers that his key won't open it.

"Evelyn, open the door or I will just go and get the spare key. I want you ... a husband has needs you know."

Silence followed for a few minutes and then she heard him returning as he put the key in the lock and fumbled with it.

She remained silent, but beads of cold sweat ran down her forehead.

"You selfish bitch, you have changed the lock, open that door or I will break it down with an axe."

Suddenly, she heard herself say.

"Go to bed Kevin, I am too tired."

This only infuriated him even more and he began to kick at the door violently.

"It doesn't make any sense, why did you bother to marry me you must have known that it is a husband's right to obtain pleasure from his wife as often as he likes."

Covering her ears, she tried to block it out, but he only increased his efforts to get in by putting his full weight against the door.

However, when he threatened to throw a brick through her window, she gave in and opened the door. Immediately, he grabbed her by the wrist and pointed a finger into her face.

"All that effort just to reach my wife so that I can poke her! A court of law would not believe it! Imagine having the lock to the bedroom door changed to keep out your own husband."

She remained silent as he pulled her hair.

"Now, don't ever act like some virginal princess in a tower again with me! A man can take his wife anytime he feels the need, that's the law of the land."

She nodded.

For several seconds he cupped her chin in his hand.

"You are lucky that you are not married to the rough farmers I meet every day on my rounds, if their wives did that to them, they would give them a good beating. Am I right?"

"Yes, you are right." She felt like a rabbit caught in a snare.

Then she lay down on the bed and tried to distance herself mentally from the whole scene as he hurriedly removed her pyjamas.

Chapter Twenty - Five

The following week brought gale force winds and torrential downpours. Rain beat on roofs and against windows while the few remaining leaves from the trees swirled around streets and clogged drains and gutters. Soaked coats, broken umbrellas, and wet feet were the norm, it was Tuesday before Evie had her car returned to her but given the extreme weather, she did not complain about forking out for the tyres and repair work. Against her better judgement, Orla went ahead with her much-touted event:

An Evening with Mrs Ryder-Lee, at the town hall.

While Iris addressed a full house, composed of the great and the good from county Meath and its environs, she was disappointed that a handful of literary giants had not managed to make it from other parts of the country. However, Evie managed to restore her boss's good humour when she learned that a group of journalists and photographers who had travelled from Dublin for the evening, were forced to spend the night in a local hotel due to storm damage and blocked roads.

Taking Iris into a small room at the interval, she said.

"This opportunity can be worth a fortune to you in terms of publicity. Invite them over to Richmond House for a literary lunch tomorrow and it will impress them.

Iris, who looked stunning in a velvet plum dress frowned.

"Will it be enough notice for cook, we don't want to make a disgrace of ourselves."

"Counting all the people from newspapers, glossy magazines and journals, there are 12, I can help out in the kitchen and we can arrange for 2 extra waitresses from the town, it's no problem."

"You are a genius, Evelyn. I think this is a major coup, fortune has smiled on me bringing together such a prestigious group at my home. I will trust you to organise it all."

Evie glowed in her rust-coloured suit with a frothy cream blouse underneath.

"Certainly, I will phone cook now to tell her the news, no doubt she will be up at dawn. Also, I think that you should make the announcement as soon as you resume your session because you have an open question time at the end and people might wander off to a local bar or back to their hotel."

Iris took out a compact from her snakeskin handbag and reapplied wine-stained lipstick.

"Make it clear to cook that no expense is to be spared and if possible, hire the best waitresses from the town. I shall rely on you to choose the wine, a vintage Bordeaux from the cellar would go down nicely with Beef Wellington.

Ideally, we should be serving venison from the estate but not at this short notice."

Evie checked her wristwatch.

"Perfect! Beef for mains, what do you want for starters and pudding?"

"Seafood chowder -and- Baked Alaska to finish."

"Consider it done! I think it best if I stay at Richmond tonight as there is a lot to be organized."

Iris rummaged around in her handbag for a small bottle of Chanel No. 19 perfume. Dabbing it behind both ears she answered.

"Yes, of course, I will not get this show on the road without you. And with this inclement weather, I will sleep better if I know that you are spending the night with us."

"Iris, there is a tiny spot of lipstick on your front teeth."

Evie handed her a tissue, and she rubbed her mouth hard.

"Now, am I presentable?"

Iris enquired as she puckered her top lip.

"Yes, you look beautiful."

Then Evie opened the door for her, but Iris hesitated for a few moments.

"I am indebted to you for this idea, it is brilliant."

The lunch went smoothly and the whole group were so taken with the charms of Richmond House and grounds, that they vied with each other to be allowed to return in the spring and take photographs when the grounds would be a mass of snowdrops, daffodils, and crocuses. In the end,

Evie put all the names into a hat and Iris drew the lucky winner, a small, bespectacled man from the quarterly publication *The Bookworm's Times*.

By four pm the group had departed, and Iris had taken to her bed with a headache. Evie was just about to lock the office when Robert rang from Waterford, where he was staying for a few days. The connection was poor as he was phoning from a public box, but they agreed to meet on the following Saturday in Phoenix Park.

"I got your letter and typing yesterday, I am delighted that you now have your own car, it means more time together." He said.

"Yes, I am looking forward to seeing you," Evie answered.

A series of clicks …

"I cannot stay overnight as I have to attend a Christmas fundraiser for the poor of the parish," Evie explained.

"Ok, but we will have the whole day –."

Crackling on the phone blocked out the remainder of his sentence.

"Lyn, are you still there?"

She felt so cherished whenever he called her Lyn.

"Yes, I can hear you clearly now."

More interference on the line like an echo of another man's voice.

"Lyn, I have something to tell you when we meet."

"Really! Give me a hint."

"It's about my work."

Ear piercing noise and then the line went dead."

She tried ringing back but got an engaged tone.

The depressing weather lasted all week and Iris stayed in bed, nursing a cold, while Evie returned to her usual office duties. Letters, cards, and phone calls congratulating Iris on her talk and subsequent luncheon, flooded into the office. Evie worked steadily through a mountain of paperwork and chatted with a researcher from Radio Eireann who planned on doing a full programme on Iris and her American background.

When Thursday evening arrived, it was still raining so she picked up Patsy Mc Ginley for his lesson. He was making faster progress than she could ever have imagined and was now able to manage a sixth class reading book, but he still needed to practise his writing and work on spellings. They were just tidying away all the books when Kevin returned home, wet and fatigued, after working for hours to save a draught mare's life. While Evie made him a hot whiskey and heated up his dinner, he chatted amicably with Patsy.

"How is Queenie?"

"Thanks to you Mister, she is in fine fettle, me ma says that you are the best man in Ireland when it comes to curing cobs."

Kevin chortled

"I am no miracle worker, but I love horses and I have picked up a lot of knowledge about them since my college days. "

Patsy's face lit up.

"I love them too, when your Mrs is finished teaching me how to read and write, I am going to save up and buy a book about them."

Suddenly, Kevin stood up and padded upstairs without a word.

"Mrs I hope that I did not insult him."

Evie glanced at the boy, who looked as if he could burst into tears at any moment.

Typical of Kevin to walk out like that.

She spoke calmly.

"Don't worry he has a lot on his mind, it has nothing to do with you."

"Thank God and his Blessed Mother."

The boy replied blessing himself just as Kevin reappeared.

"Here sonny, take this home and learn to read it."

Kevin handed him a book titled: *A guide to Irish Cobs.*

"Thanks, but – I- I am afraid that it will get- dirty – my house is not clean like this one."

Kevin patted him on the head.

"Take it, it's yours to keep forever, someone gave it to me years ago, I have no use for it as I could write volumes on horses if need be."

Patsy was speechless as he stroked the dust cover of the book as if it were a cat and Kevin returned to the table where Evie left a hot whiskey for him.

She spoke in a soft voice.

"It's a beautiful book and it will give you a whole new range of words as well as information on cobs."

Kevin's kindness toward the boy had surprised her and she was struggling with a strange urge to either laugh or cry. However, by concentrating on pouring steaming gravy from a saucepan over some pork chops, she managed to let the moment pass.

"This book is the best present I ever got, thank you, sir, all my hard work late at night doing my lessons, has paid off."

Patsy's eyes lingered on the horse adorning the front cover.

"Just enjoy it."

Kevin said as he fished out cloves from his glass with a spoon.

"The blessings of God on you both, ma told me that I am very lucky to be able to come here, some folk, treat us like dirt."

"Well, they are making a big mistake, shame on those ignorant people," Evie said.

Patsy tapped his foot on the floor.

"I have an idea I will get a brace of pheasants for you to show how grateful I am."

Kevin pulled a quizzical face.

"My dear boy, where do you intend to hunt them?"

Patsy's jaw dropped.

"Dessie – my - second father had a shotgun and so my uncle taught me how to use it after he died. Sometimes we go poaching."

Kevin, who was just about to cut up his chop into smaller pieces left down his cutlery and roared with laughter.

Patsy looked to Evie for guidance, but she just winked. Then Kevin said.

"Thanks for the offer Patsy but don't get into trouble for us, poaching will land you in hot water with the law, best to leave the poor pheasants alone, let them live, we have plenty of food."

Evie backed him up.

"Yes, my husband is right don't even dream of killing pheasants for us. Our reward is to see you happy and able to read about your beloved horses."

Patsy stood up and then sat down again with excitement.

"I can't wait to go home and read this. By the way Mrs I saw you on Monday at the big house, you were talking to some swanky men in suits in the eating room. "

She cast Kevin a furtive look.

"Patsy, the correct word is dining room and what were you doing at Redmond House?"

"Begging your pardon Mrs the boss man gives me an hour off from farm work at lunchtime, so I decided to try and find a few rabbits for me ma to cook for dinner – I never miss a shot, I use the gun belonging to my stepfather, God rest him."

"Be careful, I would prefer if you did not go near my place of work again, Mrs Higgins might report you to the Gardai not to mention our old gardener, who is very cranky."

He shifted nervously in his chair.

"I promise that I won't go near that big house again."

Kevin said with a smirk.

"I know your mother has a lot of mouths to feed but surely there are plenty of pickings elsewhere."

The boy rubbed his hands together.

"When there is a hunter's moon, I stay out all night with my uncle and we roam from here to Navan and back, I shoot snipe, rabbits, pheasants even an odd deer."

Evie put her finger to her lips.

"Enough said, just be careful that some gamekeeper does not shoot you, I hear that there are a few dangerous ones on the big estates."

"Don't worry I can run like a hare."

Patsy's face was poker straight while Evie and Kevin both chortled.

Much later, as Evie drove home on that dismal November night, having dropped off Patsy at his home, she marvelled at her husband's kindness towards the boy. Most of the time she believed that he lacked any feelings towards others and certainly within their marriage she had experienced his lack of sensitivity with her, especially at lovemaking. Yet, there was no denying his sheer joy tonight at the boy's progress with reading and writing and his spontaneous act of giving a book about horses to Patsy.

She knew that she would never forget Patsy's expression when he realized that he could keep the book.

It was a moment of grace, due to my incorrigible husband.

As she turned into the driveway of her home, the house was in darkness and she found a rough note on the table saying he had been called out to some emergency several miles away.

To the beat of some jazz music on the radio, she heated milk and poured it into a mug which she sprinkled with a generous helping of ashwagandha. Then stirring it vigorously, she listened to the steady patter of rain against the window and she wondered again if their marriage would have been different, had they had children. After all, she could not deny that he was marvellous with animals and now it seemed that he had a special way with youngsters too.

Chapter Twenty - Six

The two cars parked alongside the old, deserted cottage in the tiny village of Blanchardstown. Peering through the fogged-up windscreen of her Ford Anglia she could just make out the figure of Robert in the pelting rain, grappling with a black umbrella as he walked towards her. When he opened the passenger- door splashes landed everywhere.

"Hello, Lyn! What a downpour!"

"It's a day for ducks." She gave him a cheeky smile.

By the time he had settled his long limbs into the front seat rivulets of water were running down the interior panels. She laughed at his wet face and damp clothes and he reached over and kissed her with his cold lips.

"Oh my God! It's like kissing a lump of ice," she exclaimed.

Smoothing his drenched moustache, he replied.

"Give me an hour or so to warm up by the fire and you won't be complaining about my lips, I promise."

"I shall hold you to that," she said with a glint in her eye.

"I like your motor! I am leaving my car here until tonight as I want you to get used to driving in the city, the first time is always the worst."

"Are you sure you don't mind leaving it there all day?"

"No. It will give you confidence in heavy traffic to have someone with you, the blaring horns and errant drivers who weave in and out of lanes can be disconcerting for a new driver."

"You are so thoughtful Robert you think of everything."

He left his hand on her knee.

"No problem, you look so fresh and pretty today, I can hardly wait to get you home."

She rolled her eyes.

"You need a hot toddy before you get up to any mischief."

"Wait a second, I am supposed to be the doctor around here!" He replied.

Following a steaming plate of beef stew at an old-world restaurant near Kilmainham village, where an oil painting of Ireland's famous tenor Count John McCormack hung, alongside two princes of the catholic church, she drove to Robert's home. Leaving their damp coats on the hallstand they embraced.

Then he said. "I love that you are here for the whole day."

"Me too, the place is spotless!"

She followed him into the drawing room where a log fire was burning brightly.

"Oh, I can thank my housekeeper for that and the fire, she only left a short time ago judging by the heat from it."

He beckoned to her to take a seat while he went for drinks.

When he returned, she was sitting with her hands raised in front of the flames.

"Now my pretty lady, a double brandy for you and a double for me."

Then he pulled up an armchair beside her and they clinked their glasses.

"To good friends and more!" She said cryptically.

For a split second she saw something in his eyes which she could not name but then she dismissed it.

Just because Kevin is devious, it does not mean that all men are.

"Now, it's your turn."

She said as she raised her glass a second time.

"To 1959 and all who sail in her."

"Today is only the first of December," she teased.

"Yes, but we might as well start celebrating Christmas, every year it seems to start earlier."

The golden liquid warmed her throat as she swallowed a mouthful and then another.

He took a long swig from his glass and shifted uncomfortably in his chair. Wind rattled the bay window as they both listened to a huge log spitting and hissing in the grate.

"Do you think that the timber is in its death throes and lamenting being cut down?"

Evie asked dreamily.

"Perhaps, it sounds like the death cries of some animal that can be seen in Africa."

"A snake?" She suggested.

"A pangolin or a lizard," he replied.

For some minutes, no words passed between them, but she sensed that there was a strain on the silence which engulfed the room. She tried to break the tension and asked.

"Robert, you said on the phone that you had some news."

He sat up straight.

"Yes, I did."

"You – seem - a little..."

She did not finish her sentence because he leaned across and she smelt his heady aftershave. When his moustache brushed her face, she kissed him, and he returned her kiss.

Then he stood up and pulled her gently to her feet

"Will we go to bed or stay here?" He asked in a low voice.

She stood on tiptoes beside him and stroked his cheek.

"Let's try your big soft bed."

"I shall lead the way," he replied.

It was well past six pm when they awoke to a darkened room with only the streetlights casting a strange glow on the walls.

"I need to be home before midnight, I told Kevin that I was meeting up with you to give you typing and then later with Val."

"Good." He kissed the top of her head. "I love when your silky hair is loose around your neck and shoulders, it drives me wild."

"Well, we have seen enough of your wild side for today!"

She joked as she wrapped his dressing gown around her body and headed for the bathroom.

"Can I join you? I could scrub your back."

His handsome face reminded her of a naughty school-boy who had just lost his homework.

"No, Doctor Robert that is enough of excitement for one day, now be a good boy."

Her face shone as she left the room.

Later, when they were both dressed, Robert walked to a nearby fish and chip shop and returned with two salty bundles drowned in vinegar.

"This food is so tasty, I was ravenous."

"I know, Potts fish and chips are famous."

"Thanks for a lovely day," she said before licking salt from her fingers.

He poured beer into two glasses and handed her one.

"Thank you, Evelyn, you have lit up my life again and every time when we are apart I look forward to seeing you again - but life is about change and - now, I don't know how to tell you this."

Suddenly, a band of pain like a vice grip held her head.

I knew he had something on his mind while we were sitting by the fire.

She pushed away the remains of her fish and chips.

"Don't look so alarmed my love it is not that bad."

"Then tell me, I cannot bear the suspense."

"You know that I have a son in Africa, who is a doctor." He rubbed his eyes.

"Yes. Is he not the one who is called Roger?"

"You are right. There is a famine in the Horn of Africa and Roger is setting up temporary hospitals and relief stations with a team of colleagues to try and save lives. I have been invited out to assist them as I have a lot of experience of working in Africa.

She willed herself to stay calm and hide her shock.

"I see, remind me what countries are in the Horn of Africa."

"Somalia, Ethiopia, and Kenya."

He swallowed some alcohol, but his food remained untouched.

"When are you planning to go?"

"Next Tuesday, I am going to London to meet up with another doctor, who is travelling out with me. Then, three days later we fly out."

Evie's jaw dropped.

"Wow, you don't hang around."

"British Overseas Airways Corporation started flights from London to Africa in October, so we are lucky in that respect. However, the trip I believe entails several stops as well as many hours of flying time. It will be my first time flying to Africa and I am a little nervous."

She took three deep breaths before replying.

"What an adventure! Not to mention the poor starving people of those countries. Will you be staying for a few months?"

"I have no idea, it depends on how bad conditions are and on how my own health holds up, I am no spring chicken."

She ignored his attempt at humour as her mind was racing.

Why do I feel like the mat has just been pulled from under my feet?

When she realized that he was waiting for a response she managed a few stiff words.

"Well done for being so brave, there will be many challenges I am sure."

"I am not brave, but I don't want to let Roger down."

The pain had now moved to her chest and she felt like she might suffocate.

"Can you get me more water?"

"Certainly."

He went to the sink and filled a glass.

She drank it down in a few mouthfuls

"Robert, this is quite a shock and I am wondering where it leaves our relationship."

He reached across the table for her hand.

"I know it all came out of the blue Roger only phoned about 10 days ago and then I needed time to think it through. I phoned you as soon as I had reached a decision."

"I see but."

He released her hand.

"Look Lyn, I cherish the time we spend together but there are some monumental hurdles to be crossed before we decide about the future. From the start I have been honest with you, I have reservations about committing to a long-term relationship again and you are still married and living with your husband."

A tear fell from the corner of her right eye and ran silently down her cheek.

"Yes, I accept that all of what you say is true, but I shall miss you."

He moved to her side of the table and massaged her shoulders as he spoke.

"I am not going away forever at most it will be six to nine months and we can write regularly to each other. You see sometimes I get jealous when I realize that you are still a wife to your husband in every sense."

A rush of blood to her cheeks, made her stand up abruptly and she turned to face him.

"He takes sex from me, I endure it, because he sees it as his right. There is no reason for you to be jealous."

"I am so sorry to bring the matter up, I was wrong, what goes on in your marriage is your business."

He went to the mantelpiece and put his back to the fire.

Tapping her fingers on the table, she said.

"I intend to leave him sometime in the New Year as the first stage in my plan has been reached, as I have learned to drive and bought a car."

"Indeed, well done for being such a fast learner and for finding a lovely car."

She twisted her wedding ring as she continued.

"It will be difficult to leave my lovely house and start renting a flat from an old miser of a landlord, but it has to be done – I am hoping to find a reasonable place some-where on the north side so I can drive to work every day."

"It is never easy to leave a marriage, but you cannot just endure an abusive relationship while your life ticks away. You are too good for him in every sense and I hope that you will write often once I send you my new address."

His forehead creased with lines as he looked directly at her.

She nodded.

"Yes, but only if you promise to answer all my letters."

He ran his fingers through his hair.

"Do not doubt me, I promise."

She took her time lighting a cigarette before answering.

"I have always feared change, yet I remember reading something from a book in the library at Richmond, that to live well is to change often."

"Indeed, they are clever words but ones that are hard to put into practise. I too struggle with them."

While she pulled on her cigarette, he left the room but moments later returned, holding a small yellow box with a black ribbon tied in a bow.

"This my beautiful lady is an early Christmas present for you."

She gasped.

"But I have nothing to give you."

"But you did not know I was leaving so it is not im-portant."

She opened it with trembling fingers and there nestling in tissue paper were a pair of tiny diamond and ruby earrings.

"They are beautiful! Thank you."

She moved the box around so that they sparkled in the light while he shifted from one foot to the other.

"I know that you cannot wear them at present because he will ask questions, but once you leave him, they will complement your lovely eyes and rosebud lips."

"Sweet talker."

Quickly, she put out her cigarette and walked towards him.

He opened his arms and they embraced. Then their lips moved in unison as he undid the buttons on her blouse and moved his hand gently over her neck. Minutes later, she slipped out of her skirt and lay on the soft rug in front of the fire as he began to undress.

"Kiss me like we never kissed before," she whispered.

Then with the rain lashing against the windowpane, they made love again.

Chapter Twenty - Seven

The next few weeks seemed to pass in a haze as Evie was busy helping Iris with research on the hallowed site of Clonmacnoise, for a series of articles to be published in a Canadian magazine. Dusty old books borrowed from the well-stocked libraries of Iris's titled acquaintances filled the office as she perused them for nuggets of wisdom about the monks who once had a monastery there on the banks of the Shannon. In the end, Iris insisted that they stay at the Gresham Hotel in Dublin so that they could spend three days searching through ancient volumes held at the National Library.

She was glad that her mind was preoccupied with work as Robert's departure was a big shock. Even his brief phone call from London on the eve of his flight to Africa did little to console her. For a start, she was terrified that Kevin would walk in at any moment and she became so emotional on hearing Robert's voice at the other end of the line that she had to pretend that she had a cough. However, she accepted that he could not just sit in Dublin waiting like a love-sick youngster while she endeavoured to find excuses for travelling to the city.

After replacing the receiver, she hurried to the kitchen and drank a double brandy, to help blot out the sense of loneliness which threatened to overwhelm her.

While a voice in her head mocked her.

What if some accident befalls him in the jungle?

Unable to tolerate it any longer she turned on the radio at full blast and danced around the room to *Peggy Sue* sung by Buddy Holly.

Kevin too was busier than ever as the biting cold and heavy night frosts played havoc with sheep, cattle, horses, and pigs. In one week alone, he reported that nine calves, as well as three bullocks, had died from various illnesses. Then among his own herd of prize-winning cattle, two succumbed to pneumonia in one weekend. Filled with fury at his failure to save them he spent that Saturday afternoon chopping wood in the back yard, with his shirt sleeves rolled up to his elbows. From the landing window, she watched him for a long time, while his powerful, hairy arms, swung the axe back and forth through the air as it split and cut the wood into logs, which would fit in the grate. It seemed to her that there was a rhythm to his movements, but she knew from experience that at any moment he could grow tired of chopping wood and vent his anger elsewhere. Tension seemed to hang everywhere, like a gossamer web so she went to extra trouble that evening to cook a meal which would be pleasing to him. In the end, having searched through her stack of cookery books she decided on: Egg Mayonnaise followed by Coq-au-Vin and to finish, Black Forest Gateau.

It was well past seven pm by the time the meal was ready as it had taken her longer than expected to prepare the dessert. Fortunately, she had some home-made oxtail soup left over from the previous evening. Dressing it up with cream, brandy, and a dollop of parsley, she brought in a steaming bowl to him in the sitting room and announced that it was the first of two starters. This kept his hunger at bay and made it seem that she had worked extra hard at preparing dinner.

Later, following dinner when she had finished washing-up all the dishes, he came back downstairs in his house-coat, having enjoyed a long soak in the bath with a glass of wine.

"Thanks, Evie, for the lovely meal, it was superb."

"I am glad you enjoyed it."

She continued putting away the last Pyrex dish into the press, while she fended off an inner voice.

He has never washed or dried any item from the kitchen.

"Come and sit by the fire with me, I have a surprise for you."

She stifled the desire to say that she was tired and wanted to go to bed with a magazine.

"I wonder what the surprise might be."

"All in good time."

He opened a bottle of Beaujolais wine and filled up two glasses, then she followed him into the sitting room.

"Have the armchair."

He directed as he sat at the table and rustled through some glossy brochures. She sank into it and took a few mouthfuls from her glass.

"I am going to buy a television set for Christmas, I don't know why I didn't buy one earlier but I suppose so much happened this year that the months flew by."

"That's great news, Iris has a TV but rarely watches it and Orla is debating with herself about buying one – it's a pity that we don't have our own Irish broadcasting unit like the British but according to the *Irish Press*, it's only a year or two away."

"That Orla one needs a virile man, not a television." Kevin flicked quickly through the pages.

Exhaustion seemed to overtake her, and she struggled to keep her eyes open as the heat from the fire relaxed her. While his voice seemed to drone on and on about different makes and brands of televisions, she sipped wine and sat up straight, hoping that she would not fall asleep. Eventually, when she dozed off, he woke her.

"You should go to bed, you look pale, I want to listen to a late-night programme from London."

He stacked all his papers on the table.

She stood up and then gripped the edge of the mantelpiece as the room swayed in front of her eyes. After a few moments, the feeling passed.

"Goodnight Kevin, I think I have had too much wine."

He laughed.

"We finished that bottle over dinner and now this one is empty too, I am not surprised."

"Yes, I feel so tired."

She gave a half-smile and climbed the stairs to bed.

Much later, a noise disturbed her and when she opened her eyes, she saw a long shadow in the doorway which formed in the moonlight into Kevin as he approached the bed.

"Evelyn, it's only me, that Coq-au-Vin made me randy, move over."

She was too tired to argue.

A blast of cold air as he removed the bedclothes and her pyjamas.

Then the wine took over.

And she fell back into a deep sleep.

On the last Sunday but one before Christmas, a huge "Bring and Buy Sale" was organised jointly between the local Catholic church and the Church of Ireland, in the town hall, with all the proceeds going to needy members of both persuasions. The number of Protestants in the town and surrounding areas had been dwindling since the foundation of the state in the twenties and the parish priest believed that it was his duty to try and build bridges between the two churches. Although the members of the parish committee outwardly went along with him there were at least three older individuals who despised the Rector, George Charles Brown because of his plummy accent and penchant for having the last word whenever he was in the presence of his counterpart Fr. Gandon. Consequently, the days leading up to the annual event brought mixed reactions from parishioners. And the town gossips who were drawn to Hilary Byrne's little shop like moths to a flame, lingered to hear her excoriate the Rector and denounce all members of the Church of Ireland as "Black Protestants".

While at Richmond House, it was all hands on deck, as Evie and Mrs Higgins, spent three days in the large kitchen, helping Cook make four square Christmas cakes, six plum puddings, and dozens of mince pies, all to be donated to the charitable venture. Iris meanwhile had departed for the Christmas break to a castle in Cornwall where her younger half-sister Isobel and her latest lover, a Count, were staying.

"It's great to get a break from herself, maybe she will find a new Romeo there too."

Cook's waspish tongue spared no one, not even her own deceased husband.

Evie, who was stirring dried fruit into a big bowl of creamed butter and sugar left down her wooden spoon.

"Herself?" I don't know anyone by that name."

Cook's generous bosom heaved with annoyance.

"I should know better than to complain to you, we all know that herself treats you like a second daughter."

"Hardly, I am just an employee like everyone else here."

"You could have fooled me. Who else gets to stay in swanky hotels in the city?"

For a few minutes, there was an ominous silence, only Mrs Higgins clicked her tongue in disapproval, now and again as she assiduously lined cake tins.

Evie's patience was wearing thin and she felt so tired in recent weeks that the last place she wanted to be was standing in a hot kitchen, at Cook's beck and call.

"For the love of God, use her name, I am Mrs Ryder-Lee's personal assistant and it is part of my job to help with research or be by her side at various talks, book signings and so forth."

Cook, who was tying a muslin cloth around a bowl of pudding mixture before steaming it, suddenly snapped the string with her scissors.

"I have a name for you!"

Mrs Higgins cleared her throat.

"Stop this bickering at once, you are like a pair of cocks, crowing about nothing."

Evie felt her cheeks burning.

"I won't stop until I hear the name, she has given me."

Cook put her floury hands on her hips.

"It's Mrs High and Mighty!"

"Well at least I don't have a tongue as venomous as a viper," Evie retorted.

Cook smirked.

"Say what you like but it seems that your husband is earning a nickname too for himself among the widows of the farming community – it's "Dirty Dick" because he likes to pinch their bottoms."

Apoplectic with rage Evie picked up an egg and threw it at her tormentor, who ducked in the nick of time, allowing the egg to smash against the opposite wall where pots and pans along with other utensils hung from hooks.

Suddenly, slow, deliberate hand-clapping sounded from the back door as Brendan surveyed the mess.

"Ladies, ladies, behave yourselves! "

"Who is going to clean this up?" Cook enquired.

"Okay, okay, keep your hair on!" Evie said.

Shaking her head in exasperation, Mrs Higgins spoke.

"Mrs Butler and Mrs Moore, it's Christmas time and I think that you should both shake hands and then forget about your petty differences. I will ask the new maid Bridget to clean up the mess, I would not normally let you off the hook so lightly Mrs Moore, but I have to admit that you were provoked by Cook."

The housekeeper straightened to her full, imposing 5ft. 10 Ins and with a look of steel in her eyes, she pressed the bell on the old wallboard, and it rang throughout the house.

Cook rubbed her hand against her apron and then extended it to Evie.

"I am sorry Mrs Moore, your husband's business is none of my business, forgive me."

Evie who was still smarting from the latest news about Kevin's antics forced a smile.

"Apology accepted, Mrs Butler I am so sorry for losing my temper and flinging that egg, I am just so tired these days, I feel like I am about to come down with the flu."

"Well, there is a lot of it about, the butcher boy told me that his mother is in bed with fever and a bad cough."

The two women shook hands and then went back to their chores.

"Now ladies, no more run-ins!" Brendan grinned

"Get out of here, before I give you a job," Mrs Higgins retorted.

He went outside whistling to himself just as the young maid arrived with dusters in her hand.

"There has been a slight accident here, so I want you to get a basin of hot water and wash that wall well."

Mrs Higgins said with a hint of irony.

The day following the Bring and Buy Sale, Evie developed indigestion and a feeling of nausea. She did not touch breakfast and had chicken soup for lunch, made by Cook who was happy to show that she was not one to bear a grudge. The previous evening Evie had bought a tin of spiced biscuits at the sale, later before going to bed she munched several of them with a mug of hot milk and ashwagandha. Now she regretted her gluttony.

She left work at four pm and drove to Mai's house.

"Come in Evelyn, how good to see you!"

"And you too Mai, it's so dark at this time of year that I almost took a wrong turn at the four crossroads."

The two women hugged and then Mai led the way into her cosy sitting room.

"Daylight at this time of year is so short and in a few more days we will have the winter solstice. I am travelling to the Neolithic site at Newgrange with some academics from Dublin to see the inner chamber illuminated by the rising sun."

"It must be a spectacular sight."

Evie took the nearest chair, glad to sit down

"Indeed. Now Evelyn what can I do for you, you look very tired and pale."

Mai sat on a carved stool and studied her.

"I know, the last few weeks have been hectic as my boss has gone to England for Christmas and she makes us work like trojans before her departure. Then, the annual charity event took place in the town last night which involved a lot of baking ."

"Yes, I donated some jars of honey and preserves, the Rector's wife told me all about it."

Evie burped loudly and then spoke.

"Apologies for the indigestion! A big crowd turned out last night, I believe that the takings far exceeded other years. But I am kicking myself for buying a tin of spiced biscuits because I over-indulged and today, I have hiccups with a feeling of nausea."

Mai laughed heartily and then enquired.

"May I ask if you know the provenance of these biscuits?"

Evie shrugged.

"Mrs Ahearn – the postman's wife, who fancies herself as a baker, but she went too heavy on the spices, especially the cinnamon."

"Have you eaten today?"

"Just soup and watery tea."

"Ok. I can make up something for you."

"Mai."

"Yes."

"I have been feeling very worn out since Robert announced at short notice that he was going to Africa, to help with famine relief, he is a doctor."

Mai showed no emotion.

"Is Robert the same friend you mentioned a while back?"

"Yes, we are lovers or more to the point we were lovers."

Mai opened and closed a bangle on her wrist.

"I must say that I admire him for his decision but that does not mean that I don't understand your shock at his departure, I take it that you will stay in touch while is away."

"Absolutely, he gave me an early Christmas present, a pair of exquisite earrings."

"Good, maybe now that he is out of the picture for a while you will be able to see your relationship with your husband more clearly."

Evie gave a sardonic smile.

"Oh, I am fully aware of all the shortcomings and once the New year arrives, I will actively look for accommodation on the outskirts of Dublin. You could not possibly imagine how much confidence I have gained by learning to drive and then buying my own car."

Mai's eyes had a distant expression.

"I take it that he still insists on sex-."

Evie blinked.

" I am treated like one of his mares! But thanks to your wonder herb ashwagandha, I sleep like a log and even when he disturbs me during the night, I fall back to sleep quickly once he is spent."

"Evelyn, he is such a selfish brute, you must leave him sooner rather than later."

"I know, my skin crawls when he touches me."

Mai shook her head.

"Only last week I got a telephone call from Dublin from my friend Lavinia, a mutual acquaintance broke her pelvis when she fell down a flight of stairs at her home. It appears that she was pushed by her husband, but she is afraid to report him as he is a member of the judiciary."

"My God, that's awful but don't worry I know how to manage Kevin after all these years."

"I hope you are right, now let me sort out those herbs for you."

She disappeared into a room at the far end of the cottage while Evie studied the flames dancing in the hearth. When she returned, Evie had dozed off, but she awoke at the sound of Mai's voice.

"Sorry about that, the heat made me sleepy."

"Don't apologise, I am just glad to see that you are so relaxed in my home."

They both laughed as Evie stood up and smoothed her hair back from her face but Mai's voice was serious when she spoke.

"Now, I am prescribing peppermint tea for your indigestion and a cocktail of ginseng and liquorice, to be taken in the morning for building up the immune system. The tea should relieve the indigestion immediately, but you will have to wait for a week or so until you see the cumulative effect of the other herbs."

"Should I stop the ashwagandha?" Evie enquired.

"If you wish, see how it goes, there are some who believe that it also helps to build up the immune system as it relieves stress and worry, but it is not a soporific per se."

"Thank you for everything, how much do I owe you?"

Mai did the mental arithmetic.

"How about six shillings to me and six shillings in the donation box for abused women."

"No problem."

Evie took out her purse and left the coins on the table, along with a small present wrapped in Christmas paper.

"What is that?" Mai raised one eye.

"Evie waved a hand in the air.

"It's just a small box of fancy writing paper with envelopes, my way of saying how much I appreciate all your help in recent weeks."

"You are very welcome and thank you, Evelyn. By the way, I slipped two jars of honey from my bees into that bag along with the herbs, it will help ward off colds and sore throats during the coming months."

Evie said hoarsely.

"You are just such a generous person. Happy Christmas Mai."

"And many happy returns Evelyn, now remember to take care of yourself."

At the front door, Evie paused, and they embraced.

Outside a flurry of snow was falling.

"Looks like we might have a white Christmas!"

Evie remarked before hurrying to her car.

"Maybe, you have a safe journey Evelyn and mind yourself with that man."

Chapter Twenty - Eight

The main street was thronged with men, women, and children, all in a hurry to finish their Christmas shopping, while fairy lights twinkled amidst the baubles and tinsel on the small fake Christmas trees displayed in the shop windows. With just over three days left until Christmas, everyone was in a jovial mood and the carol singers stationed near Gillespie's drapery store were singing their hearts out with a beautiful rendition of *O Holy Night.*

Evie and Orla, sitting at a table in the big bay window of Miss Kennedy's tea rooms had a full view of the festivities. Around them, at several tables, exhausted mothers ate pastries while they took a break from buying dolls, drums, toy guns, board games, Meccano and Bunty or Beano Annuals.

"There is nothing more comforting than a hot mince pie smothered with cream."

Orla eyed the basket of tiny pies which the waitress had just delivered to the table.

"Don't I know it, but I have already gorged on Yule log and Eccles cake." Evie pulled a face.

"Look, it's the season to be happy so let's indulge ourselves."

Orla placed two on Evie's plate with silver tongs and then two on her own plate while Evie poured tea from the large Willow pattern teapot as she explained.

"Do you know that I am lucky to be able to stuff my face like this! The day after the parish fundraiser, I had a dreadful bout of indigestion thanks to over-indulging in heavily spiced biscuits, so I had to go to the herbalist for a remedy."

"Dare I ask who made them?"

"The postman's wife."

"Enough said! What herbs did you get?"

"Peppermint tea for indigestion and a mixture of ginseng and liquorice to build up my stamina as I was feeling tired like I had the flu or infection coming on."

Orla filled her mouth with a spoonful of thick cream and swallowed it. Then she asked.

"Did they work?"

"Well, the indigestion has gone, and I am not half as tired as I was."

"Great! Mrs Ryder-Lee is a gifted writer, but I saw at her recent lecture that she has shades of a prima -donna so I am not surprised that you have been feeling tired following her around."

Evie left her cake-fork on the green gingham tablecloth.

"In fairness, she is a very decent employer and is kind and very generous. You only saw her public persona."

"Maybe. By the way thanks again for arranging that talk Evelyn, I am still receiving letters and phone calls from people who attended, thanking me for arranging the night but I tell them that much of the credit must go to you."

"Not at all, you got me off the hook with that awful gossip Hilary Byrne."

Orla smiled.

"No problem! Do you know that I am looking forward to staying with my sister and her family in Bray for Christmas, lots of long walks, and time to catch up with all my nieces and nephews?"

A shadow seemed to cross Evie's face.

"Yes, it's a wonderful time of year for kids – I still wish that we had had children as I can't help thinking that Kevin would have been a great father."

"Perhaps – I hope that you have a good Christmas, have you relatives staying?"

"Kevin's mother and stepfather were planning on visiting but apparently he has shingles, so they are not travelling."

Orla raised her left eye.

"Is that a good or a bad thing, I am never sure when people talk about their in-laws what they mean?"

"Good, I think."

Evie winked before she finished the last morsel of pie on her plate.

"I have two full weeks off."

Orla craned her neck as a very tall Santa Claus, strode by the window like the pied- piper with a line of children after him.

"That's Billy Owens, I would know the lanky git a mile off!"

Evie shook her head in mock dismay.

"Orla you broke his heart."

"I was never attracted to him and he ran after me like a little lap dog."

They both laughed, drawing glances from other customers.

Then Evie continued.

"You were talking about holiday leave I am off until January the tenth. The prima donna as you call her is in Cornwall for the festive season but Mrs Higgins, with her daughter and son-in-law, are caretaking Richmond house."

"Really! Imagine having that pile at your disposal for a few weeks." Orla exclaimed.

"I know, her daughter has twin girls so they will have to follow them around to make sure that they don't damage anything."

"If I had charge of that big house, the wine would flow, because I would fill it with guests and hire an orchestra to play the best of jazz and classical music." Orla mused.

Evie gave a wry smile.

"Mrs Ryder-Lee would faint if she heard you, that is the reason she chose the housekeeper who would rather die than allow a party to take place behind her boss's back."

Orla flicked her fringe back from her forehead.

"What a waste! By the way, did you ever discover the identity of those vandals who damaged your car?"

"No, there are several corner boys who could have done it, and I have not ruled Kevin out of the frame."

Orla frowned.

"How are things between you?"

"Look, I don't want to talk about him now but suffice to say that I need to find a place of my own - things are very strained between us. I trust that you will keep this news to yourself."

Orla glanced around at the other tables and then spoke.

"I promise, I shall not tell a soul I think that you are making the right decision — I have sensed for a long time that you were unhappy in your marriage."

Evie crossed her fingers.

"Sorry I don't want to say any more at this stage, it is too raw."

Orla patted her hand lightly.

"Don't apologise, besides, it is not my business."

Then, they exchanged gifts. Orla gave her a copy of Raymond Chandler's latest novel *Playback,* while Evie's gift was a small oil painting of the hill of Tara, which she had completed over the summer.

"Wow, I cannot believe that you painted this, it is love-ly." Orla's face glowed with pleasure.

"I knew you would like it as we have had many enjoy-able walks there together and thanks for this book, I love detective stories."

Evie patted the purple and gold dust cover.

Outside, the temperature had dropped, and they hugged.

"All the best!"

As Orla spoke, her breath hung in the air for a few moments.

Two shivering girls clinging to their boyfriends, hobbled by in vertiginous heels and flimsy dresses while Evie raised her eyes heavenwards.

"Thanks, Orla, for everything, and enjoy your break."

On Christmas Eve, she woke to a world covered in white. Everything was silent, the only sound the far -off bleating of Tom Cafferty's sheep as he tried to round them up with the help of his collie dog. Dressing quickly, she went downstairs, through the window she saw Kevin removing shovelfuls of snow from beneath the jeep and when she opened the back door, a pile of slush fell onto the floor.

He shouted across the yard at her.

"What are you looking at? Hurry up and make the bloody breakfast, I must leave in twenty-five minutes, and I have to dig my way out of the drive."

She gave him a thumbs up sign.

He kept his coat and boots on while he devoured the rashers and eggs followed by a cup of tea. All she could think of was the trail of snow that he had left on the floor, but she said nothing and filled a flask with coffee.

"Take that with you, it's cold out there."

He muttered, "Thanks." Then he turned to face her.

"I don't think this snow will last, but I may be late home tonight as I am going for a few drinks after work with the lads."

She nodded, unsure of what to say because his mouth had that crooked grin that she had come to hate.

Then he said, with an air of superiority.

"Don't forget to look at the television, you know how to use it."

Her patience was running out.

"I am not stupid, it's just a matter of plugging it in and turning it on! It's been here five days."

He guffawed. "Well, you are useless at other household gadgets."

She snapped back at him. "You barely know how to turn on the fucking cooker."

He muttered something under his breath and allowed the door to bang in his wake.

She watched while he finished clearing snow from under his tyres and drove cautiously down the drive to the gate. When the jeep had disappeared, she went back upstairs and took a long look at the small photographs, still hidden in the lining of her handbag. It seemed like years since the photographer had snapped that magical moment of her with Robert.

The day flew by, there were so many last-minute preparations to be done: making stuffing, icing the Christmas cake, and putting the last remaining decorations on the tree. Then she drove at a snail's pace on the icy roads until she arrived at Goff's new home, where she found Mrs Goff and her son eating a meal of cabbage and bacon. At first, they were reluctant to accept her invitation to dinner on Christmas day but once she explained that Kevin's relations were not coming and that a lot of food would be wasted, they agreed. Later, as she was just about to turn for home, she saw their nearest neighbour Niall Coughlan, a bachelor farmer, ploughing his way through the snow with a bag of groceries.

Winding down the window she leaned across to him.

"Niall, will you please come to our house for dinner at two pm tomorrow, I have a huge turkey and ham, we would love to have your company."

He blew his nose which was red from the chilly air and then he spoke in a gentle voice.

"Musha, thanks Mrs Moore but I can't be bothering you, I am only a simple farmer."

She explained.

"I thought that Kevin's family were coming for Christmas so I ordered a lot of food now it will be wasted unless you help us eat it along with Kieran Goff and his mother."

His face lit up.

"Are they coming?"

"Indeed, they are. So, you can all play cards afterwards with my husband, he loves a game of 25."

"Count me in Mrs Moore and thank you. I have a lot of ewes due to lamb in a few weeks and when Easter comes, I will send one over to you."

She laughed.

"No need to do that at all, don't kill a poor lamb for us."

The church was packed for midnight mass as parishioners, young and old turned out to see Fr. Gandon place the figure of the infant Jesus in the crib and hear the wonderful tenor voice of Johnny Browne sing *O Little Town of Bethlehem*, followed by other favourite hymns. She was glad that she had made the effort despite the frosty conditions. It felt empowering to be able to go to mass in the middle of the night without any assistance from Kevin and listen to uplifting music.

It was long after one am when she reached the gate leading to home. Kevin had just arrived before her and his jeep zig-zagged its way up the drive. She stayed at a safe distance as it was clear that he was under the influence of alcohol. Once he had parked in a reckless manner he jumped out, opened the buttons of his trousers and urinated.

She watched with disgust as the moonlight seemed to form a spotlight around him. And for a few seconds, she imagined how the hot piddle was casting a brownish stain as it melted the snow.

The imp in her head said.

He grows more and more like one of his bullocks every day.

She stayed in her car until he was finished and held her breath while he fumbled with the key to the back door. In the end, she could stand it no longer and she opened it.

"Thanks – love—I am a bit merry, too many creamy pints!"

He followed her inside.

"It's late and I have a busy day tomorrow." She hurried towards the stairs.

He lunged at her.

"Give us a kiss!"

She felt his hot lips on her as the smell of Guinness filled her nostrils.

She pushed him away, but he grabbed her by the waist and shoved her upstairs.

"My room - or – yours?" His words were slurred.

For a split second, a faint voice urged her to turn around and kick him, but the moment passed, and she found herself heading for his bed.

Suddenly he tripped over a pair of his own shoes in the dark and fell.

"You -cunt! Did you- not tidy -this room- today?"

Then he lay on the floor rubbing his knee and groaning softly, reminding her of a child.

"Get me some wintergreen ointment now."

She went back down to the drawer in the kitchen where she kept a selection of pills and ointments for healing everyday aches and pains. When she returned, relief washed over her, he had moved to the bed and was snoring loudly. It seemed like a weight had been lifted from her shoulders. Leaving the tin of ointment on the bedside locker, she tiptoed out and closed the door gently.

And as she undressed in the safety of her own room, she uttered a silent prayer.

Thank you, God, he won't bother me tonight.

Chapter Twenty - Nine

On St Stephen's day, heavy snow fell in the morning and made driving conditions hazardous. Nevertheless, Kevin was determined not to disappoint his boss, who had invited them to dinner at four pm. And so much to Evie's annoyance they set out early for the home of Andrew and Elizabeth Boxer. It took them over an hour to negotiate the treacherous roads but eventually, they arrived at the imposing red brick home. At the front door, a group of young boys, attired in the traditional disguise of "wren boys" with painted faces and straw hats, were singing a medley of festive tunes while a hunchbacked man knocked sparks out of an old fiddle. When they finished, Kevin fished in his pocket for coins.

"I suppose now you will ask me for money to bury the poor wren."

"That's right mister, thanks."

A tall child stepped forward and produced an old hat but on closer inspection, Evie realized that it was a girl disguised as a boy with braces and long trousers.

"Good singing," she said, while the girl nodded at her.

Then the door opened, and Elizabeth emerged with a ten-shilling note which she dropped into the hat followed by Andrew who gave each of them a shilling. Suddenly, the hunchback gave a loud whistle, they all bowed and headed for the road eager to go to the next house.

When they had disappeared, Andrew exploded with laughter.

"I have no idea what all that was about! Such a motley group."

Elizabeth beckoned them inside out of the chilly air, as Evie explained the ancient practice.

"According to legend, a little wren betrayed the Christian martyr St Stephen when he was in hiding by making noises. The tradition then sprung up that the wren was hunted and killed for his part in the betrayal and so modern-day groups carry around an effigy of the bird on a pole and seek money by singing, ostensibly to bury it."

"What a strange idea!" Andrew remarked.

With a grin, Kevin added.

"Call it what you like but they did well here, you were too generous with them, less would have done."

Andrew took their coats and hung them on the Victorian hallstand.

"I will know better next time, I thought the English customs were confusing but the Irish ones take the biscuit."

Later, after a five-course meal, they moved from the long dining room to the drawing room where a coal fire burned brightly in the huge old grate.

"Now, let the fun begin!" Andrew declared.

Then he took a pack of cards and dealt them out slowly, while Elizabeth refilled their glasses with vintage port.

When she came to Evie's side of the table she glanced at the two men who were enjoying some joke among themselves and whispered into Evie's ear.

"Evelyn, you look pale, are you feeling ok?"

"I am just tired, I was very busy yesterday, I invited three locals for Christmas dinner."

"Really! Why in God's name did you do that?"

Elizabeth took a seat beside her.

"Kevin's mother and step-father could not travel from England as he has shingles and rather than waste that big turkey which I had ordered we decided to invite three neighbours who would not be able to cook a proper dinner themselves."

"No doubt it was your idea! Did Kevin not object, I know he can be set in his ways or so Andrew says."

Evie leaned in closer to her hostess.

"How true! But he loves a game of cards and they were all happy to oblige."

Elizabeth exchanged a glance with her just as Andrew said.

"Now ladies quiet please, we will start with a game of switch and then move on to bigger and better games."

By the time the carriage clock on the mantelpiece marked nine pm. Evie was exhausted and to make matters worse, following the rich spicy food served earlier, her indigestion had returned. A few minutes later, she excused herself and stumbled from the table as a feeling of nausea hit her. She had just reached the bathroom when the complete contents of her stomach exploded into the toilet bowl. With sweat rolling down her forehead, she sat for a long time on the edge of the bath to try and recover.

A light tapping on the door made her jump and she heard Elizabeth's voice.

"Evelyn, you have been gone for ages, can I come in?"

Hurriedly, she peered into the mirror and hastily powdered her face and reapplied lipstick. Then she sprayed perfume into the air before unlocking the door.

"I am fine Elizabeth, lately my stomach reacts to spicy food, that's all."

Her hostess reached for the handle of the window and opened it.

"You poor thing, no need to be embarrassed about getting sick, I won't take it personally as I have to admit that I probably went overboard with the spices in the stuffing, Andrew always complains."

"Evie shivered.

"I seem to be coming down with some sort of stomach bug, I am so sorry!"

"Not at all! I got sick at my daughter's twenty-first birthday a few years ago, she was furious, but I could not help it."

"I probably need to go home to bed and sleep it off."

Elizabeth put her hand on Evie's arm.

"Yes, go home and rest, now I will just say to the men that you feel sick because of a stomach bug doing the rounds in the area, no need to tell them that you vomited."

"Thank you for being so understanding."

Elizabeth's face swelled with pride.

"Take a seat in the study and I will organise everything without making a fuss."

On the journey home there was an eerie silence between them as Kevin sat up straight and peered through the icy windscreen to focus on the road. Snow was swirling around them in the light of the headlamps and it seemed like an eternity to Evie before they eventually reached the safety of their home.

Once indoors, he erupted into a violent rage as she was removing her coat.

"You selfish bitch! Of all nights to play a stunt like this one."

"I – don't understand."

"Oh, you understand perfectly. I knew that you were not keen on going, you whinged when I set out early for their house this afternoon because of the weather conditions but to engineer a stunt like this is unforgivable!"

She pulled out a chair and sat on the edge of it.

"Kevin, I swear that I did not do it on purpose, the spicy food just sickened me, and I vomited into the toilet, I could not help it."

He grabbed a pretty, hand-painted vase which was resting in the centre of the kitchen table complete with red carnations, that she had been given by Iris before her departure. Then he held it in his hand while he shouted.

"You showed me how little you think of my boss so allow me to show you how little I think of yours! See, how you like this!"

He flung it across the room where it smashed against the opposite wall.

Evie exploded with anger.

"You are one twisted individual if you believe that I orchestrated this whole sickness."

He shook the snowflakes from his jacket as he rounded on her.

"I don't trust you."

She gave a hollow laugh.

"Don't talk about trust because I don't trust you either."

"You ruined St. Stephen's night for everyone!"

Suddenly, a knot of indigestion gripped her again, she filled a glass with cold water from the tap and took a sip from it.

"I have to lie down, I don't feel well at all – and don't dare to bother -me during the - night when you want sexual relief."

His face turned purple as she walked by him.

"No man would glance at you a second time in that state, get the fuck out of my sight, you disgust me."

She ascended the stairs slowly.

Once undressed she got into bed and wrapped the blankets tightly around her body.

I will have to visit the doctor if this continues.

For three whole days, she ate little, just slices of toast dripping with butter and washed down by tea and in the evenings boiled eggs with brown bread. For some inexplicable reason, she had developed an aversion to Mai Dolphin's herbs, apart from the ashwagandha in hot milk which she still took every night. Even the smell of cigarettes revolted her, and she threw a half-empty packet in the dustbin.

Outside the temperature hovered below zero and dirty frozen snow lay in heaps in the garden where Kevin had dumped it after clearing the driveway and paths. He was so busy with calls to sick animals that she saw very little of him and in the evenings he brought home chips cooked in beef dripping, with cod in batter, covered by an outer later of old newspapers. The sight of him tucking into greasy food made her stomach turn and she had to hurry from the room each evening.

Yet, she found great joy in watching the robins, blue tits, and great tits which arrived every morning to pick at the breadcrumbs that she left out for them.

By Monday, she was feeling much better, the snow had almost disappeared apart from hard ridges in the centre of the road and she ventured into Redmills. It was a great relief to be out in the hustle and bustle of the town again and she stocked up with groceries for the New Year festivities. That evening she enjoyed a plate of roast chicken and peas along with floury potatoes. And to finish off, they had Christmas pudding with brandy sauce. Kevin was so happy that she was back cooking proper meals that he praised her culinary skills profusely.

"They say that you don't appreciate something until it's gone and that applies to your cooking. Evelyn, I have to hand it to you, that meal was the best that I have had in years."

"Yes, I relished every mouthful of it, my stomach seems to be back to normal."

He paused beside her on his way to watch television.

"I didn't get a chance to thank you for your present because the Goffs arrived early on Christmas day but I do like those binoculars, they will be useful at the races."

She nodded, all he had given her was a bath set containing a sea sponge, bath salts and a bar of pink soap wrapped in cheap wrapping paper.

" Evie, you know I think the world of you and I am sorry for saying that you ruined St Stephen's day on purpose."

"Forget it, I accept that you wanted to please Andrew and Elizabeth."

He grinned on his way into the sitting room to watch the television.

However, the next morning she felt worse than ever and had to rush from the breakfast table with dry retching. To complicate matters, fresh snow had fallen during the night and there was an icy nip in the air. Kevin who had the day off followed her to her room and studied her face.

"You look like death warmed up, this has gone on far too long, I will phone Dr Macey and ask him to make a house call, get back into bed and rest."

She felt too weak to argue.

"Ok, I am going to lie down."

Towards midday, the doctor arrived and tapped gently on her door.

"Come in please."

He entered, carrying his large medical bag in one hand.

"Good morning Mrs Moore, please sit up, and prop those pillows behind your back, I shall give you a thorough examination, but I will start first with your lungs and heart."

"Thank you, I have not been feeling well for weeks."

For 20 minutes, he examined every inch of her body, prodding and pressing while he tested for any ominous signs. Then he asked.

"How is your menstrual cycle?"

"I think it's ok, I have never had a regular one, some months I don't have a period at all if I am stressed or busy."

He frowned and pulled a chair alongside her bed.

"When did you last have a show of blood?"

She thought for a moment then replied.

"In early November I had a light period which only lasted a day and I have had none since, but I am not surprised as I have been feeling so run down."

He rubbed his chin with his chubby hand.

"I thought so, Mrs Moore you do not have any illness."

"Then what is causing all this sickness, are you saying that I am imagining it?"

"No, my dear lady, it is the most natural state of all, you have conceived."

It seemed like she had been struck with a hammer on the head as his words began to rattle in her ears.

"Am I going to – have --a baby after 10 whole years?"

"Yes, you have all the signs - your breasts are tender when examined, you have nausea and indigestion, this is part and parcel of pregnancy, not just in the morning but in some people, it can last all day. Then there is the lack of menses…"

Her head felt like it might explode as questions raced through her mind.

Could it be that I conceived one of the times when I made love with Robert?

"Mrs Moore, are you listening?"

Or was I already pregnant with Kevin's baby by then?

"Mrs Moore, you must try to snap out of your shock."

"Sorry, I am just -flabbergasted, after all these years."

"It is not as unusual as you think, I had a patient some years ago who finally conceived after 13 years of marriage – and she had a beautiful baby boy."

"I see- I am just stunned."

"Of course, now I would like to do an internal examination when you are ready -."

"Do I have to have one?"

He suppressed a snigger.

"Come now don't act all virginal, that baby did not grow there by its own accord."

She wanted to hit him but instead, she said.

"Right."

He rummaged in his bag for gloves while she braced herself for an invasive internal test.

Afterwards, when she had rearranged her nightdress he nodded.

"Yes, I am correct, you are pregnant, but I am not sure how far on you are -."

A light knock on the door and Kevin entered without being invited.

"Is it all right to come in now? Is it serious?"

Evie watched as her husband approached her bedside, it all seemed like a dream.

"No, Kevin it is not serious, in fact, your wife is healthier than ever I would say."

"Eoghan, do not talk in riddles!"

With a big grin on his face, the doctor slapped Kevin on the back and chortled.

"Congratulations! You are going to be a father, you have done it!"

Kevin looked from Evie to the medic and back again.

"Is Evelyn pregnant?"

"She certainly is - but I will refer her to an obstetrician to determine the due date and to make sure that she receives the best possible care for the remainder of her pregnancy."

Kevin sat on the edge of the bed and rubbed his forehead for a few seconds.

"This is a lot to take in after all those years- my dear Evie, I always knew that I would put you up the spout."

"Indeed. Aren't you going to give your wife a hug?"

Dr Macey said while he snapped his bag shut.

Evie tensed as Kevin leaned over and kissed her on the mouth.

Then for the benefit of the doctor, she said.

"I am so shocked I can hardly speak."

"Well, it proves that I wasn't firing blanks after all."

Kevin moved triumphantly to the window and looked at the branches of the trees which were laden with snow.

The doctor tittered.

"No one would ever accuse you of firing blanks, you have a torso of perfect proportions."

Evie could scarcely believe her own ears.

"You both forget that I am the one carrying the baby, don't I get any credit?"

"Of course, you are wonderful!" Kevin turned around and gave her an indulgent smile. And then added. "Where would we be without the fairer sex?"

The doctor wrote a prescription before commenting.

"This medicine will help with nausea, but I suspect that you are over the worst of it and that it will settle in the next few weeks."

"What about the fatigue? I was taking herbs to build my system up."

"Cut them all out, I am recommending a gentle tonic which will solve that problem."

Out of the blue, a terrible thought struck Evelyn as she sat bolt upright in bed.

"Dr Macey, is it possible that I could miscarry?"

He looked from her to Kevin and back again.

"Anything is possible, a miscarriage can occur up to twenty weeks, after that point the loss of a baby is called a stillbirth."

"But what are my chances of losing it?"

"No one can predict, Mrs Moore you are not exactly a young woman but you are not an older woman either so you will just have to hope and pray – I see no reason to worry."

Kevin's expression was inscrutable.

"Is having – relations banned?"

Evie gasped while the doctor put the top on his fountain pen and got to his feet.

"It depends on what you mean, if you are a couple who enjoy vigorous relations, I would tell you to tone it down at least until the 20-week stage has passed – but if there is spotting of blood at any time, that could be very serious and you may have to abstain – if and when that happens, the obstetrician will advise you."

"We like a bit of nooky – don't we Evelyn." Kevin winked at her.

Evelyn shook her head in disapproval.

"My apologies Dr Macey for my husband's coarse talk, he is in shock so you will have to excuse him."

"Of course – I was young once too – your husband is a red-blooded male and he is just asking questions which other men might be too repressed to ask."

She bit hard on her lip.

Fuck you, you male chauvinist.

Kevin smirked.

"Thank you, Eoghan, how much do I owe you?"

The doctor smiled.

"Let's just say there is no charge this time, it's my way of saying congratulations to a good friend and his wife."

Kevin strode towards the doctor and shook his hand.

"Thank you Eoghan, have a whiskey with me in the kitchen before you go, it will help you face this awful weather. I dare say I will have a string of sons yet."

The doctor rubbed his eyes.

"Indeed, I would love a glass, thank you. Now Mrs Moore do as I say, and you will be fine. Kevin will get this stuff from the chemist."

"Sure thing, I will drive in shortly."

Kevin patted the end of the bed but the look on his face reminded Evie of a cat who had just eaten all the turkey.

You smug snake.

"Thank you, Dr Macey."

Evie tried to sound grateful, but she hated the way the two men seemed to be bonding over her pregnancy.

"You are welcome, I shall phone the consultant, he is an old acquaintance, I am sure that he will see you early in the New Year."

She gave him a shallow smile as he left the room with Kevin on his heels.

Then she waited for a few minutes and listened at the top of the stairs. When she was satisfied that they had settled down with their drinks, she went back into the bedroom and stared at her reflection in the mirror.

Who is the father?

Did the ashwagandha relax me so much that I finally conceived a baby with Kevin after all these years?

Or is it Robert's child?

Placing her hand on her belly, she whispered.

"No matter what lies ahead, I will look after you, my precious baby."

Chapter Thirty

Evie rose shortly after midday. It was New Year's Eve and the medicine which Dr Macey had prescribed was beginning to work. She had managed to eat fried eggs followed by tea and toast that morning. It was the only food that Kevin was able to prepare as he had lived on fries during his student days.

She found the kitchen in a mess, with dirty dishes piled in the sink and on the table, it was the first time she had ventured downstairs since Monday. Kevin had insisted that she stay in bed, fussing around her with hot drinks, Lucozade, grapes, and a stack of magazines from the local newsagent.

"Your wish is my command."

He declared, on that first evening after news of her pregnancy had been confirmed.

In a total state of shock and worn out with exhaustion she had been too weak to comment. The following day when she asked to have the radio brought up to her room he had rushed out and bought her a yellow transistor radio.

Given that she was starting to feel better she would have to put a stop to his over-protective behaviour. She knew that if it continued much longer it would become just another way for him to control her. She had so many decisions to make now that she was pregnant, her plan to leave him and make a clean break had to be reviewed. Until the consultant confirmed the due date of the baby's arrival, she could not even try and guess who had fathered the tiny being growing in her womb.

Opening the back door, she stood and sucked in the clear, icy air. Fresh snow had fallen overnight and Radio Eireann had announced that roads were in a dangerous condition. She decided to go for a walk to help her think more clearly and had just put on her coat when Kevin's jeep crawled up the driveway. It shuddered to a halt and she was surprised to see a middle-aged woman in a long fawn coat and plaid headscarf emerge from the passenger seat.

Who the hell is she?

The woman followed Kevin into the kitchen.

"Evelyn, this is Lizzie."

Evie remained dumbfounded.

"Lizzie, this is my wife Evelyn, she is expecting a baby and as I explained earlier, we need someone to help out with the housework."

She moved closer to Evie, grabbed her hand, and then pumped her arm.

"Mrs Moore I am delighted to meet you, you can rest assured that I won't leave a spot of dust anywhere and I am great at ironing, especially at starching the collars of shirts."

Evie withdrew her arm slowly.

"Yes. -It's good -to meet you."

Kevin stamped his feet on the mat to remove the snow from his boots.

"Lizzy will come in every morning from ten am to one pm."

"I -see."

Evie could feel her cheeks reddening.

Already, he is doing everything his way without consulting me.

"Mrs Moore, I hope you have a son that is every bit as handsome as his father."

Lizzie winked at Kevin as he chuckled and then addressed her.

"Lizzie, please sit down, I feel blessed to have found you."

Trying to hide her annoyance, Evie filled the kettle with water and put it to boil on the gas cooker.

"I will make some tea, it's nippy outside."

" Ladies, I have to go now duty calls, but Lizzie I will drop you home later, say six pm."

"Thank you, Mr Moore. I will have everything done by then."

"You can put your feet up Evelyn while Lizzie does the work."

He kissed the side of her cheek and then he left.

"You are so lucky to have such a lovely man – a real gentleman."

Lizzie remarked as she removed her coat and hat.

Stacking up narrow slices of Christmas cake on a plate, Evie said.

"He has his moments. Lizzie, where do you live?"

"I live in a cottage near Fairhill, it's about two miles from Railway street."

"And how did you meet my husband?"

"Paddy-Joe, my auld fellow injured his back a few weeks ago and is not able to work so I am glad of any extra money I can make. We keep a few cows and cattle and that's how Mr Moore came to hear that I was looking for work when he called to treat a bullock with the runs."

Evie measured two teaspoons of tea leaves into the pot and then poured boiling water on them.

"Do you mean that your beast got diarrhoea?"

"Aye, that's the word. Anyway, just tell me what you want done and once I have the tea swallowed, I can start work."

Although she knew that she should at least feel some sympathy for the plight of Lizzie, Evie felt nothing. She was stunned that this stranger, whom she had not chosen, was going to be in her home every day.

"Right, I can show you around and tell you how I like things done."

"I am sure that we will get along like a house on - fire -!"

Evie raised an eyebrow as she poured the tea.

"Mrs Moore, sorry for mentioning - fire, I know it's no laughing matter given that your man suffered serious pain after rescuing the Goff family from that fire."

Evie felt her chest tightening.

"Look here, I don't wish to talk about it."

The woman eyed Evie from the corner of her eye.

" I had four kids myself, my three grown lads are in England on the buildings and my youngest, who is a bit soft in the head lives with us, but some women go through hell while they are expecting – they don't feel right at all and it can even do things to their head – they don't think straight."

"That's just rubbish, it's like something a man would say."

Evie stirred sugar into her tea with gusto.

The imp was whispering in her inner ear

What is she implying?

Undeterred, Lizzie continued in the same vein.

"Look at my sister, she was married 3 years before her belly had a baby in it and in the end that was due to my advice."

"Really?"

"Yeah, I told her that she should always lie down for an hour or two after her man had done the business – and just a few months later it worked -."

Evie tut-tutted.

"That is just more hearsay."

Lizzie gave a loud sigh.

"I am telling you it's true, if I had met you years ago, you would have five or six wee ones running around by now. The whole country felt sorry for Mr Moore – to be ten years married and not even a daughter!"

Evie swallowed a mouthful of tea and then in an icy tone she said.

"My reproductive system is none of your business, when you are finished relaying gossip there is cleaning to be done and a dinner to be prepared."

The imp chastised her.

You sound like some high and mighty lady of the manor from the turn of the century.

That evening, after Kevin returned from leaving Lizzie home, they sat down to a meal of baked ham with turnips, roast potatoes, and white sauce.

"It is great to see you able to enjoy your food again."

Kevin commented as he poured more sauce onto his meat."

"Yes. I am feeling a whole lot better."

"By the way, the lads at work send their congratulations about the baby. You are as flat as a pancake, but soon you will have a bump, you must be thanking me now for insisting on having my conjugal rights, it just goes to show that I was correct -."

At any other time, she would have retorted with caustic words, instead, it gave her a great sense of power to know that he might not be the father.

You stupid fool.

She remained silent as he told jokes about sleepless nights and the patter of tiny feet.

Afterwards, they moved into the sitting room where Lizzie had lit a big log fire so that they could watch television and see the folk at the BBC in London welcome in the New Year.

"You never congratulated me for hiring Lizzie, it must be a great feeling that you can just pile up all the dishes after tonight's dinner and know that she will do them in the morning."

He lit a slim cigar while she chose a chair opposite him.

"I know you meant well but we really should have interviewed a few candidates and then decided on someone, Lizzie is a bit of a loud-mouth and only time will tell how good she is at housework."

She saw surprise register in his eyes.

"For fuck sake- you are never happy, I try to help you by finding a good housekeeper and all you can do is complain."

Evie straightened her back.

"Look here, she will need to be paid a fair wage, so why not pick the best person for the job and can we even afford her?"

Kevin harrumphed.

"When did you ever worry about money?"

She narrowed her eyes.

"Don't start, I have always done my best, my salary is not as good as yours but-."

He interrupted.

"Andrew gave me a raise at Halloween so it's not a problem."

You sly fox, now you tell me!

"Ok, but I am just saying that if she does not prove suitable it will be impossible to let her go, she should have been asked to work here on a trial basis for a week or two."

He sniggered as he walked to the TV set and adjusted the knobs.

"Listen to yourself, you sound like Mrs Ryder-Lee, full of notions."

"Time will tell."

Shaking his head, he turned up the volume to drown out her voice.

Soon her eyelids grew heavy and she went to bed.

Towards dawn, she awoke to find him beside her in bed loosening her night attire.

"Can you not leave me alone?" She asked sleepily.

He moved her onto her back.

"Who knows, I might even plant another baby in there."

"Don't be ridiculous!"

"Shut up woman."

She struggled but he placed his hand firmly on her forehead and stared into her eyes.

"If this position is going to hurt the baby, I will do it from behind like the homosexuals."

Filled with fear, she shouted.

"No, get on with it!"

"That's my woman!"

Later, once he had returned to his own room, Evie got up and stood by the window observing the night sky, where hundreds of distant stars twinkled in the inky blackness.

And she thought about Robert, far away on the African continent helping the sick and the dying.

At exactly two pm on the following Monday, she was shown into the rooms of the elderly obstetrician in Merrion Square, Dublin, by his po-faced secretary.

"Aah Mrs Moore, take a seat."

The consultant, a big heavy man with gold-rimmed spectacles, nodded in her direction and then hurried from the room while she sat on the edge of a chair. Her hands were shaking, and she put them on her lap so that he would not notice her nervousness.

He returned with a dusty file and proceeded to his desk, where he scribbled something in red biro on the inside cover. The walnut clock ticked away the seconds while her anxiety mounted as she studied the ceiling mouldings which were filled with intricate patterns.

Then, he closed the folder and threw it onto a stack of files on the floor.

"Now Mrs Moore, any history of still-birth, miscarriage, abortion, I must know everything."

He did not look up but took out a new folder and started to write her name in neat letters on a loose page.

"No. This is my first time to conceive."

He looked over his glasses at her.

"You are Eoghan's patient, he rang me about you."

"Yes."

"Were you having regular intercourse with your husband?"

"Yes, but – does that matter now that I am pregnant?"

"Mrs Moore, if you want me to see you through this pregnancy, you will answer all my questions."

She nodded.

"Eoghan told me that you are one of these uptight women who complained to him earlier in the year about your husband's natural desire for sex."

"I – I did not complain."

That pig Macey has twisted everything.

He tapped his fingers on the table.

"Come now, are you calling my colleague a liar?"

"No, but I just meant that my husband was – rough with me and -not sensitive to my needs in the bedroom department."

He glowered.

"Do you hear yourself? Bedroom department indeed. Eoghan is correct, you are acting like some prudish spinster from Victorian times."

A tiny tear threatened at the corner of her left eye.

"I just wanted to feel loved and treasured."

"Your husband is a young, red-blooded male, by all accounts a fine veterinarian who works hard, surely he is entitled to a bit of relief at the end of the day."

"I – came here – because I am carrying a baby - not to talk about my sex life."

"You are a typical woman! Don't you see that they are all interconnected?"

"What are you saying?"

She dug her nails into her wrist as she was on the verge of running out of the stifling room.

"If you had not been so repressed about your own body and so repulsed by your husband's sexual appetite, I know you would have conceived years ago. Eoghan says you are a strong, healthy woman."

Suddenly, a laugh emerged from her throat.

"How can you be so sure?"

"Because the mind and body are inextricably linked. If you are as tense as a cat on a hot tin roof, when your husband is doing his business you are not going to be receptive to having your egg fertilised."

Don't let him get to you.

"So, it is all my fault that I did not have a baby sooner! I did not come here to be blamed!"

Suddenly, he stood up and pointed at a screen.

"Go behind that and pee into the bottle provided, then undress. I am highly esteemed in my profession I was merely trying to explain your years of so-called infertility."

When the examination was over, she took a seat back at his desk.

"Going on your cycle, which you say is irregular, the cloudy colour of your urine, and the results of my physical tests, I estimate that you conceived approximately around the last day of October/early November so that means your baby is due roughly in the last week of July or early days of August."

Her head was starting to spin.

Oh my God! I had sex with both Robert and Kevin at that time.

"Mrs Moore, are you listening?"

She ignored him as the voice inside was getting louder.

I may never know who fathered my child.

"You seem preoccupied, can you not hear me?"

"Yes. I am just -trying to take in all you told me."

He gave her a strange look.

"You have just been told the due date of your baby, yet you don't seem happy. Is there something which you are not telling me?"

She twisted her wedding ring.

"Of course not, after 10 years of childlessness I am just stunned but excited."

"If you say so. Now, I shall write to Eoghan and I shall review your condition in 8 weeks.

Where do you want to give birth?"

"I don't know what you mean."

He sighed. "You are a private patient so I can look after you in any of the maternity hospitals here in the city."

"The Rotunda hospital suits me as it is easily accessible from Meath."

"Ok." He made a note in his file.

"Now, you may go, I am running late this afternoon."

She stood up.

"Thank you, doctor."

He muttered something but did not look up from her file where he was writing notes.

She had just reached the door when he called her back.

"Mrs Moore, one minute."

"Yes." She turned to face him.

"For your husband's sake, you must accommodate your husband's appetites more, I believe that you asked Eoghan about sexual relations during pregnancy and I can tell you now that you are a healthy woman so there is no need to deprive him."

"I did not ask that question - it was Kevin who asked it."

"Now, now, Mrs Moore, let go of your phallophobia- or he may find relief elsewhere."

"My what?"

"Your fear of a penis."

"How ridiculous! I am not afraid of any man's penis, I have- enjoyed."

A warning rang in her ears.

He is goading me – could he suspect that I am not telling everything?

"Mrs Moore, have you something more to say to me?"

She smiled cynically.

"Absolutely nothing, goodbye."

"Don't forget to pay my secretary on the way out."

She opened the door quickly and hurried down the long hallway.

Chapter Thirty - One

Darkness had fallen by the time she arrived home from her appointment with Dr Robin Shaw.

"When is my baby due?" Kevin asked, as soon as she opened the back door.

"End of July, the first days of August.

" She walked past him into the kitchen.

"A summer baby, that's wonderful, anyone would think that we planned the pregnancy."

Shut up man, I don't even know if it's yours.

"Yes."

She kicked off her shoes and removed her coat.

"You don't sound too enthusiastic."

He eyed her abdomen.

"I am tired, that's all."

She rested her hands on the table.

"Is the baby doing well?"

She looked out the window at the lights twinkling from across the fields.

His face was turning red with anger.

"I will phone the obstetrician if you don't tell me."

Suddenly the room seemed to swim in front of her eyes, and she sat down quickly.

"I feel a bit dizzy - get me water please."

When she had emptied her glass, she said.

"That's better, now to answer your question the baby is absolutely fine, and the pregnancy is a normal one."

"Excellent, that's all I want to hear. Lizzy left a full dinner ready do you want it?"

She shook her head.

"No. I had a meal in a little restaurant off Merrion Square, I was ravenous."

He smiled and gave her shoulder a pat.

"Well, you are eating for two. Now, I have to make a call to a farm near Killeen."

"Right. I might go to bed, I feel exhausted."

He grabbed a coat from a rack and opened the door, allowing driving rain to soak the floor.

"I can hardly contain my happiness, Evelyn, at the thought of having a son."

She raised her eyebrows.

"Or a daughter?"

"Yes, yes, a daughter but I am hoping for a son."

He grinned like a child who had just been caught with his hand in the sweet jar.

"Bye!"

When the door closed, she sighed loudly. She could not wait to tell her news to someone, she decided to phone Mai Dolphin, who was delighted to hear the good news.

"That is wonderful, but men are such fuss pots it will do you good to talk to me. Come for tea tomorrow evening."

"Thank you, I will be there at four pm," Evie replied.

Then she wrote a short letter to Val and a second to Robert. In the former, her surprise and joy about the pregnancy spilt onto the page but in the latter, she was careful not to reveal anything which might even hint at a pregnancy. She was having doubts about her plan to leave Kevin, now that there was a baby expected, and she certainly did not wish to involve someone else who was thousands of miles away. Keeping the letter to him bright and breezy, she invented stories of hair-raising slides with Orla along the ice down the Hill of Tara on a make-shift sleigh, followed by snowball fights with Patsy McGinley. She was careful to thank Robert for the bulging letter which had arrived at Richmond House just before Christmas, in which he described a hazardous journey across dusty terrain in Somalia, along with his son, where they planned to set up an emergency centre. Then, out of the blue, she put down her fountain pen and shook uncontrollably as she tried to clarify her thoughts.

If the baby is Robert's, it could not have happened at a worse time, he is in his element in Africa.

When she became aware of the distant glow of Kevin's headlamps at the main gateway, she hurriedly hid away everything before switching off the light.

She could not endure any more talk from him about his "son" for that day.

Arriving at Mai's house the following afternoon, Mai had a delicious array of cakes and sandwiches spread out on a table alongside pretty china adorned with yellow and cream roses.

"This is exquisite! Thank you so much for going to all this trouble."

Mai hugged her.

"It is no trouble at all, just my way of congratulating you on your delightful news."

When they had eaten, Evie said.

"You have no idea how good it feels to get away from Kevin for a few hours, he is obsessed with this baby and with making sure that I don't overwork."

"Really? Tell me more."

"He has a woman coming in seven mornings a week to cook and clean, I feel I am in her way as she polishes and cleans like a lunatic, moving at the speed of a tornado around the place."

Mai exploded into laughter.

"Well, at least he is not treating you like a skivvy and won't you be going back to Richmond House soon?"

"Next Monday but I know that he will not want me to work for much longer there either."

Mai put logs on the fire and then returned to her seat.

"That's ridiculous, given that you are healthy."

Evie got up from her chair and stood with her back to the window, where rivulets of rain were running down the glass.

"Mai, I am in an awful state as I don't know who the baby's father is."

Mai gazed at the flames as she took a few minutes before speaking.

"Look here, you could presume that it is Kevin's or is the other party likely to see that you are pregnant and cause trouble?"

"He – Robert is in Africa for some months to come so I don't have to tell him -at least until he returns."

"I see, you were all set before Christmas to leave Kevin-."

Evie stroked her belly.

"I know but now it's more complicated, I would like to talk to some doctor who would not report my questions back to Kevin – I had an appointment with a pompous jackass in Dublin yesterday, called Robin Shaw but I know that every word I said will go back to Dr Macey and then Kevin."

"I can understand you want to have an unbiased professional opinion about everything."

"I want to talk about – you know- who might have fathered the baby."

Mai leaned towards her in a conspiratorial fashion.

"There is a retired man in Dublin who could talk with you, a professor emeritus and a friend of my late husband. He is also discreet – but don't build up your hopes, he will not be able to give you a definitive answer about the baby's paternity."

Evie's face relaxed.

"Yes, I understand – but I need to know if there was any chance that Kevin impregnated me - 10 years is a long time -otherwise that makes Robert the father."

Mai's face relaxed into a smile.

"I will make arrangements for you to talk with him, it cannot do any harm."

"Thank you, you are so helpful and such a wise woman."

Throwing her hands into the air, Mai exclaimed.

"Less of that moniker! Is that not the name that eventually led to some women being burned at the stake as witches?"

Evie nodded.

"Probably, but this is 1959! And people are better informed."

On Friday evening Kevin arrived home with a large brown cardboard box bedecked with a massive red bow. Emblazoned on the front, the word: *Ivanov's* caught her attention.

She ignored it and continued clearing dishes away as she said softly.

"Lizzy made a beef pie for dinner followed by marmalade pudding would you like some?"

He burped.

"No, I had fish and chips on my way home from the city, I am not hungry."

"Ok. Did you have to go to Dublin on a call?"

He laughed.

"No way! I went to buy you a present."

Her head was thumping.

"A present?"

"Yes, this is for you to tell you how much I love you and to show you how excited I am about my baby."

"I am stunned."

"Don't be, you deserve it. Now open the box."

He left it on the table where it seemed to burn a hole in her eyes.

"Thank you, this is a surprise!"

He put his arms on her shoulders and touched the top of her head with a light kiss.

Then stepping away from him she said.

"I cannot wait to open it, pass me the scissors from the drawer."

With her fingers trembling, she cut first the ribbon, then the tape and finally lifted the lid to reveal a shroud of tissue paper. Tearing at it excitedly, her heart sank when she saw that it was a fur jacket.

Too shocked for words she bent her head and stroked the fur.

Several mink animals suffered and died to make this awful piece.

"Well, what do you think?"

Kevin's eyes seemed to drill into her brain.

"The fur is so soft and shiny – it must have cost you a small fortune."

"Don't worry about the money, take it out of the box."

Slowly, she took it out and stared at it, as a tear threatened to slide down her face.

"It won't bite you, just put it on."

She shivered a little as she slipped it around her shoulders and put her arms into the sleeves.

Did he do this to torment me? He should know by now that I don't like fur.

"You look lovely! Like a countess."

"Thanks, Kevin."

He frowned.

"Don't you want to go upstairs and see yourself in the long mirror?"

"Yeah – of course."

Her finger fiddled with the expensive button near the collar.

"You don't sound very enthusiastic about it, is there something wrong?"

"No, just that I am sad when I think of all the poor mink who were killed to make this jacket for me."

He gave a long, low whistle.

"Evelyn, when will you grow up? Those mink would have died anyway they are reared in special farms to supply the fur trade, they were not killed because of you."

She put her hands into the two small pockets of the jacket.

"Kevin, you are always so good to animals and despise animal cruelty – I fail to see how you can reconcile- all your good work with the fur trade."

She watched as his eyes narrowed and his lips tightened. For a couple of minutes, she stood still waiting for him to explode but instead, he shook his head.

"A typical sentimental woman! The fur trade, at least the fur farms nowadays are subject to strict rules about living conditions and indeed about – how they kill the animals."

She forced a smile.

"You are the expert."

He kicked the leg of the table with his boot.

"Goddamit! Evelyn, why do you have to take the good out of everything, I have just spent a large sum of money on a mink jacket for you and you throw it back in my face."

You should not have said anything.

She put her arms around him, but he remained unresponsive.

"I am so sorry."

"You have ruined my surprise. No matter what I do you destroy it."

She touched him gently on the hand.

"Forgive me, I do appreciate all the effort you put into buying this jacket, it is a lovely present, thank you – thank you."

She kissed him on the forehead.

He pushed her way and studied her for a moment.

"Evelyn Moore, you are an ungrateful wife, who would drive any man insane. I know that we have had our ups-and-downs but I thought that we could start all over again now that we are going to have a baby- I am trying really hard to do the right thing by you."

"I know, this is all my fault – how can I convince you that I am sorry?"

He pursed his lips, reminding her of a small boy who had just had his cowboy outfit stolen.

She stroked the glossy fur.

"Kevin, it's gorgeous, I feel like Princess Grace in it, thank you."

"Really?" His voice was dripping with cynicism."

"I must go up and have a good look at myself in the mirror."

She went upstairs, inwardly cursing herself for creating such a fuss about the dead animals.

In her own bedroom, she adjusted the mahogany mirror to study her reflection from every angle.

Apart from the suffering of the poor animals, it makes me look like some boring, old matron.

She removed the jacket and only then realized that Kevin had been watching her from the doorway.

He moved closer.

"So, what do you make of it now?"

She turned to look at him, but words were slow in coming.

"I – like it- no I mean I- love it."

He came closer and stared at her hair.

"Thank you, again Kevin."

Then he took a pair of sharp scissors from his pocket and brandished them in her face.

" I will cut off those black tresses and leave you bald if you don't admit that you were wrong – how dare you insult me."

Her body shook as she said.

"I know I was wrong, forgive me, you are a generous man. I am tired."

His eyes dropped to her stomach.

"You can thank that little one that I am letting you off the hook this time."

She swallowed hard as he rubbed his head.

"Now, I feel one of my headaches coming."

"Sorry."

"Sorry, my foot!" He looked disdainfully at her before leaving the room.

Chapter Thirty - Two

Outside, a row of giant sequoia trees, heavy with frost, stood like ghostly sentinels at the edge of the parkland, while watery sunlight caught the tiny crystals hanging from the dream-catcher, which Iris held in her hands as she swept into the room.

"Evelyn, I hear that congratulations are in order! How wonderful!"

"Has news of my pregnancy spread already?"

Iris left the dreamcatcher on her desk and smiled.

"Indeed, Brendan overheard some women talking this morning when he went to buy my newspapers."

Evie got up from behind her desk.

"More like gossiping - the village drums are out."

Iris hugged her.

"My dear Evelyn, it is a great start to the New Year, your very own baby on the way."

Evie wiped away a tear.

"Thank you, I am still in shock and a bit dazed if the truth be told."

"I am surprised after ten whole years, but I want you to have this dreamcatcher, which I got in New York some years back- a friend gave it to me when I was under a lot of stress."

"It's beautiful."

Evie fingered the feathers and then twirled it around so that the crystals caught the light.

"It will banish your worries the feathers allow only good dreams to descend on you as the webbing absorbs terrible dreams at night and then clears them in the light of day- they originated with native American tribes."

"It is a beautiful thought Iris I shall treasure it."

"You are very welcome."

A gentle tap on the door and Iris said.

"Come in."

A young girl in a black dress with a starched white apron entered, bearing a tray of food.

"Ah Kathleen, leave the tray on that small table in the corner, we can look after ourselves."

The girl did as she was told and then headed for the door.

"Thank you, Kathleen, how are you getting on with my other staff?"

"Fine – I am helping in the kitchen this morning and tomorrow I have to learn about housekeeping."

"I am glad to hear it, convey my thanks to Mrs Butler for making these pancakes so quickly."

"Yes. Mrs Ryder-Lee. I will."

Having given a nervous smile, she left the office.

Iris remarked.

"That girl is a smart young one, she is going to England in April to start her training in general nursing."

"Really? I was introduced to her before Christmas, but she seemed shy."

Evie answered as she arranged the china and cutlery on the table.

Once Iris was seated, she explained.

"Kathleen is a granddaughter of the gardener, he asked me if there was any casual work as she needs to save towards the cost of her training."

Pouring the tea slowly through a tiny silver sieve Evie said.

"Iris, you are so kind to everyone."

"Not at all, it will give the housekeeper a chance to get some extra jobs done, in a big house like this the work is never-ending. It was fine back in the last century when up to thirty servants worked here but those times are gone."

"I know, now Iris you must tell me about your break in Cornwall?"

Evie took a seat facing her boss who poured honey onto a golden pancake and then cut it into tiny slices.

"Inspiring! Oh, I could write a book here and now about a family of smugglers on the Cornish coast except that I have other literary commitments to meet – and I don't wish to stand on my agent's toes."

Evie raised her eyebrows in mock horror.

"Yes, Mr Hadleigh would not take kindly to that idea."

"Now, eat this delicious food before it goes cold."

Iris passed a dish of pancakes with an ornate silver cover.

Silence followed, apart from the sound of crows calling to each other when they swooped low to collect the crusts of bread which Cook had thrown out for them on the other side of the house, near the back door.

"Evelyn, can I take it that Kevin is delighted with your pregnancy or is there a – problem?

It seemed to Evie that the question hovered in the air for a few seconds before landing at her feet. Her head was thumping with anxiety.

This is her discreet way of asking about the baby's paternity.

She swallowed a mouthful of tea and then spoke in a firm voice.

"Iris, he is delighted – there is nothing to be gained by complicating things if you know what I mean-."

"Good- it is not my business – all I care is that you are safe and now that you are expecting -a baby -I mean his baby I hope that he will be good to you."

Evie sighed loudly and then gave her boss a weak smile.

"He bought me a mink jacket last week and he has a woman named Lizzie in seven mornings a week, doing all the housework."

Iris reached across the table and left her hand on Evie's arm.

"You deserve it – long may it last."

Evie cleared her throat.

"I was, as you know, hoping to leave him, but the pregnancy has delayed my plans – now I am wary of doing something rash which I might regret – and rearing a child on my own will not be easy."

"You know that I shall help you no matter what decision you reach but take some more time Evelyn and enjoy all the little luxuries while you can as it may not last much longer- I don't trust that Slippery Jack."

Evelyn's tense features relaxed, and she laughed like a child.

"I love the name, it suits him."

Iris rolled her eyes.

"Don't mind me, as you were speaking an image of the tubed mushrooms which grow on the wet parts of the estate came into my head. They have a brown cap which is characteristically slimy in wet conditions and it seems this coating must be removed before eating or so my dear husband told me, he studied biology and mycology as a young man."

Evie nodded.

"Iris, I appreciate your discretion so much because if the slightest hint about the baby's paternity-."

Iris put her long, manicured finger to her lips.

"Enough said, I shall take your doubts to the grave with me, we shall not mention it again unless you wish to do so."

Evie took out a crisp cotton hankie and blew her nose loudly to hide her emotion.

Saturday, to everyone's relief, brought a thaw in the icy conditions, and the winter sunshine beamed through the windscreen as Evie drove to a little old-world hotel on the outskirts of Dublin. Mai had arranged for her to meet with Clive Harte: professor emeritus. She found him in a corner of the lounge bar, smoking a cigar while immersed in the *Irish Times*, oblivious to groups of chattering women all around him.

He was a tall, angular man with dancing eyes and a warm handshake.

"Please call me Clive, I cannot bear to be addressed as anything else, there is a lot of pomposity attached to academia."

Evie laughed, feeling instantly relaxed.

"Then you must call me Evelyn."

He folded away his newspaper.

"Evelyn, shall we order afternoon tea? "

"Yes, there is a waiter on the way over."

When he had taken their order, Evie said.

"I am so grateful to you Professor -I mean- Clive for agreeing to meet with me, I know that your time is precious."

He stubbed out his cigar.

"I am happy to help out, Mai's husband was a dear friend of mine and I value her friendship too. She has given me the bones of your story and may I say that anything you tell me will be treated in the strictest of confidence."

"Thank you so much, I - am unsure about - who is the father of my baby-."

He smiled at her.

"I am not here to pass judgement."

"Yes, I know that – my husband is a difficult man, he studied veterinary medicine but too many years among farmers has made him coarse and selfish, especially in the bedroom so when I met a widower who was kind, generous and loving towards me I slept with him - ."

"Where is he now?"

"He is abroad at least for another few months, so he has no idea about my pregnancy."

"I see, and your husband has no knowledge of your affair?"

"None but I am worried as I don't know what to do -."

"Do nothing that you will regret -now have you conceived before – any history of miscarriages?"

"No none, I was taking herbs around the time I conceived."

"Yes, Mai told me what she had prescribed for you and it is possible that they helped you to relax and so you finally conceived with your husband – a major element of such herbs is the placebo effect whereby a patient may have such a strong belief in the efficacy of such plants that the desired outcome is achieved anyway."

Evie sighed.

"I have heard that it's some sort of a psychological phenomenon if I am not mistaken."

The professor nodded.

"You are not far off the meaning."

Just then a taciturn waiter returned with a silver tray groaning under the weight of tiny sandwiches and fancy tea cakes. When he had poured the tea into delicate cups and laid the table he departed.

"Now, talking about infertility, we are still learning – it was believed that it was caused solely by physical factors but then some wonderful work was done about the impact of the mind on the body and now we accept that it is a complex area."

Evie nibbled the corner of a salad sandwich before speaking.

"In that case, the fact that I was generally happier because of my relationship with Robert may have inadvertently helped me to fall pregnant with Kevin's baby."

"Indeed -who knows?"

"It seems somewhat ironic that an affair could have finally helped me to conceive with Kevin, after all these years."

"Absolutely, but you are certainly not the first and you won't be the last to have this experience."

"Clive, in simple terms -do you believe that this baby is my husband's?"

"It does not matter what I believe – it is what you believe but I must ask did you always have unprotected sex with your lover?"

She wiped her mouth with her napkin.

"Never, he is a doctor and we always took precautions but there was one time when we threw caution to the wind."

"I see – look there is no way at this stage to determine who the father is- we are researching methods of determining paternity which will be accurate but I believe that it will take several more decades before we crack it -there are a couple of expensive tests which can be done after the baby arrives, for example, comparing blood types of baby and putative father but this is not an accurate one by any means."

"I am more confused than ever," Evie said.

"Look here Evelyn, I am not a betting man but if I were, I would put all my money on your husband, he is probably the baby's father and if you take my advice you will dwell no more on the paternity of the child, just take it that the child is of the marriage and then enjoy your pregnancy."

A party of middle-aged ladies arrived and took the next space to them.

Evie leaned across the table.

"I had decided to leave him before this happened but now with the baby coming it is more complicated."

He lowered his voice.

"Do you harbour a desire to have a future with the absent doctor?"

"Not a marriage per se – with the baby on the way I am so confused."

"You have to put your baby first but take a little more time."

"What if I got a solicitor to fight for financial support?"

"If you seek justice through the courts, problems may arise – the matter of why you bailed out of your marriage and a baby on the way, will give rise to questions about paternity. Even if you can answer these, there is nothing to say that a judge will look favourably on you and even if he is sympathetic, Kevin could promise to pay you the sun, moon and stars but simply not deliver on his promises."

"But if we separated on genuine grounds - say incompatibility?"

"Evelyn, there is as yet no legal separation in this state and civil divorce is a long way off so you could end up in a no man's land – wait another month or two and see how things unfold with him."

"Kevin still demands his conjugal rights from me, and I cannot abide him touching me."

He shook his head.

"If I had a penny for all the women who have confided in me about their husband's lack of sensitivity or finesse when making love, I would be a rich man. Ireland is very repressed in sexual matters aided and abetted by the church and its attitude to women and sexuality. Sadly, many Irish men still believe that women are there solely to provide pleasure and relief for them."

"Yes, Ireland is still so backward, have you worked abroad?" Evie asked.

"Indeed, I worked in France and North America, it was refreshing - both men and women had a much healthier attitude to sexuality."

Evie nodded.

" I can still recall Sr Mary at my convent school telling us to keep our legs together and think of the fires of hell when in the company of a boy as he had only one thing on his mind. "

Clive tapped his fingers on the table.

"The damage such comments did to young people is incalculable as it was the only attempt at sex education."

"Iris often reminds me that some of our greatest writers are still banned in this country because they wrote openly about sex."

He chuckled.

"Yes, Iris is absolutely right and last year our very own Brendan Behan highlighted this fact."

Evie stood up and excused herself.

"Clive please excuse me I need to visit the ladies room."

"Certainly, take your time."

On the way back she caught the eye of the waiter and paid the bill at the counter.

When she returned to her seat Clive teased her.

"It is rather unusual to have a lady pay the bill for me."

She laughed.

"I would feel very uncomfortable if I did not cover the cost of the food, after all, you have shared not only your valuable time but considerable knowledge with me."

He waved his hands in the air.

" While you were gone an idea came to me, might I say that if your husband continues to exercise his conjugal rights against your will as your pregnancy advances, all you have to do is fake a bad back."

"Really!"

"Yes, a small percentage of women suffer severe back pain during the last few months of pregnancy and refrain from sexual intercourse."

"Thank you for telling me."

He readjusted his gold tiepin.

"I had a patient some years ago, a French countess who had three children, but she managed to excuse herself from intercourse for four to five months during each pregnancy as she complained vociferously about back pain, her husband was by all accounts a curmudgeon despite his blue blood. Eventually, she left him."

She winked.

"Thank you so much Clive for that tip."

On the way home, she stopped at a sweet shop in the tiny village of Ochill and bought a large box of Cadbury's Dairy Milk chocolate and a bag of toffee's. In the last few days, she had developed a craving for sweets while the chocolates were a peace offering for Orla. She had not been in contact with her since before Christmas as she dreaded telling her that she was pregnant, now that she knew Orla had given up a baby for adoption. Then, she sat back in her seat and gazed at two chestnut ponies in a nearby field while she resolved to phone a few auctioneers in Dublin on the forthcoming Monday, about the cost of renting a small cottage on the northside of the city.

Only the previous evening she had arrived home from work to find Kevin along with Timmy Baxter, a local handyman, clad in white paint-spattered overalls stripping the wallpaper from the fourth bedroom. It had been cleared of furniture and tins of paint for walls and ceiling in royal blue and white respectively were stacked up in the corner.

Furious that Kevin had made no effort to consult her she exploded.

"What in God's name is going on here?"

The handyman gave her a sideways look and then continued with his work, while Kevin pretended to be taken aback by her anger.

"Darling, I am having this room converted into a nursery, it was supposed to be a surprise, but I am sorry that you are annoyed with me."

She had counted to ten before replying while the imp in her brain goaded her.

Look at him! Butter would not melt in his mouth!

Then, the words rolled off her tongue.

"Do not paint the walls in blue, I may have a girl and then they will need to be repainted in pink. Just bring back those tins to the hardware shop and buy a neutral colour like yellow."

Kevin winked at his partner in crime.

"Timmy, pay no attention to my wife, she is like all pregnant women not thinking straight."

"Don't talk down at me!"

Evie felt a tear rolling down her cheek and she ran from the room.

Much later, when the handyman had departed, Kevin burst into the sitting room where she was watching a film on television.

He strode over to her and caught her by the wrist.

"If you ever try and make little of me like that again in front of someone you will regret it."

"You are hurting me, let go!"

She managed to free her hand, but he caught her by the hair and pulled it hard instead.

"No man would tolerate your attitude I try to do something nice for you and you throw it back in my face as always."

"I am sorry, but you should have told me about your plans, I thought that we would convert the bigger room with the large window into a nursery as it faces south and is warmer."

He released his grip on her hair and sneered.

"There you go again! You want everything your way, well too bad, the nursery is nearly finished now so get over it."

"You are nothing but a mini-Hitler."

The words were barely out of her mouth when she regretted them.

She heard an inner voice say.

Calm him down before he kills you with a blow.

He towered over her and was about to strike her on the face with his hand when she pleaded with him.

"Please don't hit me, I am so sorry I did not mean it, Kevin I admit I am an ungrateful wife."

He spat in her face before moving to the sideboard. Then to her horror, he took a swipe at the Waterford glass bowl and vase resting there. They flew across the room and crashed to the floor near her feet.

"Now, tell me again that you are sorry because I don't believe you."

He was foaming at the mouth and she decided to humour him for the sake of the baby.

"Kevin, I beg your forgiveness, you were right earlier when you said that I am not thinking straight because my hormones are all over the place."

"Too right, now let this be a lesson, don't ever make little of me again. I love you Evie, but you make me do awful things, things which I would never do if you were a normal, loving wife."

"I promise Kevin that I won't upset you like that again."

He approached her and planted a cold kiss on her lips.

"Evie, I am sorry too. Now make me a ham sandwich and a cup of tea, my head feels like it could explode at any minute, I didn't take my tablets this morning."

Cursing inwardly, she nodded.

Suddenly, a light tapping on the windscreen brought her back to the present. A young boy grinned at her as she rolled down the window.

"Sorry, Mrs my football went under your car, can you move it "

She nodded.

"Certainly, it is time for me to move off anyway."

When she reached Redmills, she drove directly to Orla's home. Contrary to her fears, Orla was delighted with her news and hugged Evie tightly.

"To be honest I heard about it, you know what this town is like for gossip."

"Indeed, Orla, I was concerned that in some way my news might."

Orla interjected.

"Your news might upset me because of my history?"

Evie nodded.

"Not at all, don't think like that. I have moved on with my life, I am not really a maternal person, I adore literature and books and I really believe that I made the best decision for the child's needs. Now, I bought you a copy of Dr Spock's bestseller, *The Common Book of Baby and Child Care*. "

"Orla, you are so thoughtful, it's on my shopping list for next Saturday's trip into Dublin when I plan to buy a few smart maternity outfits in Arnotts."

Orla chuckled.

"I have heard that Molly Flanagan's maternity dresses are like sacks."

"Yes, she gets off lightly because her shop is the only one in town which stocks maternity wear."

"True! Orla, I can barely wait for my trip to the city as I want to buy wool and baby knitting patterns in Clery's store for matinee coats, blankets, hats, and bootees."

"Aah! That sounds lovely, I hope that Kevin is treating you with respect."

Evie chewed on her thumbnail.

"I want to tell you everything, a leopard never changes his spots and I need to be honest with you just as you have been with me."

"Thank you, Evie, first, let me get a pot of tea along with some cream buns."

Evie's voice sounded hoarse.

"You are such a good friend to me that I hope you will agree to be the baby's godmother in due course."

"Oh Evie, thank you so much, that is a great honour but what will Kevin say?"

"To hell with him, I shall have my own place by then."

Chapter Thirty - Three

Easter was late that year, falling on the last weekend of April. And to make matters worse it was a wet, cold spring, farmers complained that grass growth was at least three weeks behind other years while early plants and flowers struggled to make an appearance. Kevin had been busier than ever, high mortality rates during the lambing season and an outbreak of pneumonia among several herds meant that cows, calves, and bullocks were dying like flies. Even Evie began to feel sorry for him when he was called out night after night. Every Easter Monday, he attended the horse racing at Fairyhouse racecourse where the Irish Grand National took place. And this year was no exception, once breakfast was over and he had complemented Lizzie on the large fry which she had cooked, he turned to Evie who was finishing a piece of toast.

"Evie, you won't believe it but one of the horses running in the 2.20 today has a very interesting name."

"Really, what is it?"

She asked, aware that Lizzie who was dusting in the hallway was straining to hear every word.

He clapped his hands with glee.

"He is a young gelding from Skinnadre's Stud and his name is "Eve's Boy.""

"Remember that Eve can be short for several names apart from mine like Evangeline, Evanna, and even Yvonne."

"Yeah, I know but don't you think that it's a good omen given that you are expecting a baby?"

She drummed her fingers on the tablecloth.

"I don't know."

"Well, I view it as a sign that we are going to have a son and I will be betting a couple of pounds on that horse."

She gave a loud forced laugh.

"Kevin Moore, I never thought that you would believe in omens."

He patted her hair gently as he passed by.

"You can mock all you like but just wait until I return tonight with my winnings."

"I do hope that you are correct, but I won't hold my breath."

After his departure, she stroked her belly, she was by now experiencing regular tiny movements from the baby and it filled her with great joy.

His comments worried her, once news of her pregnancy had sunk in, he had become increasingly convinced that the baby was a boy. And certain that fortune was at last smiling on him, he spent his free weekends away at poker games or so he told her but sometimes she wondered if he had another woman. Since his head injury, every free minute of his time seemed to be spent at some form of gambling if not cards it was horse racing, which he followed assiduously. And she often drove past the main bookmakers in the town to check if his jeep was parked outside as he liked to place bets there on English races.

"Mrs Moore -a penny for your thoughts."

Evie jumped.

"Sorry, Lizzie I was not aware that you were speaking to me."

"Expecting a baby does strange things to a woman's head – some craythur's can't think straight at all."

Lizzie held a packet of Robin starch in her hand as she stood at the sink, grinning.

Counting to five, Evie stretched her neck from side to side.

"That's nonsense, there is nothing wrong with my brain, pregnancy is a state of health, not some incurable disease."

"I know what I know."

The older woman replied as she turned her back and began to mix some starch with water.

Evie stuck out her tongue at her back like a bold child.

"I am having a friend over for a late lunch, so you might do some scotch eggs and poached salmon. A few fresh brown scones would also be nice."

Lizzie turned around quickly, her face red with indignation.

"What time do you call a late lunch?"

Evie glared back at her.

"In this case, it is two-thirty pm to be precise but there is no need for you to get annoyed about it. I would prepare it myself except that I know we might get in each other's way – two women in the same kitchen never works."

A mischievous voice whispered to her.

She should not be here every morning – acting like she owns the place and making snide remarks.

"Look here, Mr Moore pays me to do the housework and cooking – consider it done - but I will be leaving as usual at one pm."

Evie shook her head, sometimes she felt that Lizzie was spying on her and reporting everything back to Kevin.

"Fine, if I had my way you would not be here so often."

Lizzie's eyes blazed.

"Hah! But you are not the boss!"

Evie bit hard on her lip, as she refrained from firing back insults.

Despite herself, she shouted.

"Fuck you."

Then she hurried out of the room and went upstairs to have a long soak.

Mai arrived at two pm bearing a willow basket full of herbal gifts which she had made.

"It is so good to have you finally visit my home."

Evie held the back door open for her.

Mai's eyes glistened with tears.

"And I am delighted to be here! You look well and may I say that your bump has grown since we met a few weeks ago."

Evie laughed.

"I know, I feel as big as an elephant already!"

"Now, while I take off my jacket have a look through the contents of this basket, I hope you find them useful."

"Wow! I am bowled over with all these beautiful gifts!"

Evie removed tissue paper from small bottles and jars.

"I can explain them quickly to you."

Mai put on a pair of glasses and then proceeded to look over the rim of them while she spoke.

"Elderflower water is an old-fashioned skin tonic but a good one, here are two herbal teas; Cowslip and Camomile, both are relaxing after a long day. Then there is a witch hazel poultice which I made this morning, you should apply it to those haemorrhoids you have been enduring, morning and evening. Next is a bottle of non-alcoholic wildflower wine and finally, I have included my herbal foot soak for your swollen ankles and feet, always a problem in the last few months of pregnancy."

Evie hugged her.

"Thank you so much, Mai, it is like a treasure trove of gifts, every one of them made by your skilled hands."

"You are so welcome I just hope that you find them useful."

Evie tapped her stomach.

"That surely is an understatement, after all, I attribute my pregnancy to your wonderful knowledge of herbs and in particular to that one you call ashwagandha!"

Mai pulled out a chair and sat down, then with a big smile she said.

"People have accused me of some outrageous things in my life including black-magic, but this is the first time that I have been found guilty of causing a pregnancy!"

Evie chuckled.

"You know what I mean, I believe that your herb helped me to relax and so I finally conceived, ten years is a long time to be married and childless. Something about it obviously worked even if it was just the placebo effect."

Mai nodded.

"You are with child now and that is all that matters."

After lunch, they took a stroll to the head of the road and then turned into a laneway which was seldom used apart from farmers leading cattle to and from the fields.

"It's like Heaven here, just listening to the birds singing all around us." Evie's face glowed.

They sat down on a low stone wall near a stream where the gurgling of the water made its own music while Mai shielded her eyes from the sunshine as she took in her surroundings.

"Nature is wonderful, but some people manage to make a snake-pit of this world. Tell me, how is Kevin treating you now?"

"He has outbursts of temper if things don't go to his liking and he shouts and roars like a spoiled child, never of course if Lizzie is around as he loves to play the part of the perfect gentleman in front of her."

"I see. What about his nasty habit of pinching/bruising you?"

Evie looked directly at her.

"Oh, he still pulls my hair and grabs my wrists if I step out of line, but I don't intend to endure his tantrums for much longer. And thanks to your friend Clive I don't have him grunting and groaning over me like some randy bull either."

Mai's eyes followed a Peacock butterfly who whooshed by her, disorientated after emerging from hibernation.

"I – don't understand -how did Clive stop your husband's nocturnal visits to your bed?"

Evie sighed.

"I didn't get the chance to tell you earlier but I followed some unorthodox advice which he gave me. Once February arrived, I feigned a bad back, which has become shall we say increasingly problematic as my bump grows."

"And does he believe you?"

"At first he was very sceptical, but I did so much yelping with pain whenever he tried to have his way with me that he insisted Dr Macey examine my back."

"So, did you fool him?"

"Indeed, I did, Clive had told me about some French countess who simulated a bad back during all of her pregnancies to get a break from her curmudgeonly husband – when Macey poked and prodded my spine like he was dissecting some sort of earthworm I really acted like I had a few damaged discs in my back."

Mai rocked from side to side with laughter.

"Fair play to Clive for thinking of that ruse!"

"Indeed. Macey was so convinced by my performance that he prescribed three different lotions and rubs for my back as well as some gentle walking to keep me from getting stiff."

"Great but what about Kevin?" Mai enquired.

"Put it this way, he has not made any sexual demands on me since – and that suits me fine."

Mai hesitated for a moment and then added.

"You know that he may – seek out other women."

Evie raised her eyebrows.

"Of course, the thought has occurred to me but even when I was having sex with him, I could never be sure that he was not fooling around with tarts too. I always had my doubts."

"I am sad to hear that."

"Look, it's water under the bridge now and I am no saint either - my niggling concern is still who actually fathered my child, Kevin or Robert but as I told you some weeks ago, I am choosing to believe that it is Kevin's."

"Yes, there is no point in torturing yourself at this stage."

"Indeed, after all the weeks of searching for a nice place to rent I have finally found a two-bedroom flat with bathroom and kitchen cum living room on Worthing Lane near Phoenix Park. The price is within my budget, it is on the first floor of an old Victorian house, the landlady lives on the ground floor and another tenant on the top floor so there will be people around all the time if Kevin tries anything."

Mai's mouth opened and then closed.

"I admire your courage I appreciate that it is not easy having to walk out on your lovely home and you in the last months of pregnancy."

Evie stared into the middle distance.

"Yes. I have put down a deposit and I will be getting the keys next week. Then on Friday morning after he has left for work, I shall pack a suitcase and bring most of my belongings."

Mai frowned.

"What if Kevin tries to stop you, that maid he employs will spill the beans."

"Yes, but by the time she tracks him down on his rounds, it will be too late. I have confided in Mrs Ryder-Lee, I am taking the day off and Brendan her chauffeur will help me move the stuff into the flat. However, she has insisted that I stay at her home for a few weeks at least until Kevin gets used to the idea that I have left him."

After a long sigh, Mai's jaws relaxed.

"Thank heavens that you have a very generous and kind lady as your boss, she is right it is better to be safe than sorry. Your husband won't dare to create an ugly scene outside Richmond House as he will just make a spectacle of himself."

"Exactly. Mai, please do not feel offended that I did not ask for your help with moving but I have a different favour to ask of you."

"Certainly, Evelyn I will do what I can, I have to confess that I was taken aback for a moment or two that you did not involve me given my special interest in helping women from troubled marriages but once I heard that you have Mrs Ryder-Lee and her chauffeur on board, it all makes sense."

Evie left her hand on the older woman's shoulder.

"Thank you, Mai. I have continued exchanging letters with Robert but I have not told him about my pregnancy. However, on Thursday a card arrived at the office with a London postmark, to say that he had to come home earlier from Africa than anticipated - he has a problem with his right eye which will need surgery."

"Oh, my goodness, that it a surprise development."

"Well, I need to tell him the truth – I must finish with him- at least in the short term until I sort myself out – as the baby comes first."

"Absolutely, but how can I assist you?"

"I want to meet him somewhere safe where I have back-up – so that if he takes it badly and insists the child is his - I can ask him to leave. I am wary of meeting him in Dublin as I will be alone, my cousin Val returned to live in England last week."

Mai pulled some primroses close by and then sniffed them before answering.

"You are welcome to use my home, I can go off in the car for an hour or so to give you time to tell him - but I think he will guess that something is wrong once you say that you want him to meet you at a friend's house."

"Yes, that is true, but I cannot think of any better way of breaking the news to him."

Mai leaned across and hugged Evie.

"Don't worry, it will work out, he is a reasonable and educated man by all accounts, and did you not tell me last year that he has two grown-up sons?"

"Yes. Thank you for agreeing to help me, Mai. I had thought about asking my friend Orla, but her house is in town where anyone could see us."

"Evelyn, I am happy to be able to help, you are like a daughter in many ways and I hope to be able to support you by babysitting and so forth. Your baby is the main priority at this stage, in a year or two you will look back at this time and marvel at how brave you are."

Evie wiped away a tear.

" I don't feel brave I feel scared but if I don't leave before the baby arrives it would be impossible to go after it is born as Kevin would never let me take his child from him. He believes that I am giving up work for good from next Friday and has warned me that my place is at home."

"What an awful man, he is sick in the head." Mai's face reddened with anger.

"He is controlling everything relating to the baby, the nursery, cot, pram, and even the food I eat which must be what he deems nutritional. I suppose seeing him so obsessed with being in charge even before the child arrives has been a real wake-up call for me."

Mai looked closely at her and then smiled knowingly.

" It will all work out, and all your friends will help you. You are not alone."

Chapter Thirty - Four

That evening Kevin returned home late from the races. A whiff of whiskey filled the air as he flung open the door of the sitting room where Evie was soaking her feet in a basin of Mai's balm. Jubilantly, he pulled a roll of pound notes from his pocket and waved them in front of her face.

"The horse romped home can you believe it?"

She looked up at him. "Do you mean "Eve's Boy?"

He sat down on the couch beside her.

"Yeah, I told you it was a sign that my luck has changed – he was a complete outsider but the favourite fell at the third last jump from home and then a loose horse put the other favourite off his course."

"That's amazing."

He studied her feet as she removed them from the water and dried them with a towel.

"How much did you win?"

He laughed.

"Fourteen pounds and ten shillings to be precise."

"Well done! But I suppose it's a case of you win some you lose some!"

He glowered at her.

"Typical of you, you are never happy, you are never able to live in the moment."

She sat up straight

"Hang on a minute, I was just making an observation about gambling, I didn't mean anything else."

He grabbed her hand tightly.

"Are you implying that I have some sort of a problem?"

"For heaven's sake Kevin, I am over six months pregnant, I have enough on my plate."

She pulled her hand free.

He threw the notes across the coffee table.

"I hope that you have a boy in that womb of yours, God forbid that I would have to tolerate another female in this house, a carbon copy of you."

She stood up but he pushed her back onto the settee.

"You are such a bitch and I only thinking of the baby - I was going to say that you could open a fund for him to cover his university fees."

"Hang on a minute the baby has not even been born yet!"

He lifted his right foot as if he were about to kick her in the shin.

"An apology, I want an apology." He shouted.

He has been drinking all day, be careful.

"I am sorry, so sorry, it is great that you are thinking about the baby's future already."

He shrugged his shoulders and then lit a cigarette, blowing the smoke in her direction.

"By the way, the baby will be called Frederick after my dear father, it is such a pity that he died so young."

She looked at him wide-eyed.

That's what you think.

"And what if it's a girl?"

"Maggie after my grandmother."

She blinked slowly but refrained from answering.

"Where the hell did you get that mixture?"

"Do you mean the foot soak?" She asked.

"Yeah, I could smell you before I saw you."

"Mai Dolphin gave it to me, it's great for swollen ankles and legs, common in pregnancy."

He looked at her from under his lashes.

"Like that weak back of yours, sometimes I think it's all in your head, a way of stopping me from having my rights but you are not the only female on the planet."

"That's not fair, even the doctor confirmed that bad back pain can happen as the body adjusts to carrying the extra weight of the foetus."

He stubbed out his cigarette on a crystal fruit bowl in the centre of the small table.

"I saw a basket in the kitchen, filled with potions, no doubt that - old witch gave them to you."

"She is no witch, and she does not make potions - her creams and treatments are most efficacious."

He grabbed her by the upper arm.

"Do you know that Betsie Meagher, lost six young calves from pneumonia in the past few weeks all due to that stupid woman with her herbal concoctions?"

"I don't understand why you are blaming Mai."

"Auld Betsie is not the brightest – she swears she heard the banshee when her husband died – anyway, she got some concoction for her joint pain - from the witch and made the calves swallow it."

Evie tried to stand - but he tightened his grip on her arm.

"I doubt if Mai undertook to treat calves with pneumonia - can you stop squeezing my arm."

He let her arm go.

"No, she did not treat the beasts directly, but she should never have given that bottle of -purple muck to Betsy at all – it seems that Betsy suffers from rheumatism – and the witch gave her a bottle of cumin oil mixed with something else to rub on her knees."

"So, it must have cured her rheumatism, or she would not have decided to give it to the calves."

Evie said with a malicious grin.

Kevin shouted.

"Don't get smart with me! Instead of seeking veterinary advice for those animals Betsy tried to save money and made the poor calves drink it, she got it into her head that cumin would clean out their lungs!"

Evie took a deep breath and rubbed her stomach.

"Stop shouting at me, I am sorry about the loss of the calves but that's what happens when ignorance takes over, poor Betsy has obviously had no education, you cannot blame Mai for what happened."

"Thanks to that auld wan, my reputation is at stake."

"Hardly! Everyone knows you are a great vet."

He coughed loudly.

"I wonder! Betsy only called me when it was too late, the calves all died a couple of days afterwards from pure neglect – now Betsy is blaming me for letting them die but it was all down to that stinking fish who should not have given her the oil at all."

"But Mai could never have foreseen that Betsy would treat calves with it!"

Kevin's shoulders heaved with fury.

"She needs to fuck off back to the city as she hasn't a clue about the people who live in the country or how they think – because of the damp, late spring a lot of beasts have died anyway. "

"Yes, I know that the hard weather was awful for the poor animals," Evie said.

He looked at her with disdain.

"What do you know really about my life? Sitting over in Richmond house like a lady, typing a few letters – the boss hauled me in last week to dispel rumours which he had heard relating to my cavalier attitude with young calves."

"I am sorry, but really Andrew should know better than asking you to explain about those calves – he has only been the boss for a short time."

He banged the coffee table with his fist.

"At the end of the day it's a business and he has invested all his money into the practise so he has to be sure that I am pulling my weight as well as my colleagues – he has two other vets employed now because his business is expanding and he hopes to keep it that way."

Evie tightened her earring.

"I see, so he has big plans."

"Yes, but big plans mean more pressure on me."

Calm him down, say something to humour him.

"Would you like something to eat or drink?"

She managed to stand up and was about to move away from him when he sneered.

"You are like an elephant at this stage that baby will come early, mark my words."

He lunged at her and left his big hand on her belly.

A feeling of repulsion seemed to spring up from her chest and she shivered.

"The least you might do is let me have a feel of my own baby, you know, and I know that your back is not bad at all, it's just an excuse to stop me from riding you."

She looked him in the eye.

"I am telling the truth, even the doctor believed me."

He allowed his hand to slip down and forced it between her legs.

Her heart was beating furiously.

He is going to rape me.

Suddenly, he drew back and pulled hard on the gold earring dangling from her left ear until she screamed.

"Stop."

"I would have my way with you every night if I desired you as your bad back would not stop me. But the truth is that you disgust me with that belly like a balloon."

She swiped at his hand and the earring fell to the floor.

Then his mood changed.

"Get me a brandy and soda."

Appease him for the sake of the child.

"Ok. Coming right up."

He followed her into the kitchen and waited in the doorway while she located a bottle of Hennessy brandy in a cupboard.

When his eye fell on Mai's basket, he strode across the floor and grabbed it. Then opening the back door, he went outside into the gathering darkness.

She watched from the window as her heart hammered in her chest and she saw a light in the main shed where he kept his tools.

Next came the sound of glass breaking followed by swearing and then silence.

She waited with bated breath.

A few minutes later he returned.

"That's the end of those stupid creams and potions. Don't ever let me see you using them again – while you are carrying my baby."

She nodded.

"Ok, I heard you."

Then a thought struck him.

"Was that witch here today in my house?"

She hesitated.

"Well?"

"Yes. She was here."

He kicked the back door shut with his foot and sat on the edge of a chair.

Evie left a glass of brandy and a decanter of soda water in front of him.

"Sorry, we are out of ginger ale, but I can get some tomorrow. I am going to bed now I feel tired."

He took a nip of neat brandy, then he pointed his finger at her.

"Before you rush off to your bed – note that I want you to cut all contact with that woman – she is a charlatan."

She nodded.

"Ok."

"Secondly, write out your formal resignation tonight for your boss, I will check it in the morning."

Her throat felt dry.

Just humour him for the moment.

"She knows that I am leaving soon."

His top lip twitched.

"By the way, I had a phone call from mother, she will be staying for eight weeks after the baby arrives to help you, as Dr Macey says you are very highly-strung and will struggle to cope."

Slowly, as his words sank in, hatred bubbled up inside her and she grabbed a pile of newspapers resting on the worktop and flung them across the room.

An inner voice reminded her.

When you leave him – none of them can control you.

Yet she could not resist shouting.

"How dare that misogynistic old doctor pass judgement on me."

He gave a low whistle and stood up as he clapped his hands slowly.

"What a performance!"

She was about to answer when she felt the baby kick and her hand automatically went to her belly.

"Look at you, your hormones are ruling you."

Go to bed – no point in arguing -I am within days of leaving him.

"I need to lie down now - my back is killing me."

She walked slowly across the room, deliberately dragging her hip.

"Yes, mind that precious baby you have on board."

Climbing the stairs, she heard him humming Elvis Presley's *Hard- Headed Woman.*

Chapter Thirty - Five

It was long past ten o'clock on that first Saturday morning in May when Evie absent-mindedly tapped the boiled egg with her spoon and removed the cap. Egg white slipped down the shell, along the blue willow patterned eggcup, and onto the table-cloth.

"Lizzie, how many times have I told you that I like my eggs hard-boiled?"

Evie enunciated every word.

The imp in her brain shocked her.

You grow more and more like your husband every day.

Lizzie turned around quickly to face her accuser.

"I can't remember every detail, your husband prefers them runny, besides, they have more nourishment in them like that."

"Are you just too lazy to bother cooking them my way?"

"I am not lazy I work hard here trying to please you."

Evie shoved the egg across the table and poured herself some tea from the pot on the table.

"Where is the tea cosy? You know I don't like cold tea."

"There!"

Lizzie plonked a red and white knitted cover on the teapot.

The voice was back again.

You are as cantankerous as him.

"Can you toast some white bread, please? I seem to have a permanent longing for it."

Lizzie made a face.

"That toaster is not working properly, it takes ages to brown the bread – can you do it yourself, Mr Moore asked me to tidy the garage on top of my usual jobs."

"Suits me fine, I only asked because I can't get near anything while you are bustling around the kitchen."

Lizzie gave her a dagger look as she headed for the door into the hallway.

Evie could not resist having a go at her.

"Lizzie, when my baby arrives, I won't be needing you every morning – I think that three or four mornings will suffice."

The older woman turned back suddenly.

"Mr Moore has already promised me that I can continue to work here every morning – this is your first child, and you will need all the help you can get – he says that you are inclined to be moody and he is worried about how you will cope with all the sleepless nights."

Evie felt the blood drain from her face.

"How dare you talk about me in such a disparaging manner - do you report back every tittle-tattle to him?"

"It's not like that - he just asked me to keep an eye on you because of your bad back and your sensitive nature."

Evie stood up and looked Lizzie directly in the eye.

"Who do you think you are?"

"Just the housekeeper - but Mr Moore is so kind and generous that I want to do my best — you are lucky to be married to him, he adores you and he is so excited about the baby."

Evie cleared her throat.

Be careful- do not let anything slip.

She checked the wall clock.

"I thought you were busy, off you go."

Lizzie bristled.

"If you are finished talking Mrs Moore."

Evie ignored her and went to the window, gazing into the distance where cattle were contently grazing. She had lost her appetite.

He wants Lizzie here — so that he can control me even when he is out?

It was a dry, sunny day and rows of late spring flowers were now in full bloom in the garden. She searched the sky for swallows, only three had arrived so far to rebuild the old nests in the ruins of a stone shed at the back of their garden. After several deep breaths, she made a fresh pot of tea. She had to keep up her strength today of all days as she had arranged to meet Robert in the late afternoon at Mai's house. The thought of it filled her with dread and it was the reason that she had been so edgy with Lizzie earlier. Her head ached as she tried to imagine his reaction to the news that she was almost 7 months pregnant.

Will he understand when I insist on cutting all contact with him -at least in the short term?

She opened the back door and allowed the gentle breeze to caress her face while she walked outside with her cup of tea. A sweet medley of bird song from the hedgerows filled her with awe and she paused at a cherry tree swathed in pink blossoms where a blue-tit was warbling. Then she heard a strange humming noise and looking in every direction, her eyes fell on the old, gnarled apple tree where a swarm of bees had landed high up on the branches. Enthralled she listened carefully to them, by closing her eyes she was able to distinguish different sounds, some bees were making piping noises, others were emitting whooping signals and more still were making a low, buzzing vibration.

Mai, who was a keen beekeeper had told her a lot about bees and if she remembered correctly, a swarm of bees arriving in a garden was regarded as an unlucky omen. For a second she felt a chill go through her despite the weak sunshine and she moved on quickly to a row of primroses, chiding herself for her silly thoughts.

On this of all days, I can't pay heed to foolish old beliefs.

Then she saw Lizzie running towards her.

"Mrs Moore – Mrs Moore you are wanted on the phone -."

Lizzie said breathlessly.

"Calm down and tell me who wants me?"

Evie threw the contents of her cup across the grass.

"I wanted to take a message, but he said he has to talk to you now as it is important -."

"What is his name?"

"He did not give his name he just said that he is a doctor."

Evie felt her chest tighten as she wondered if something had shown up in routine tests.

"Here, take this."

She thrust the empty cup into Lizzie's hand and then ran to the old pantry which Kevin had converted into an office.

Picking up the receiver she said nervously.

"Hello. Who is this?"

"Evelyn, do you not recognise my voice?- It's Robert."

"Robert, you gave me the fright of my life, I thought that my doctor had found something bad in my tests."

"Tests! Have you been sick?"

She hesitated.

"No - just routine ones I will explain when I see you."

"Good."

She could hear him exhale loudly but she continued.

"I asked you not to phone here."

"Yes, but it's an emergency I wanted to tell you that I might be late."

She lowered her voice.

"Luckily, Kevin is at work."

"Evelyn, the clutch in my car was sticking this morning so I am waiting in the garage now while they fix it, but it will be ready about three o clock."

"Ok, I will ring Mai and tell her."

"I should be in Redmills about four-thirty but I was so annoyed about the car this morning that I forgot to bring the piece of paper with directions for your friend's house."

"It's easy, as you leave Redmills, take the north road heading for Cavan, then take a right onto the Bog road for another mile, then a left and Mai's house is on the left up an old winding lane but if you do get lost just ask for the herbalist's house, everyone knows it."

"Thanks, Evelyn, I can hardly wait to see you and have you in my arms again."

"Robert as I said in my letter, I have something to tell you – also I am leaving Kevin next week, but he has no idea."

" That is great news but you take care, Evelyn."

A short, loud click and then another click -.

"Robert -did you hear a click?"

"No. Goodbye."

She did not answer as her whole body went stiff with fear and she dropped the phone.

Did the click come from within the house or from the exchange – was Lizzie listening in on one of the extensions?

She flung open the door of the office leading to the hallway.

Her eye picked out the black Bakelite phone sitting peacefully on the hall table.

Next, she headed for the stairs, taking the steps two at a time.

There was a second extension in Kevin's room.

The door was closed but she opened it wide.

Her eye picked out the phone which was undisturbed, then the unmade bed and Kevin's dirty clothes still strewn across the floor from the night before.

From the bathroom across the landing where the door was ajar, a light scraping sound came. Gripped by a mixture of foreboding and curiosity she stood at the bathroom door and watched Lizzie, who was kneeling as she scrubbed limescale from the sides of the bath.

Lizzie turned around slowly.

"You look white in the face Mrs Moore – were you given bad news?"

"No, nothing like that – he is just someone connected with Richmond house, he happens to be a doctor."

Lizzie got to her feet.

"Would you like a cup of tea with a nice slice of fruit cake, you had no breakfast."

"No, I am fine, carry on with your own work."

"All right so, Mrs Moore."

She smiled at Evie and then shook white scouring powder along the edge of the bath and proceeded to scour it vigorously with some steel wool.

Evie went slowly downstairs and made a mug of strong coffee which she sipped slowly.

She went over the whole episode again in her head - the click on the line must have come from the main telephone exchange in Dublin. It was unlikely that Lizzie, who was well into her fifties, would have managed to run across from the bedroom and arrange to be scrubbing the dirty bath in that short space of time.

It only took me about four minutes to check the hallway, run upstairs and enter the bedroom.

She felt cross with Robert for daring to phone her at her home but the voice in her head was pragmatic.

After living for years with a bully you are suspicious of everyone Lizzie did not hear anything.

Chapter Thirty - Six

That afternoon she left the house at four pm. She had phoned Mai earlier about the change in plans and Mai had agreed to leave the house key under a basket of turf near the front door.

She took the longer route to the cottage which bypassed the town hoping to avoid meeting Kevin on his rounds. Now and again, she glimpsed milky sunshine reflecting on the river through breaks in the trees. Near Moran's farmyard, at least six cattle had escaped from a field and were fleeing in every direction along the straight narrow road. She pressed the brakes hard bringing the car to a sudden stop. Two bullocks with steam coming from their nostrils were rushing towards the vehicle.

Sweat dripped from her forehead.

On either side of the car were steep dykes.

She pumped the car horn, and a series of loud honks panicked the beasts. They turned within yards of the car and headed back up the road towards the farm.

Then to her relief, she saw the figure of J.J. Moran and his collie dog in the distance. She switched off the engine and waited while they rounded up the cattle.

When her breathing slowly returned to normal the thought struck her that everything seemed to be going against her.

What if Robert is angry that I did not tell him earlier – and insists that the baby is his.

A rap on the car made her look towards the front passenger's side and she wound down the window.

"My name is Marty Moran, Daddy told me to tell you that the cattle are all back in the field."

She studied the young boy.

"Where did you come from?"

He grinned.

"I squeezed through a hole in the hedge, you can drive on now."

"Thanks."

She started the car and moved off at a snail's pace, she was taking no chances as she wanted to get to the cottage safely. When she reached the red and white Stop sign at the end of the road, a quick flash of Lizzie scrubbing the bath on her knees came into her mind.

Yet there was something different about this image than the one she had witnessed earlier.

She pulled up onto the grass margin at the side of the road and wracked her brain.

Then it came to her like a bolt from the blue.

Lizzie had not been wearing her trademark navy crossover apron when cleaning the bath – the one she always wore when tackling cleaning jobs. She was still in the smaller, neat apron she wore when preparing food.

She roared at her reflection in the mirror.

"Why did I not notice it earlier – Lizzie heard every word I said on the extension and raced from the bedroom across to the bathroom before I got to the top of the stairs."

She checked her wristwatch which showed 4. 50 pm. The journey had taken her much longer than expected.

It was possible that Robert was already waiting at Mai's house, she must hurry and keep the meeting with him brief. Kevin spent most days out on calls but when he returned to the surgery in the evening Lizzie would tell him everything. It would not be safe for her to be under the same roof as him once the truth was out. Later, she would confide in Mai about her fears and spend the night at her house.

Blessing herself she revved the engine and pulled out onto the road. A truck passing in the opposite direction seemed to appear from nowhere and the driver blew angrily at her as he swerved to avoid a collision. She shivered, it was the second mishap of the afternoon.

The quicker I get off these roads the better.

Five minutes later she turned into the lane leading to Mai's cottage where young rabbits were cavorting in the tufts of grass growing along the side, she slowed the car to second gear.

I must put the baby first.

She rounded the last bend and saw Robert's Volkswagen Beetle parked near the front door. Stopping beside it, she jumped out but there was no sign of him. Then she peered through the windows and saw a newspaper and his hat lying on the back seat.

It was obvious that he had been tempted to take a walk and look at Mai's dizzying array of herbs and flowers which attracted countless birds and insects.

She crunched across the gravel to the old wooden gate that led into the garden.

It creaked noisily as she opened it.

There was a stillness about the garden which surprised her, she had expected it to be filled with birdsong on that lovely evening. There wasn't a sound apart from a big bumblebee which whooshed past her and landed on some French lavender. The garden had been so cleverly designed by a professional from Dublin that it had several pathways twisting and turning, through tall plants and shrubs like a labyrinth, but only one opened out in the very centre where a stone seat was placed near an image of Buddha.

She called out.

"Robert – Robert –."

Still, silence prevailed but from the corner of her eye, she saw a movement in the tall pampas grass at the bottom of the garden. She would sneak over there and surprise him, Mai had shown her a short cut. She turned to the left and went under a small arch covered in ivy which separated the main garden from the vegetable patch.

In the distance, sticking out between the tall rows of rhubarb, and young apple trees she saw the tip of a leather shoe.

Smiling she hurried on but as she got nearer, she saw the shape of Robert – he was lying on his side.

He was not moving.

Something was wrong.

She ran the last couple of yards.

His eyes were closed.

A bluebottle fly was hovering above him.

His white shirt had tiny spots of blood.

She knelt over him and turned his head.

She suppressed a scream in her throat and whispered.

"Talk to me, Robert."

She tried to recall lessons from her first aid class long ago on how to check for signs of life.

Then she heard a voice, a voice which seemed to come from far away but was familiar to her.

It was getting closer.

She turned around and saw a man approaching, he was backlit by the sun and for a few seconds, she did not recognize him.

Then she realized that it was Kevin.

"Get help -he is not breathing -."

He lunged at her and grabbed her by the collar of her dress.

There was a strong smell of whiskey.

"Look what you made me do – Lizzie told me everything - – he is dead-."

"No – no -no."

She struggled to free herself, but he held her arm in a vice-like grip

Then he frog-marched her back towards the cottage.

She tried to look back at Robert, but he roared.

"Forget about him."

There was spittle coming from his mouth and his breathing reminded her of the cattle she had encountered earlier.

Tears streamed down her face.

"That's right – cry your heart out for your lover -."

She spluttered.

"I -I did -not- plan to get involved with him."

He gave her a slap on the jaw.

"Don't give me your lies – no wonder you were frigid with me – saving your energy for him."

She saw the hate in his eyes and fear left her unable to speak coherently.

"I – I-."

"Is that his spawn in your belly?"

She did not reply.

If you admit that you are not sure he will kill you.

He swung his foot in her direction.

"Tell me the truth you whore – is it his or mine?"

"I swear that the baby is yours – he did not even know that I was expecting -."

He pulled the last of the pins from her bun so that her hair fell around her face.

"Look at you – another Mary Magdalen – opening your legs for every auld fellow."

"Please Kevin – the baby is yours."

"How can I believe one word that comes from your filthy mouth?"

My life and my baby's life hinge on what I say next.

"Because it could not possibly be his – I did not sleep with him around the time I conceived – if I thought it was his I would have told him earlier, but I only arranged to meet him today to tell him about my pregnancy."

He put his two hands around her neck and looked into her eyes.

"Swear to me on that baby's life that you are telling the truth."

"On our baby's life, I swear that I am telling the truth."

He took his hands away as he rubbed a tear from the corner of his eye.

She massaged her neck.

I need to keep him calm and convince him that it will all work out.

"I know that you will make a great father – we are a family now with our very own baby on the way."

He eyed her suspiciously as he shouted.

"This is all your fault – if you had not thrown yourself at that piece of shit on the ground – none of this would have happened."

"I am so sorry I promise that I will spend the rest of my life making amends to you."

She was shivering all over.

"Then why did you tell him on the phone that you intended to leave me."

Tell him it's a lie or he will kill you now.

Kevin, that's not true, Lizzie is mistaken, I said that I -would have to – leave you if you found out."

He coughed up phlegm and then his eyes seemed to bore a hole through hers.

"You are such a bitch that you don't know the truth from lies anymore."

"Kevin, I know where the key is hidden, we can ring for help."

He looked past her like he had seen a spectre.

"Help? Are you mad?"

"Kevin we can say that it was an accident – you happened to stop here to buy herbs and when you saw Robert, you assumed that he was intent on robbing the place -a good barrister will get you off the hook, everyone in Redmills will vouch for your impeccable character."

He prodded her in the ribs.

"Move along quickly- you are talking rubbish."

She nodded.

"Ok – I can phone for the ambulance and the Gardai and when they arrive, they will understand that it was not planned."

He caught her by the elbow and hurried her through the archway.

Evie held her breath as he located his shotgun from under a pile of logs, she guessed he had concealed it after firing at Robert earlier.

Then minutes later, when she stooped to retrieve the key from beneath the basket of turf, he gave a menacing laugh.

"You are not ringing for help- I have unfinished business here – that charlatan must die too"

Her blood ran cold.

"What do you mean?"

"We will wait inside until that witch returns -the one you call your friend- she cannot have gone far."

"But she had nothing to do with me and – him."

He pinned her against the wall with his two arms.

"She connived with you in making a fool of me – allowing you to meet up with your lover in her house – this is the second time that she has crossed me."

Her heart felt like it might explode.

"I swear – she is innocent – I never met him here before."

As soon as the words were out of her mouth, she regretted them.

He poked a finger into her face as he slurred his words.

"I don't believe you – otherwise you did -it in the streets of Dublin like two dogs – go on admit it you bitch."

She shook her head.

"Please don't harm her."

Suddenly, he stepped back and walked to a nearby bush.

"Do you really think that your pleas- for mercy matter now?"

He said over his shoulder as he unzipped his trousers and relieved himself

She saw a chance to escape and took it.

Running for all she was worth she took off down the laneway and at the first bend she turned left and crossed over a broken-down fence into the overgrown ruins of an old stone shed which was hidden from view – only a few weeks earlier Mai had mentioned it to her on one of their walks. She cowered down behind the furze bushes and then she heard him shouting as he ran past.

"Come out Evelyn I have the gun – I will shoot you."

She cowered closer behind the tall ferns, her fear was so great that she could not hold her urine any longer and it trickled down her leg.

His shouts grew fainter, but she knew that he would double back and search every inch of the laneway, he would work out that she had not gone far.

Then she heard the unmistakable sound of a gunshot from further down the lane.

Pigeons in the trees beside her took off in fright leaving a trail of grey feathers that fell to the ground beside her.

Dear God – he is firing into the hedgerows

Then another shot rang out followed by another but now she was confused because the shots seemed to be coming from different directions.

Inching her way deeper through the undergrowth her ankle ached, and blood trickled down her arm from a wound, but she had no time to stop. A voice in her head willed her onwards.

Run for your life - to the bog you can hide there.

When she saw stacks of turf in the distance, convulsive gasps escaped from her body.

Reaching the edge of the bog she slithered over a low bank.

A red cow speckled with white mooed with fright as she ran past her.

A few moments later, she stopped.

All around her was a vast expanse of purple heather and wildflowers interspersed with gorse bushes showing yellow buds.

She had lost all sense of direction.

She decided to make for the very centre of the bog where she could hide.

The deeper she went the more uneven the ground.

She had to watch every step.

Then she saw a mass of tiny blue plants growing near rows of turf left to dry in the wind. If she made it to the far side of them there were several bushes where she could lie flat and hide.

Beneath her feet, she felt marsh.

Water filled her shoes.

She lifted her right foot slowly, but the other foot slipped

Suddenly, the ground seemed to be looming towards her.

White cotton flowers were everywhere.

She rubbed her eyes.

The last thing she felt before slipping into unconsciousness was the cold water from a bog pool seeping into her clothes.

Chapter Thirty - Seven

Jack Madden at 77 years of age still knew every inch of his farm, given to him by the Land Commission, he took great pride in it. Three times a day he walked it to check on his sheep, cattle, and six cows. He was a bachelor and he often mused how the cows were like children to him, he took extra care of them and when each one produced a calf, he felt heartbroken when the time came to sell the calves on to other farmers. That evening he was on a mission, his favourite cow, a red one with white speckling called Daisy was missing. His land bordered the bog and as he suffered from rheumatism, he was not as vigilant about maintaining his fences as he used to be. His cows loved to escape into the bogland and nibble at sweet herbs and wildflowers but only 12 months earlier he had lost a cow after she fell into a large bog-hole and broke her pelvis.

When he came to the outskirts of his farm he climbed up onto the top of a ditch and scanned the surrounding areas for a glimpse of his errant cow.

His eyes could not pick out anything unusual, in the distance, he saw the unmistakable outline of a fox making his stealthy way through some heather where he had noticed grey partridges nesting only a week earlier. Then, he heard the distant sound of a shotgun followed by the warning cry of a curlew. He looked to the left where a small group of curlews rose in panic from the wetlands and soared high into the sky, their raucous screams alerting other birds who quickly followed them into the blue evening sky.

Jack continued to walk along the ditch for some minutes until he spotted the shape of an animal on the other side. Lifting the peak of his old cap he realized that it was not his cow but Christy Farrell's jackass.

He laughed out loud at his own foolishness.

Then he heard someone shouting wildly and he looked around.

It was the local vet.

He was gesticulating at him to come down from the ditch.

Jack's heart felt heavy.

He must have found poor Daisy drowned in a pool of water.

He inched down the grassy slope carefully to avoid exacerbating his hip pain, while Kevin Moore screamed at him.

"Hurry up you old fool."

When his feet reached the ground, he realized that the vet had a shotgun behind his back.

"Mr Moore, don't tell me that you found poor old Daisy and shot her, I had no time to say goodbye."

To his astonishment, he saw the barrel of the gun pointed at him.

"Shut up about your bloody cow! I want your shotgun, where is it?"

"It's in the kitchen but why do you want it?"

"Start walking back to your house I need it for two old whores who made a fool out of me."

Jack felt a sharp pain in his back as the double-barrel gun prodded him.

He took a few steps and then stopped, turning around to face his captor.

"Mr Moore, you don't look well and you are acting like a crazy man, put down the gun and I can get someone to help you."

Jack saw rage in the vet's eyes and acting on an impulse he wrestled with him for the gun.

When the younger man got the upper hand, he kneed Jack in the groin and knocked him sideways.

He was just getting back onto his feet when he heard the shot, and the ground came hurtling towards him.

There was a sharp pain in his arm and his shoulder was pumping blood, he could hear Moore warning him that if he did not stand up that he would shoot a second time.

"Help me! I am losing blood -."

"This is your last chance - get up."

Jack tried to stand but now his whole body was in shock and he fell back onto the grass.

"You old fucker-look, look what you are making me do."

Jack heard him reloading the gun and started to whisper.

"Our Father-."

Then from far away – a roar – reminding him of a lion he had seen on the television in his neighbour's home.

Suddenly a shot rang out.

He could smell his own blood.

He felt faint.

Numb with fear he vomited.

When he opened his eyes, someone was towering over him.

He blinked.

A familiar face but not the vet's.

"Sir, in the name of God I am doing my best- I am going to bind up your shoulder to stop you losing any more blood."

He tried to answer but he was too weak.

He looked into the young boy's kind eyes and then he tried hard to concentrate on the boy's words."

"Don't worry, I will run like a hare and get help to bring you to hospital, once I tie up this wound."

"I know you – you are the tinker woman's lad."

At that point, he passed out.

Much later, just as the town clock was chiming midnight Evie who had been knocked out, finally came around. When she saw a hazy figure with a white uniform and a white cap, she tried to sit up, but her neck and throat hurt, and she sank back into the bed.

The figure, who had a kind voice was coming closer.

"No one can harm you now Mrs Moore, you are in hospital."

Suddenly, an image of Kevin chasing her with a gun flashed before her.

She began to shake all over.

"My husband – he was out of control -."

The nurse moved nearer.

"I promise you that it is all over, he won't harm you anymore."

A silent tear rolled down her cheek.

"Try to sit up, let me help you."

She looked into the eyes of the young nurse.

"I am pregnant -and why have I got a drip attached to me?"

"Yes, we know that you are pregnant, your baby is fine, but Dr Sheehy put you on a drip to prevent you becoming dehydrated- now let me adjust the head of this bed."

In a few minutes, Evie was sitting up in a comfortable position with pillows supporting her back.

The nurse sat on a chair beside her.

"Do you feel pain anywhere apart from your neck?"

"My ankle feels tight."

"Don't worry about that – the doctor said that it is sprained so we have strapped it but in a few days it will be better."

Evie nodded. "I need to know about my friend Mai -you see my husband was like a mad man, threatening to kill her. And there was someone else -."

"Your three friends are unharmed. They waited all evening down at reception until they were satisfied that all your tests came back clear."

"Three friends? "

"Yes, Mrs Mai Dolphin, Mrs Ryder-Lee, and a lady called Orla- I have forgotten her surname."

A faint smile crinkled the corner of Evie's eyes.

"Are they still here?"

"No. They had a quick look at you, but you were still asleep, so the doctor told them to go home and come back in the morning."

Suddenly, she sat bolt upright in the bed.

"Oh my God, poor Robert. It's all coming back to me now, he is dead, my husband killed him."

The nurse's expression changed.

"I am sorry Mrs Moore, you seem a little confused, your friend Robert is still clinging to life, but your husband is dead – he went on a shooting spree."

Evie took in the news slowly and then her head shook vehemently.

"He cannot be dead he was chasing me when I fell into a hole in the bog and he told me that Robert was dead."

She saw a tall man in a white coat and with a stethoscope in his pocket approach the bed.

"My name is Dr Brian Sheehy I am sorry to confirm that it is true, Mrs Moore, your husband is dead."

Then, the still figure of Robert lying on the ground seemed to rise before her eyes.

"Robert, my friend Robert I saw him lying on the ground – so he is badly wounded but alive, thanks be to God."

The doctor exchanged a quick glance with the nurse.

"Yes, he is breathing but I am sorry to tell you Mrs Moore that he lost a lot of blood, he was shot in the lower back, my colleagues are working on him as we speak, we will know more within the next 24 hours."

She gripped the sheet with her two hands.

"I saw spots of blood on his shirt and I think his moustache was covered in something like phlegm, I hope he was not choking to death."

"Don't fret, he is alive."

The nurse said calmly, then she held Evie's hand as she said in a gentle voice.

"Take a deep breath now another -and another."

Evie clung to the young woman's strong hand which emitted a smell of antiseptic.

" I remember- Kevin, was acting like an escaped lunatic, he had shot Robert and then set a trap for me, but I escaped – the last thing I saw was water- he wanted to kill Mai."

The doctor cleared his throat.

"Your husband fired shots at random into the hedgerows when he was searching for you, he must have been running out of fire and approached a neighbour called Jack Madden – we think he wanted him to get his gun and hand it over."

Evie clenched her teeth.

"Please tell me- everything."

" He shot the poor farmer in the shoulder. He was about to fire a second time when a young itinerant boy called Patsy Mc Ginley, who happened to be hunting rabbits in the area heard the commotion and ran to the scene. When he heard Mr Madden begging for his life he shouted at your husband to stop but he turned his gun on Patsy, fortunately, the young boy was faster, and he returned fire and so your husband died instantly."

She let out a scream.

"Mrs Moore, your husband was out of control, he was on a murderous rampage, if that lad had not killed him, he would have killed the old man -."

She nodded grimly.

"I understand - Patsy probably saved at least three if not four lives- firstly the farmer, then Mai Dolphin, he was planning to wait until she returned home and shoot her – and Robert, he thought Robert was dead – and God only knows what he intended to do to me."

The doctor rubbed his hands together.

"Young Patsy is a hero."

"Is he hurt? I am teaching him how to read and write and I have grown fond of him, he is a good lad."

"No, he is in shock, but we are keeping him in hospital for the night in the same ward as Jack Madden, who has a nasty shoulder injury."

"Will Jack recover?"

She asked as her teeth chattered.

"Yes."

"Who found me?"

"When Mrs Dolphin returned home and discovered your friend lying in her garden with a bullet in his back she phoned for an ambulance and the Gardai, but Patsy Mc Ginley had already notified them about your husband and Jack Madden. The Gardai then sent out a search party to find your good self – you had passed out, but you came around by the time an ambulance took you in here- you were frantic, we sedated you while we cleaned you up and performed all the tests."

Evie removed her wedding ring and flung it across the floor.

"I never want to see that again. When I think of the mayhem that man has caused -."

The doctor exchanged a look with the nurse.

"Now, you have had a terrible shock especially for a lady in your condition so I am giving you a light sleeping tablet which will help you sleep."

She took it from him and swallowed it with a little water.

"I feel exhausted – I take it that it won't harm my baby?"

His face lit up.

"The answer is no, your baby is well and a big, healthy one by all appearances."

She frowned.

"I – feel weak."

"Mrs Moore, you are expecting a baby, and you have been through a horrendous time."

She looked from one white-coated person to another.

"I need the truth - I want to be sure, is Kevin really dead? I think he was going to kill me too after he had ended Mai's life but please don't tell me lies just to soothe me."

"Mrs Moore, your husband died instantly, I am not in the habit of making up lies. You and your baby are safe now."

Evie lay back on the bed and stroked her stomach.

'Kevin was obsessed with the baby, he thought it was a boy but he – was abusive to me and I don't know how he would have reacted if I had a girl."

"You need not worry now he is gone, please get some rest."

The doctor smiled at her sympathetically.

"A boy or a girl – I don't mind at all but he."

Evie's eyelids closed, and her head relaxed to one side.

The nurse winked at the doctor.

"She is asleep poor lamb, Mrs Dolphin told me that Kevin Moore was nothing but a bully who abused his wife."

The doctor checked his watch.

"It's very late – I am going off duty, but I can tell you that Kevin Moore isn't the first street- angel and house -devil I have encountered, and he certainly won't be the last."

The nurse tucked in the bedclothes around Evie.

"I know but Mrs Moore's troubles are over, now she can get on with her life and enjoy her baby with the help of her friends."

He sighed.

"That brute is gone, and by all accounts, I would say that Mrs Moore is one lucky woman to have escaped his murderous intentions."

"Dr Sheehy."

"Yes, Nurse Coleman."

"Do you think that the patient now in theatre will make it? I overhead Mrs Moore's friend's whispering and it seems there is a strong possibility that he is the baby's father."

The doctor tut-tutted.

"Nurse Coleman, you know that we do not tolerate gossip in this hospital among staff about their patients, do not let matron hear you speaking like that. Suffice to say that the man in question is clinging to life by a thread. The bullet was lodged in his lower spine and, there is only so much my colleagues can do. His fate lies in the lap of the gods."

Epilogue

FIVE YEARS LATER

On a sunny afternoon in June, with a perfect blue sky and a shy breeze rippling the delicate ivory cloth on the table set with crystal glasses, not far from the magnificent Victorian conservatory, Richmond House looks resplendent. At a distance, in the parkland under the shade of giant sequoia trees skittish red deer, whose ancestors roamed free for thousands of years are observing the movements of the humans on the freshly mown lawn sloping down to the river. Every now and again the voices of people milling around in the sunshine reach their ears. The leader of the herd is poised for flight yet something different about today's gathering causes him to linger, perhaps it is the dizzying medley of strange scents coming from these male and female humans, maybe he is entranced by the notes of the harp floating through the air. He sniffs as the hazy figures take their seats among the rows of chairs facing a small platform, the silhouette of a woman in a cloud of blue silk and large brimmed hat is climbing the steps to the loudspeaker, he is familiar with her smell and her low voice. In the long stretch of a summer's evening, she sometimes crouches among the trees observing the wildlife and instinctively he knows that she poses no threat to buck, doe, or fawn.

Suddenly, a booming sound followed by a series of blinding flashes alarms the stag. Adrenaline courses through his body and he takes flight, followed by the rest of the herd, they head for the forest at the perimeter of the demesne where they blend into the undergrowth.

Of those humans present for the official opening of a voluntary refuge centre for abused women, one woman is struck by the swift movement of the herd. Their dash for safety through the sprawling estate resonates with her own desperate attempt through the bog to escape her husband's murderous mindset, years earlier.

She feels a slight tug on her arm, and she smiles down at her little daughter Audrey, whose titian curls and sapphire eyes lend her an angelic look. Yet, she is mischievous and strong-willed with a sharp intelligence and a dimple on her chin that reminds Evie of her own mother. The little girl points up at the speaker and with whoops of delight, she says.

"I see Aunty Iris and over there I see Uncle Robert and my other aunties, Mai and Orla."

Evie puts her fingers to her lips.

"Shush. Sit down, you must stay quiet, have a look at the pictures in the new book I put in your bag."

Audrey nods and proceeds to do as she is told while Evie concentrates on Iris's speech.

"Ladies and Gentlemen, it is both an honour and a priv-
ilege to have the official launch of our first refuge centre for
abused women here at Richmond House. For the last twelve
months, we have operated from a temporary dwelling in
Dublin and we currently have eight women residing there.
Thanks to the trojan efforts of our committee chaired by
Mai Dolphin and to the generosity of our benefactors we
have now been able to buy an old house near Dublin which
will become our permanent centre for women seeking to get
away from violent husbands and partners. For obvious reasons we do not wish to make public the location of this new
oasis and therefore we decided to have the public opening
here. Now, I shall hand you over to Mai."

Following loud applause and another flash of cameras,
Mai took to the stage.

"Thank you, Iris, your generosity knows no bounds
and you have been a tower of strength since I first mooted
the idea of this centre five years ago. There are so many individuals who have been instrumental in helping to make
my dream of a centre for battered women a reality that
I cannot possibly mention everyone. However, it behoves
me to single out two extraordinary people who have been
the cornerstones of this project. The first is Evelyn Moore,
herself a former victim of domestic abuse. Despite personal
tragedy, she has shown remarkable courage in bringing the
skeleton of spousal abuse out of the cupboard and into the
realm of public consciousness, through open discussion, an
interview on *The Late Late Show* and her brutally honest

account of her marriage as featured in the programme on Radio Eireann called *Escape.*

Please be upstanding and give this brave lady the recognition she deserves."

Evie nods while the cameraman from Radio Telefis, Eireann, swings the cumbersome machine in her direction, as fifty chairs are pushed back, and their occupants stand to applaud her. Then, minutes later, when everyone is seated again. Mai continues with her speech.

"The second person I wish to commend is Dr Robert Nash. Again, despite personal suffering and the fact that he is confined to a wheelchair since that tragic shooting in Redmills five years ago, he has not shown any bitterness or indulged in self-pity. Instead, he has thrown the full weight of his mighty intellect behind this cause and has managed to bring the esteemed support of the medical profession on board, by highlighting the heretofore unspoken wars which raged in many homes, behind closed doors, irrespective of class. Not only has he succeeded in this mission but he has also contributed the proceeds of his bestselling book: *Adventures of an Intrepid Traveller in Africa,* towards the cost of running the centre on a day-to-day basis.

Again, I ask you to please be upstanding and show this man the respect he has earned so admirably."

From her place in the front row, Evie stands and claps vigorously but her eye is locked on Robert, who is sitting up straight in his wheelchair, at the edge of the row and smiling warmly at her.

Before Mai leaves the platform, she adds.

"Finally, I would like you all to give a standing ovation in absentia, to Mr Patsy Mc Ginley. He is apprenticed to a farrier down in Cork, but he needs no introduction because he has already been honoured by the town of Redmills for his quick thinking in saving the lives of at least three people sitting among us. And in recognition of his heroism, a local fundraising group are enabling him to follow his ambition to help heal horses."

When the applause ends and the photographers from the local and national newspapers signal that they are happy with the day's shoot, the merriment begins. Three waiters hand out glasses of champagne while the guests mingle, and a string quartet gives a wonderful rendition of Tchaikovsky's: *The Dance of The Sugar Plum Fairy*.

Evie and Robert slip away from the crowd and take the well-worn path under the yew trees, which is beyond the walled garden and away from prying eyes. Now and again, Evie pushes the wheelchair when the ground gets rough to avoid gnarled roots of trees which are exposed. When they come to a clearing, where they have a full view of the Boyne river meandering by, far below, Robert stops his wheelchair and takes her hand in his.

"Lyn, we have achieved more than we ever dreamed of with this project, and now it is time for you to consider tying the knot with me. God knows we are not just best friends, but lovers and I think of Audrey as my own little daughter."

She squeezes his hand tightly and plants a kiss on his cheek, although still handsome he now has a white moustache.

"Robert."

He lifts his head towards her.

"Yes."

"We have had this discussion before, I am still wary of committing to another marriage why not just continue the way we are, a piece of paper means nothing."

"Whatever you want my love."

Suddenly, a child's voice echoes through the ancient trees and they turn to see Audrey racing towards them.

Then laughing excitedly, she stops at Robert's chair and climbs onto his lap.

"Uncle Robert, I met the sugar plum fairy in the woods, and I told her that I want you to be my Daddy."

He kisses her on her forehead and then replies.

"My lovely little girl I would like nothing better."

A tear threatens to slide down Evie's face.

"Audrey, Robert is the best Daddy in Ireland and from now on you can call him by that name."

The child laughs and slides to the ground.

Robert's face glows as he swings his wheelchair around and claps while Audrey does a little fairy dance and shouts at the top of her voice.

"Daddy, Daddy, Daddy."

The End

About the Author

A nne Frehill has had short stories and non-fiction published in a range of magazines.

She has also contributed to Sunday Miscellany on RTE Radio 1, and was included in a book relating to the same programme, edited by Marie Heaney comprising the best writing from 2003 and 2004. Since the start of the Pandemic, she has written regularly in a local online newsletter, on a range of topics.

Anne has an abiding interest in history, folklore, sociology and nature. And is passionate about animal welfare and care of the earth. She lives in Meath in the heart of farming country.

Please Review

Dear Reader,

If you enjoyed this book, would you kindly post a short review on Amazon? Your feedback will make all the difference to getting the word out about this book.

To leave a review, go to Amazon and type in the book title. When you have found it go to the book page, please scroll to the bottom of the page to where it says 'Write a Review' and then submit your review.

Thank you in advance.

Printed in Poland
by Amazon Fulfillment
Poland Sp. z o.o., Wrocław

74869453R00261